The Unfinished Revolution

KATHLEEN
GERSON

The Unfinished Revolution

How a New Generation Is Reshaping Family, Work, and Gender in America

OXFORD
UNIVERSITY PRESS
2010

OXFORD
UNIVERSITY PRESS

Oxford University Press, Inc., publishes works that further
Oxford University's objective of excellence
in research, scholarship, and education.

Oxford   New York
Auckland   Cape Town   Dar es Salaam   Hong Kong   Karachi
Kuala Lumpur   Madrid   Melbourne   Mexico City   Nairobi
New Delhi   Shanghai   Taipei   Toronto

With offices in
Argentina   Austria   Brazil   Chile   Czech Republic   France   Greece
Guatemala   Hungary   Italy   Japan   Poland   Portugal   Singapore
South Korea   Switzerland   Thailand   Turkey   Ukraine   Vietnam

Published by Oxford University Press, Inc.
198 Madison Avenue, New York, NY 10016

www.oup.com

Oxford is a registered trademark of Oxford University Press.

Library of Congress Cataloging-in-Publication Data
Gerson, Kathleen.
The unfinished revolution : how a new generation is reshaping family,
work, and gender in America / Kathleen Gerson.
    p.   cm.
Includes bibliographical references and index.
ISBN 978-0-19-537167-3
1. Family—United States.   2. Work and family—United States.
3. Professional employees—United States.   4. Women employees—United States.
5. Male employees—United States.   6. Sex role—United States.
I. Title.
HQ536.G47 2009
306.872—dc22   2009012789

9 8 7 6 5 4 3 2 1

Printed in the United States of America
on acid-free paper

CONTENTS

ACKNOWLEDGMENTS

L IKE GROWING UP, writing a book is a long and unpredictable process that depends on the generosity of family, friends, and colleagues as well as strangers. Having reached the end of the path for this one, I can only marvel at my good fortune for the support so many people have given me along the way.

To start at the beginning, the research project on the Immigrant Second Generation in Metropolitan New York, conducted by Philip Kasinitz, John Mollenkopf, and Mary Waters, helped me to identify my sample. (The leading funding source for this project was The Russell Sage Foundation, led by Eric Wanner.) Jennifer Holdaway introduced me to the intricacies (and quirks) of Atlas.ti. Two gifted research assistants, Stephanie Byrd and Jordana Pestrong, conducted a portion of the interviews, and their contributions greatly enriched insights gleaned from my own forays into the field. Eleanor Bernal transcribed the interviews with her usual intelligence and good cheer, and Courtney Abrams helped organize and code the transcripts for computer analysis. Sarah Damaske provided both heroic help in compiling the references and insightful feedback on early drafts. Most important, the young women and men who agreed to spend their time with me and my assistants have my deep gratitude and respect. We entered their lives as strangers, and they opened their doors and shared their most private experiences and thoughts with us. My hope is that the interview process gave them at least a portion of the insight and enjoyment that their participation gave us.

A wide and deep network of colleagues and friends listened to my developing thoughts, provided essential feedback, and offered moral support. A writing group with Lynn Chancer, Ruth Horowitz, and Arlene Skolnick served as a forum for thoughtful discussions and constructive criticism. Many other colleagues inspired me with their own work and their reactions to mine. Among these, I am especially grateful to Rosalind Barnett, Cynthia Epstein, Jennifer Glass, Sydney Halpern, Lynne Haney, Sharon Hays, Rosanna Hertz, Jerry A. Jacobs, Pamela Stone, Viviana Zelizer, and Eviatar Zerubavel. My students, especially Michael Armato, Stephanie Byrd, Sarah Damaske, Adam Green, Pamela Kaufman, Allen Li, and Louise Roth, also offered valued feedback. Over the years they have taught me as much as I taught them.

The Council on Contemporary Families provided an opportunity to work closely with a remarkable group of academics and practitioners who collaborate at the intersection of research, policy, and clinical practice. My thanks go to all my fellow board members and especially to Stephanie Coontz, Joshua Coleman, Carolyn and Phil Cowan, Paula England, Frank Furstenberg, Steven Mintz, Mignon Moore, Barbara Risman, Virginia Rutter, Pepper Schwartz, Arlene Skolnick, and Pamela Smock. It was a pleasure to organize a CCF conference on "dilemmas of work and family in the twenty-first century" with Janet Gornick and Joan Williams and then to publish a selection of these presentations in *The American Prospect*, working with Robert Kuttner.

During the course of this project, I benefitted from stimulating reactions to a number of presentations of my work-in-progress. My thanks go to colleagues at the Charles Phelps Taft Center for Research at the University of Cincinnati, the Institute for the Study of Status Passages and Risks in the Life Course at the University of Bremen in Germany, the MacArthur Foundation Research Network on the Transition to Adulthood, the National Opinion Research Center at the University of Chicago, the New York Chapter of the Stanford Institute for Research on Women and Gender, the Sloan Center for the Study of Myth and Ritual in Everyday Life at Emory University, the Sloan Work and Family Research Network, the Working Group on Wealth and Power in the Post-Industrial Age, and the Departments of Sociology at Harvard University, University of Pennsylvania, University of California at San Diego, University of Southern California, and Vanderbilt University. I am also grateful for incisive blind reviews from Stephanie Coontz, Sharon Hays, Pamela Stone, Eviatar Zerubavel, and two anonymous reviewers as well as for thoughtful comments from Naomi Schneider at the University of California Press and Elizabeth Knoll and Joyce Seltzer at Harvard University Press.

It has been an unqualified pleasure to work with the team at Oxford University Press. David McBride and Niko Pfund inspired me with their enthusiasm and professionalism. Keith Faivre handled the editing and production stages with an unerringly deft touch. To put it simply, James Cook has been the best editor imaginable. Through every stage in the publication process, he has gone above and beyond the call of duty, offering wise advice, masterful editing of the manuscript, much-appreciated help with the title, and unstinting attention to large and small details at every turning point. In an age of declining budgets and overburdened editors, I have been exceedingly fortunate to have James as an editor and a friend.

Since this book is about families, writing it has provided me with an opportunity to savor my own. Rose Blum successfully raised my sisters and me with unwavering grace and dignity at a time when single motherhood was rare and women's options were far too limited. Now in her ninety-third year, she remains as warm, courageous, and life-affirming as ever. She taught me that a love of life, an indomitable spirit, and a sense of humor will not only help you prevail over life's difficulties but also give you the courage to make a difference in the world. My two sisters, Linda and Betty Gerson, are testament to the wisdom of her outlook. Through their friendship and example, they have given me a lifelong appreciation for the meaning of sisterhood.

John Mollenkopf, my partner-in-life for three decades, has made this book possible on every level—from his careful reading and brilliant editing of the manuscript to our constant discussions about gender, work, and family both as urgent public matters and personal conundrums to his devoted parenting, inspired cooking, and optimistic outlook. When it comes to being an equal partner, he has walked the walk as well as talked the talk. For sharing this journey with me, I thank him from the bottom of my heart.

Finally, my daughter, Emily, a child of the gender revolution, has inspired me in too many ways to name. She taught me to appreciate the joys and challenges she has faced growing up and to treasure the gift of unconditional love. It is an honor beyond measure to be her mother, and I could not be more proud of her. I am confident that Emily and her peers will work to create a more humane, equal, and just world for the generations to follow. Now it is up to the rest of us to help them succeed.

The Unfinished Revolution

CHAPTER ONE | The Shaping of a New Generation

I T IS A COOL, clear morning in Oceanside Terrace, a working-class suburb where American flags are almost as plentiful as family pets. As Josh answers the doorbell, I anticipate the story he will tell. His brief answers to a telephone survey tell a straightforward tale of growing up in a stable, two-parent home of the kind Americans like to call "traditional." He reported, for instance, that his dad worked as a carpenter throughout his childhood, his mom stayed home during most of his preschool years, and his parents raised three sons and were still married after thirty years.

After we settle into overstuffed chairs in his parents' cozy living room, where he is home for a brief visit, the more complete life story Josh tells belies this simple image of family life. Despite the apparent stability and continuity conveyed in the telephone survey, Josh actually felt he lived in three different families, one after the other. Anchored by a breadwinning father and a home-centered mother, the first did indeed take a traditional form. Yet this outward appearance mattered less to him than his parents' constant fighting over money, housework, and the drug and alcohol habit his father developed in the army. As Josh put it, "All I remember is just being real upset, not being able to look at the benefits if it would remain like that, having all the fighting and that element in the house."

As Josh reached school age, his home life changed dramatically. His mother took a job as an administrator in a local business and, feeling more secure about her ability to support the family, asked her husband to move out and "either get straight or don't come back." Even though his father's departure was painful and fairly unusual in this family-oriented neighborhood, relief tempered Josh's sense of loss. He certainly did not miss his parents' constant fighting, his father's surly demeanor, or the embarrassment he felt whenever he dared to bring a friend home. His parents' separation also provided space for his mother to renew her self-esteem through her work outside the home. Josh missed his father, but he also knew a distance had always existed between them, even if it now took a physical as well as an emotional form. He came to accept this new situation as the better of two less-than-ideal alternatives.

Yet Josh's family life took a third turn a year later. Just as he had adjusted to a new routine, Josh's father "got clean" and returned. Although his parents reunited, they hardly seemed the same couple. The separation had triggered a remarkable change in both. Being away had given his father a new appreciation for his family and a deepening desire to be a "real family man." Now drug-free, he resolved to become thoroughly involved in his children's lives. Josh's mother displayed equally dramatic changes, for taking a job had given her a newfound pride in knowing she could stand on her own. As his father became more involved and his mother more self-confident, it lifted the family's spirits and fortunes. In Josh's words, "that changed the whole family dynamic. We got extremely close."

In the years that followed, Josh watched his parents forge a new partnership quite different from the conflict-ridden one he remembered. "A whole new relationship" developed with his father, whom he came to see as "one of my best friends." He also valued his mother's strengthening ties to work, which not only nourished her sense of self but also provided enough additional income for him to attend college.

Now twenty-four, Josh has left home to begin his own adult journey. As he looks back over the full sweep of his childhood, he sees that, while the actors did not change, the play did. In fact, at some point in this series of events, he lived in all three types of households—traditional, single-parent, and dual-earner—now dominating the debate about family change. To Josh, however, these pictures of discrete family types do not do justice to the flow of his family experiences. Not only did Josh live in each of these family forms, but the static nature of these categories misses the importance of the turning points when his parents faced difficulties and fashioned new ways of connecting to each other, their children, and the wider world. For Josh, these transitions produced "three different childhoods, really."

As Josh considers his options for the future, he draws inspiration from the flexibility his parents were able to muster in the face of enormous personal and social challenges. He hopes to avoid the problems of his parents' early marriage, but he admires their efforts to fashion more personally satisfying and mutually supportive bonds. He, too, wants to build a marriage that is flexible enough to weather the difficulties that will surely come, even if he cannot foresee what exactly they will be. Yet his highest hopes are colliding with his greatest fears. The few close relationships he has had with young women have underscored his desire to build the flexible, egalitarian, and sharing partnership his parents finally created. After a series of dissatisfying construction jobs, he now plans to become a teacher and hopes this occupational choice will allow him to integrate satisfying work with ample time for children and family.

Yet Josh's early forays into the worlds of work and dating have also left him worried about the obstacles looming on the horizon. On the one hand, the pressure to put in long workweeks just to earn a decent living seems to leave little time for life beyond the world of work. On the other, the chance of finding a fulfilling relationship that is intimate, enduring, and equal seems "iffy" at best. Although he wants to "have it all" and plans to "reach for these golden rings," he fears that building a happy marriage and striking a good balance between work and home will remain just beyond his grasp.

———

Josh's story exemplifies how the tumultuous changes of the last several decades require us to think in new ways about families, work, and gender. Josh recounts how a family pathway unfolded as his parents developed new responses to a set of unanticipated crises. In a rapidly changing world, their efforts to let go of rigid, fixed roles—and replace them with more flexible forms of providing emotional and financial support—made the crucial difference.[1] Yet Josh also recognizes that his parents' "happy ending" was not inevitable and their lives could have followed a less uplifting path. These experiences have given him high hopes for his future, but also left him with nagging doubts about his own ability to overcome the barriers likely to block the way.

Josh and his peers are children of the gender revolution.[2] They watched their mothers go to work and their parents invent a mosaic of new family forms. As they embark on their own journeys through adulthood, they take for granted options their parents barely imagined and their grandparents could not envision, but they also face dilemmas that decades of prior change have not resolved. Shifts in women's place and new forms of adult partnerships have created more options, but they also pose unprecedented conflicts and challenges. Is it possible to meld a lasting, egalitarian intimate bond with a satisfying work life, or will gender conflicts, fragile relationships, and uncertain job prospects overwhelm such possibilities? Like Josh, all of the young women and men who came of age during this period of tumultuous change must make sense of their experiences growing up and build their own adult paths amid new options and old constraints; their strategies will shape the course of work, family, and gender change for decades to come.

Growing Up in Changing Families

Whether they are judged as liberating or disastrous, the closing decades of the twentieth century witnessed revolutionary shifts in the ways new generations grow to adulthood. The march of mothers into the workplace, combined with the rise of alternatives to lifelong marriage, created a patchwork of domestic arrangements that bears little resemblance to the 1950s Ozzie and Harriet world of American nostalgia.[3] By 2000, 60 percent of all married couples had two earners, while only 26 percent depended solely on a husband's income, down from 51 percent in 1970. In fact, in 2006, two-paycheck couples were more numerous than male-breadwinner households had been in 1970. During this same period, single-parent homes, overwhelmingly headed by women, claimed a growing proportion of American households.[4] To put this in perspective, not all female-headed households consist of a mother only, since many parents cohabit but do not marry. Nevertheless, in 2007, 33 percent of non-Hispanic white children and 60 percent of black children lived with one parent (up from 10 percent and 41 percent in 1970).[5] As today's young women and men have reached adulthood, two-income and single-parent homes outnumber married couples with sole (male) breadwinners by a substantial margin.

Equally significant, members of this new generation lived in families far more likely to change shape over time. While families have always faced predictable turning points as children are born, grow up, and leave home, today's young adults were reared in households where volatile changes occurred when parents altered their ties to each other or to the wider world of work. These young women and men grew up in a period when divorce rates were increasing and a rising proportion of children were born into homes anchored either by a single mother or cohabiting but unmarried parents.[6] Lifelong marriage, once the only socially acceptable option for bearing and rearing children, became one of several alternatives that now include staying single, breaking up, or remarrying.[7]

This generation also came of age just as women's entry into the paid labor force began to challenge the once ascendant pattern of home-centered motherhood. In 1975, only 34 percent of mothers with children under the age of three held a paid job, but this number rose to 61 percent by 2000. This peak subsided slightly, with 57 percent of such mothers at work in 2004, but even this figure represents an enormous shift from earlier patterns. More telling, among mothers with children under eighteen, a full 71 percent are now employed.[8]

In fact, the recent ebbs and flows among working mothers with young children point to the competing pushes and pulls women continue to confront in balancing the needs of children and the demands of jobs. Even as women have strengthened their commitment to paid work, they have had to cope with unforeseen work-family conflicts. Growing up in this period, children observed women's massive shift from home to work, but they also watched their mothers move back and forth between full-time work, part-time work, and no job at all.[9]

Finally, the rising uncertainty in men's economic fortunes has also reverberated in their children's lives. During the closing decades of the twentieth century, the "family wage," which once made it possible for most men (though certainly not all) to support nonworking wives, became a quaint relic of an earlier time.[10] Whether at the factory or the office, a growing number of men faced unpredictable prospects as secure, well-paid careers offering the promise of upward mobility became an increasingly endangered species.[11] Fathers who expected to be sole breadwinners found they needed their wives' earnings to survive. Like a life raft in choppy seas, second incomes helped keep a growing number of families afloat and allowed some fathers to change jobs if they hit a sudden dead end on a once promising career path. As more fathers could not live up to the "good provider" ethic, however, many left their families or were dismissed by mothers who saw little reason to care for a man who could not keep himself afloat. The changes in men's lives and economic fortunes provide another reason why many members of this generation experienced unpredictable ups and downs.

Coming of age in an era of more fluid marriages, less stable work careers, and profound shifts in mothers' ties to the workplace shaped the experiences of a new generation. Compared to their parents or grandparents, they are more likely to have lived in a home containing either one parent or a cohabiting but unmarried couple and to have seen married parents break up or single parents remarry. They are more likely to have watched a stay-at-home mother join the workplace or an employed mother pull back from work when the balancing act got too difficult. And they are more likely to have seen their financial stability rise or fall as a household's composition changed or parents encountered unexpected shifts in their job situations.

These intertwined changes in intimate relationships, work trajectories, and gender arrangements have created new patterns of living, working, and family-building that amount to no less than a social revolution. Yet this revolution also faces great resistance from institutions rooted in earlier eras. On the job, workers continue to experience enormous pressures to give uninterrupted full-time, and often overtime, commitment not just to move up but even stay in place. In the home, privatized caretaking leaves parents, especially mothers, coping with seemingly endless demands and unattainable standards. And the entrenched conflicts between work and family life place mounting strains on adult partnerships. The tensions between changing lives and resistant institutions have created dilemmas for everyone.

In all of these ways, the children of the gender revolution grew to adulthood amid unprecedented, unpredictable, and uneven changes. They now must build their lives in an irrevocably but uncertainly altered world.

The Voices of a New Generation

What are the consequences of this widespread, but partial, social revolution? Where some see a generation shortchanged by working mothers and fragmenting households, others see one that can draw on more diverse and egalitarian models of family life. Where some see a resurgence of tradition, especially among those young women who want to leave the workplace, others see a deepening decline of commitment in the rising number of young adults living on their own. Whether judged to be worrisome or welcome, these contradictory views point to the continuing puzzles of the family and gender revolution. Has the rise of two-earner and single-parent households left children feeling neglected and insecure, or has it given them hope for the possibility of more diverse and flexible relationships? Will the young women and men reared in these changing circumstances turn back toward older patterns or seek new ways of building their families and integrating family and work?

To resolve these puzzles, we need to take a close look at the young women and men who came of age in this turbulent period. Through no choice of their own, they grew up in rapidly changing times, and their experiences are crucial to deciphering the contours and unexpected consequences of gender, work, and family change. Their lives also provide an opportunity to view the inner workings of diverse family forms, including two-income partnerships and single-parent homes as well as homemaker-breadwinner households, from the vantage point of the young people most directly affected. This generation lived through a natural social experiment, and their biographies make it possible to illuminate processes of social change and human development that remain hidden during more stable historical periods.

Poised between the dependency of childhood and the irrevocable investments of later life, young adulthood is a crucial phase in the human life
course that represents both a time of individual transition and a potential
engine for social change.[12] Old enough to look back over the full sweep of
their childhoods and forward to their own futures, today's young adults are
uniquely positioned to help us see beneath the surface of popular debate to
deeper truths. Their childhood experiences can tell us how family, work, and
gender arrangements shape life chances, and their young adult strategies can,
in turn, reveal how people use their experiences to craft new life paths and
redefine the contours of change.

Regardless of their own family experiences, today's young women and
men have grown up in revolutionary times. For better or worse, they have
inherited new options and questions about women's and men's proper
places.[13] Now making the transition to adulthood, they have no well-worn
paths to follow. Marriage no longer offers the promise of permanence, nor
is it the only option for bearing and rearing children, but there is no clear
route to building and maintaining an intimate bond. Most women no
longer assume they can or will want to stay home with young children,
but there is no clear model for how children should now be raised. Most
men can no longer assume they can or will want to support a family on
their own, but there is no clear path to manhood. Work and family shifts
have created an ambiguous mix of new options *and* new insecurities, with
growing conflicts between work and parenting, autonomy and commitment, time and money. Amid these social conflicts and contradictions,
young women and men must search for new answers and develop innovative responses.

The Lives of Young Women and Men

Each generation's experiences are both a judgment about the past and a
statement about the future. To understand the sources of these outlooks and
actions, we need to examine what C. Wright Mills argued is the core focus of
"the sociological imagination"—the intersection of biography, history, and
social structure.[14] This approach calls on us to investigate how specific social
and historical contexts give shape to the transhistorical links between social
arrangements and human lives, paying special attention to how societies and
individuals develop. Such an approach is especially needed when social shifts
erode earlier ways of life, reveal the tenuous nature of certainties once taken
for granted, and create new social conditions and possibilities.

Following in this tradition, I examine the lives of a strategically situated group to ask and answer broad questions. How, why, and under what conditions does large-scale social change take place? What are its limits, and what shapes its trajectories? How do social arrangements affect individual lives, and how, in turn, does the cumulative influence of individual responses give unexpected shape to the course of change?

Using this pivotal generation as a window on change, I interviewed 120 young women and men between the ages of eighteen and thirty-two. As a whole, they lived through the full range of changes taking place in family life. Most lived in some form of nontraditional home before reaching eighteen. Forty percent had some experience growing up with a single parent, and another 7 percent saw their parents separate or divorce after they left home. About a third had two parents who held full-time jobs for a significant portion of their childhood, while 27 percent grew up in homes where fathers were consistent primary breadwinners and mothers worked intermittently or not at all. Yet even many of these traditional households underwent significant shifts as parents changed their work situation or marriages faced a crisis.

With an average age of twenty-four at the time of the interview, they are evenly divided between women and men, and about 5 percent (also evenly divided between women and men) openly identified as either lesbian or gay. Randomly chosen from a broad range of city and suburban neighborhoods dispersed widely throughout the New York metropolitan area, the group includes people from a broad range of racial, ethnic, and class backgrounds who were reared in all regions of the country, including the South, West, and Midwest as well as throughout the East.

About 46 percent had a middle-class or upper-middle-class background, while another 38 percent described a working-class upbringing and 16 percent lived in or on the edge of poverty (including 10 percent whose families received public assistance during some portion of their childhood).[15] The group contained a similar level of racial and ethnic diversity. In all, 55 percent identified as non-Hispanic white, 22 percent as African-American, 17 percent as Latino or Latina, and 6 percent as Asian.[16] As a group, they reflect the demographic contours of young adults throughout metropolitan America.[17]

Everyone participated in a lengthy, in-depth life history interview in which they described their experiences growing up, reflected on the significance of these experiences, and considered their hopes and plans for the future. Focusing on processes of stability and change, the interview sought to uncover critical turning points in the lives of families and individuals, to discover the social contexts and events triggering these changes, and to explore how people imparted meaning and adopted coping strategies in response. Their life stories provide a surprising view on the social revolution this generation has inherited and whose future course it will shape.

The View from Below

What have young women and men concluded about their experiences in changing families? In contrast to the popular claim that this generation feels neglected by working mothers, unsettled by parental breakups, and wary of equality, they express strong support for working mothers and much greater concern with the quality of the relationship between parents than whether parents stayed together or separated.[18] Almost four out of five of those who had work-committed mothers believe this was the best option, while half of those whose mothers did not have sustained work lives wish they had.[19] On the controversial matters of divorce and single parenthood, a slight majority of those who lived in a single-parent home wish their biological parents had stayed together, but almost half believe it was better, if not ideal, for their parents to separate than to live in a conflict-ridden or silently unhappy home. Even more surprising, while a majority of children from intact homes think this was best, two out of five feel their parents might have been better off splitting up.

The following pages reveal a generation more focused on *how well* parents met the challenges of providing economic and emotional support than on *what form* their families took. They care about how their families unfolded, not what they looked like at any one point in time. Their narratives show that family life is a film, not a snapshot. Families are not a stable set of relationships frozen in time but a dynamic process that changes daily, monthly, and yearly as children grow. In fact, all families experience change, and even the happiest ones must adapt to changing contingencies—both in their midst and in the wider world—if they are to remain happy. No outcome is guaranteed. Stable, supportive families can become insecure and riven with conflict, while unstable families can develop supportive patterns and bonds.

Young women and men recount *family pathways* that moved in different directions as some homes became more supportive and others less so. These pathways undermine the usefulness of conceiving of families as types. Not only do many contemporary families change their form as time passes, but even those retaining a stable outward form can change in subtle but important ways as interpersonal dynamics shift.

By changing the focus from family types to family pathways, we can transcend the seemingly intractable debate pitting "traditional" homes against other family forms. The lives of these young women and men call into question a number of strongly held beliefs about the primacy of family structure and the supremacy of one household type. Their experiences point instead to the importance of processes of family change, the ways that social contexts shape a family's trajectory, and people's active efforts to cope with and draw meaning from their changing circumstances.

What explains why some family pathways remain stable or improve, while others stay mired in difficulty or take a downward course? *Gender flexibility* in breadwinning and caretaking provides a key to answering this question. In the place of fixed, rigid behavioral strategies and mental categories demarcating separate spheres for women and men, gender flexibility involves more equal sharing and more fluid boundaries for organizing and apportioning emotional, social, and economic care. Flexible strategies can take different forms, including sharing, taking turns, and expanding beyond narrowly defined roles, in addition to more straightforward definitions of equality, but they all transgress the once rigidly drawn boundaries between women as caretakers and men as breadwinners.[20]

In a world where men may not be able or willing to support wives and children and women may need and want to pursue sustained work ties, parents (and other caretakers) could only overcome such family crises as the loss of a father's income or the decline of a mother's morale by letting go of rigid gender boundaries. As families faced a father's departure, a mother's frustration at staying home, or the loss of a parent's job, the ability of parents and other caretakers to respond flexibly to new family needs helped parents create more financially stable and emotionally supportive homes. Flexible approaches to earning and caring helped families adapt, while inflexible outlooks on women's and men's proper places left them ill prepared to cope with new economic and social realities. Although it may not be welcomed by those who prefer a clearer gender order, gender flexibility in earning and caring provided the most effective way for families to transcend the economic challenges and marital conundrums that imperiled their children's well-being.

Facing the Future

What, then, do young women and men hope and plan to do in their own lives? My interviews subvert the conventional wisdom here as well, whether it stresses the rise of "opt-out" mothers or the decline of commitment.[21] Most of my interviewees hope to create lasting, egalitarian partnerships, but they are also doubtful about their chances of reaching this goal. Whether or not their parents stayed together, more than nine out of ten hope to rear children in the context of a satisfying lifelong bond. Far from rejecting the value of commitment, almost everyone wants to create a lasting marriage or marriage-like relationship.

Their affirmation of the value of commitment does not, however, reflect a desire for a relationship based on clear, fixed separate spheres for mothers and fathers. Instead, most want to create a flexible, egalitarian partnership with considerable room for personal autonomy. Whether reared by homemaker-breadwinning, dual-earner, or single parents, most women *and* men want a committed bond where they share both paid work and family caretaking. Three-fourths of those reared in dual-earner homes want their spouses to share breadwinning and caretaking, but so do more than two-thirds of those from traditional homes and close to nine-tenths of those with single parents. Four-fifths of the women want egalitarian relationships, but so do over two-thirds of the men.

Yet young women and men also fear it may not be possible to forge an enduring, egalitarian relationship or integrate committed careers with devoted parenting. Skeptical about whether they can find the right partner and worried about balancing family and work amid mounting job demands and a lack of caretaking supports, they are developing second-best fallback strategies as insurance against their worst-case fears. In contrast to their ideals, women's and men's fallback strategies diverge sharply.

Hoping to avoid being trapped in an unhappy marriage or deserted by an unfaithful spouse, most women see work as essential to their survival. If a supportive partner cannot be found, they prefer self-reliance over economic dependence within a traditional marriage. Most men, however, worry more about the costs equal sharing might exact on their careers. If time-greedy workplaces make it difficult to strike an equal balance between work and parenting, men prefer a neotraditional arrangement that allows them to put work first and rely on a partner for the lion's share of caregiving. As they prepare to settle for second best, women and men both emphasize the importance of work as a central source of personal identity and financial survival, but this stance leads them to pursue different strategies. Reversing the argument that women are returning to tradition, men are more likely to want to count on a partner at home. Women, on the other hand, are more likely to see paid work as essential to providing for themselves and their children in a world where they may not be able to count on a man.

The rise of self-reliant women, who stress emotional and economic autonomy, and neotraditional men, who grant women's choice to work but also want to maintain their position as the breadwinning specialist, portends a new work-family divide. But this division does not reflect the highest aspirations of most women or men. The debate about whether a new generation is rejecting commitment or embracing tradition does not capture the full story, because it does not distinguish between *ideals* and *fallback positions*. Young adults overwhelmingly hope to forge a lasting marriage or marriage-like relationship, to create a flexible and egalitarian bond with their intimate partner, and to blend home and work in their own lives. When it comes to their aspirations, women and men share many hopes and dreams. But fears that time-demanding workplaces, unreliable partners, and a dearth of caretaking supports will place these ideals out of reach propel them down different paths.

Drawing a distinction between ideals and enacted strategies resolves the ambiguity about the shape and direction of generational change. One-dimensional images—whether they depict resurgent traditionalism or family decline—cannot capture the complex, ambiguous experiences of today's young women and men. New generations *neither* wish to turn back to earlier gender patterns *nor* to create a brave new world of disconnected individuals. Most prefer instead to build a life that balances autonomy and commitment in the context of satisfying work and an egalitarian partnership.

Yet changing lives are colliding with resistant institutions, leaving new generations facing alternatives that are far less appealing. While institutional shifts such as the erosion of single-earner paychecks, the fragility of modern marriage, and the expanding options and pressures for women to work have made gender flexibility both desirable and necessary, demanding workplaces and privatized child rearing make work-family integration and egalitarian commitment difficult to achieve. Young women and men must reshape family, work, and gender amid an unfinished revolution. Whether they are able to create the world they want or will have to fall back on less desirable options remains an open question. Their struggles point to the social roots of these conflicts. They also make it clear that nothing less than the restructuring of work and caretaking will allow new generations to achieve the ideals they seek and provide the supports their own children will need.

PART ONE | Growing Up in Changing Families

Beyond Family Structure

Whether they judge family changes to be good, bad, or somewhere in between, analysts and advocates engaged in the controversy over what is best for children commonly focus on family "structures." Some argue that any family form diverging from the two-parent, homemaker-breadwinner household represents decline, while others counter that new family forms actually represent creative adaptations to new social contingencies. But both perspectives focus on family *structure* as the crucial arena of contention. Are children better off when parents are together or apart? Do they suffer when mothers hold a paid job or stay home? Do all children need two married biological parents, or can they thrive with a diverse combination of loving caretakers?

Those who worry about the erosion of "traditional" families continue to argue that permanent marriages, especially marriages with a clear division between a home-centered mother and a breadwinning father, are the only way to ensure a child's healthy development. The most strident voices assert that children are bound to suffer when women do not devote their lives to their care and (heterosexual) couples are no longer compelled to marry and stay together for their sake. But even less extreme versions of this perspective insist that working mothers, single parents, and both straight and gay cohabiting couples promote moral decline by allowing adults to pursue narrow self-interest at the expense of new generations.[3]

More progressive voices, including most feminists, counter that family life is adapting, not declining, as it always has in the face of new social and economic exigencies.[4] Children face new risks because an irreversible but still unfolding revolution has left families without the supports they need, not because adults have become more selfish. Since mothers in the workplace and new, more voluntary forms of adult relationships are inescapable responses to deep-seated social shifts, the danger lies not in individuals abandoning the right values but rather in our collective failure to restructure workplaces and families to meet new needs. This perspective locates the crux of the current crisis in our tendency to give lip service to "valuing children" while failing to support real children or the people entrusted with their care.[5] Blaming single parents and working mothers merely creates scapegoats for conditions with far deeper social roots.

In the polarized "family values" debate, these contending views point to different causes and different solutions, but they share a common focus on family structure. Are biological parents together or apart? Does a mother work or stay home? For the young people who spoke with me, however, these conventional categories hold far less significance. Instead, as Figure 2.1 shows, my informants had diverse reactions to similar family arrangements.

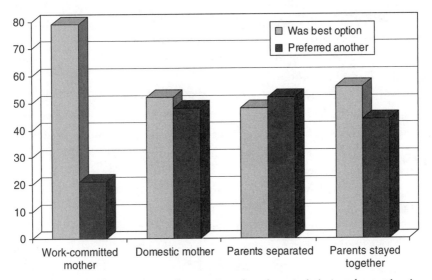

FIGURE 2.1 Children's views of parents' work and marital choices, by mothers' work status and parents' marital status.

While almost eight out of ten of those with a work-committed mother see this as the best option, those whose mothers did not work in a committed way are more divided in their outlooks, with close to half wishing their mothers had pursued a different path. When it comes to whether parents had stayed together or not, my interviewees are also divided. While a slight majority of those who lived in a single-parent home wish their biological parents had stayed together, a significant minority believe a parental separation, while not ideal, provided a better option than the alternative. Even more surprising, while most of those who lived with both biological parents agree this was the best arrangement, about four out of ten feel their parents might have been better off apart. More often than not, generalizations drawing an unwavering causal arrow between a household's form and a child's well-being shed limited light on my informants' experiences.[6] To understand their outlooks, we need to look beyond the black box of these conventional categories and focus on the reasons for—and the consequences of—their parents' strategies and choices.

Mothers—and Fathers—at Work and at Home

As members of the first generation to watch a majority of their mothers join the paid workforce, most of my interviewees had mothers with some work experience, but only about half had mothers who worked in the sustained way once reserved for men's careers.[7] The rest subordinated part-time and intermittent jobs to their domestic duties. Yet whether or not a mother became strongly committed to work, these patterns evoked divided and ambivalent responses from the children.

Children reared by a home-focused mother are especially divided, with almost half concluding it would have been better if their mothers had worked in a committed way. While 45 percent believe this arrangement gave them special advantages, the rest disagree, concluding their mothers made unnecessary and ultimately counterproductive sacrifices. In contrast, almost four out of five of those with work-committed mothers consider this the better—if not perfect—alternative. Few have misgivings about a mother's commitment to work, and those who do are more likely to focus on the circumstances surrounding a mother's choice than the fact they held a paid job. All in all, most do not believe they were—or would have been—better off had their mothers stayed home.[8] Even though we can never know whether these conclusions are "correct" in a strictly testable way, what counts is their *belief* in them.

HAVING A HOME-CENTERED MOTHER

Why are children with a home-centered mother so divided? Gender provides some of the explanation, with more than half of men but less than 40 percent of women concluding that a mother at home was the best arrangement. Yet, among women as well as men, those voicing the strongest support reported that their families enjoyed an increasingly rare convergence of circumstances that made traditional arrangements not just possible, but "good" for everyone. Most crucial, their fathers were able to provide a stable financial base. Adam grew up in an affluent, white suburb, where his father's career as a dentist allowed his mother, who trained to become a nurse, to enjoy a far better life than she could have achieved on her own:

> My mom appreciates my father a lot. She lives a much nicer life than she did when she was growing up. They live an ideal life almost, and I don't think either one of them takes advantage of it or believes in it more.

This logic made even more sense when a mother's domesticity helped a father succeed at work. Andrew's parents' "traditional marriage" worked to everyone's advantage, he reasoned, because his mother's decision to put her teaching career on hold helped his father rise to the vice presidency of a major corporation:

> It was a very traditional marriage where mom gave up her career, stayed home, and raised the kids, and dad went on with his career.

And it worked because dad's career really took off. So I wonder if the marriage would not have been as successful if dad hadn't been as successful at his job.

A mother's domesticity seemed even more preferable when she faced especially limited job opportunities. Nate believed his Latina mother's foreshortened education, poor job prospects, and failing health left her happier—and better off—at home:

> My mother dropped out at twelfth grade, and she used to work as a home attendant part-time, but staying home and taking care of the kids, that's what she liked most. So she stopped working when she got diabetic. She was more relaxed at home.

When fathers had promising work prospects and mothers did not, their children are especially likely to believe everyone benefited when a mother stayed home. Growing up with a hardworking father who rose up the ladder in hospital administration and a mother who seemed happy to leave her dead-end job in a public welfare agency, Jason did not worry about his mother's well-being conflicting with his own:

> Staying home and taking care of us, I know she enjoyed that. She's a great mother, but I think she enjoyed it, too. So I never wished she worked. I never wished she didn't work, either, but she was working as a mother, as a quote unquote housewife.

Yet others harbored strong doubts about a mother's home-centered life. In these cases, mothers did not find domestic life a welcome respite from the world of work. Reared on a farm in the rural Northeast, Hannah listened to her mother regularly complain—and blame her father—about lost chances and roads not taken:

> I hear about this ad nauseam! My mother was the first woman in the state to be in agricultural engineering, so she was in the vanguard and had a lot of opportunities. She was offered a grant to study, and it was this fabulous opportunity, but she chose to marry my father, giving up the scholarship. Her life would have gone in a totally different direction, and she looks back now and blames my father for giving up this opportunity.

For some, a mother's domesticity created undue financial pressures for their husbands. Megan worried that her mother's desires for a higher standard of living left her father, who worked as a salesman of stationary products, feeling embattled and inadequate:

My mother was always dissatisfied that she didn't have more stuff. She wanted my father to be more ambitious, and he wasn't an ambitious man. As long as he was supporting the family, it didn't matter to him if it was a bigger house or a bigger car. But forty years of being married to a woman saying, "Why don't we have more money?"—I think that does something to your self-esteem.

Finally, many children believed they would have been better off with a work-committed mother, even if their parents appeared satisfied. Reversing the argument that stay-at-home mothers benefit their children, these young women and men felt their mother's single-minded devotion came with too many strings attached. Hannah rued the double-edged quality of her mother's unabated attention:

> She would become way too into her children's lives and spend way too much time paying attention to what we're doing, and it became really oppressive. If I made the mistake of telling her anything, it would be all over town, as if I just won some blue ribbon or something.

Connie agreed. Even though her father's jobs as a driver and supervisor at a trucking company kept her family afloat, having a mother without a paid job felt out of tune with the times. Her friends' employed mothers seemed to provide a better model as well as more financial support:

> A lot of the kids, their mothers had already gone to work. It felt odd to me that, "Well, what does your mother do? What do you mean she stays home? What does she do?" And we didn't have the money that my friends had, either.

As they considered the pressures facing their frustrated mothers and financially pressed fathers, the children of domestic mothers often concluded that the costs ultimately outweighed the benefits. Despite her mother's devotion and her father's success as a stockbroker, Lauren gradually decided her father had been "an absentee parent" and her mother found domesticity a dead-end street without a viable route to personal happiness:

> I liked having her around. But I would have liked her to have had more enjoyment from it or more of a career track. My brother and I would have been okay. As a kid, you don't realize your parent's unhappy. I thought she just wanted to be a mom and carpool, and it turns out, she didn't want to do that at all.

In the end, when mothers seemed unhappy at home or too involved in their children's lives, the cost of their "sacrifices" outweighed the presumed benefits.

SUPPORT AND SYMPATHY FOR WORK-COMMITTED MOTHERS

Having a work-committed mother evoked much less ambivalence than having a home-centered mother. Even though juggling jobs and families brought its own set of pressures, women and men largely agree that employed mothers provided a wealth of benefits, with four out of five reaching this conclusion.[9] Like those who wish their mothers had worked, these children often believe that their mothers were ill suited to a life of domesticity or that their fathers were unable—and, in some cases, unwilling—to provide a sufficient and steady income. Some are grateful their mothers' jobs provided a cushion against the insecurities and vagaries of a labor market that left many fathers without the stable jobs and generous incomes needed to support a family on one paycheck. Others are grateful their mothers' jobs provided support amid the uncertainties of parental breakups that left them without a father's financial contributions. Dolores lived in a close-knit Latino family, with her grandmother nearby to help out. When her father lost a series of jobs as a cab driver and then a travel agent, her mother's steady, full-time work as a seamstress kept the family from falling into poverty:

> In my early childhood, my dad was going on and off with jobs, so my mom was the core. It seemed totally natural. She didn't want to be home, and it kept the family stable.

Although Josh's father did well as a carpenter, his mother's additional paycheck from her steady job as an office manager made it possible for him to go to college:

> I had a lot of opportunities other people didn't have, just because my parents were willing to pay for my education. And that was because of the two of them.

Mothers' jobs were obviously critical when fathers made no contributions at all. Faced with the challenge of rearing a child on her own at eighteen, Samantha's mother got a GED, went to college, and landed a job in data processing. As the child of a single parent, Samantha felt cherished and inspired by her mother's devotion to providing them both with a better future:

She was working as long as I can remember. I remember her telling me she wanted something better for me. She wanted to be able to give me something better after everything we had been through. She lived her life for me. Always.

Without diminishing the financial significance, children found additional reasons beyond money to appreciate a mother's paid work. These children also concluded their mothers would have been dissatisfied and overly attentive had they *not* had another place to direct their energies. Rachel knew her mother needed another outlet for channeling her volatile temperament:

I've heard all that stuff about how children need a parent at home, but I don't think that having her stay home, particularly considering her temper, would have been anything other than counterproductive. Even though her sort of high-end administrative job is significantly below her talent and intelligence, it's better than the boredom and anger if she was at home.

Patricia reached a similar conclusion about her mother, who ran a successful business forecasting design trends:

I honestly don't think I could deal with my mother twenty-four hours a day. She'd be very smothering. Even with her job, she'd be like, "Oh, I don't have time to cook you brownies." I'm like, "Mom, I wouldn't eat them anyway." If I had to deal with someone like that all the time, I'd go crazy.

Despite the popular fear that employed mothers deprive their children of essential maternal attention, no one cited a mother's job as a cause of neglect. To the contrary, they were more likely to see working as an indication of a mother's love. Nancy did not believe her mother's nursing career had any costs for the family:

My mom would definitely be working, pay or no pay, because she just loves to work. But I didn't feel we were lacking in anything. Any extracurricular activity, she would be there. She was very supportive, very generous, just always there, and she still is, no matter how much of a devil me and my brother are.

Young women and men reared by work-committed mothers generally perceive clear benefits, which outweigh vague, hypothetical losses. Most are proud of their mother's work and appreciate how it allowed her, like fathers, to be a "good" parent. But this widespread support for working mothers does not tell the whole story, because children also focus on the *context* in which their mother's work unfolded. The central issue is not whether their mother held a job, but whether she received the support she needed at the workplace and at home.[10]

When mothers had good work opportunities and substantial help at home, their children harbored few "ifs" or "buts" about their situation. Watching her single mother move up the ladder at a large bank, Isabella took even more pride than her mother did in this accomplishment:

> I was always proud of my mother. I'm sure when she started out she never imagined she would become executive treasurer of a bank. She always says there's tons of them in the company, but I say to her, "Mom, you're one of them!"

Having a father who shared the domestic load also relieved a child's concern. Raised in a two-earner home in a working-class, African-American neighborhood, Serena took pride in knowing her parents were equal partners in most ways:

> She never felt overburdened because she was raising three kids and working at the same time. I think because my father was equally involved, it lessened the burden, so that made a big difference.

A mother's work also seemed unproblematic when at least one parent had a flexible work arrangement and a child had access to good child care. As a firefighter, Daniel's father was able—and eager—to do far more than just fill in at home:

> She wasn't home to take care of us all the time, but my father was always around for us. He's a firefighter and had a lot of free time. And if she'd been home and been miserable, that would have made me miserable. And I was always happy.

And Kristen enjoyed playing with friends and learning the alphabet in a preschool while her mother worked full-time as a secretary:

> I really enjoyed preschool. They taught me the ABC's. And I had a lot of friends. I got my social skills. So it was a good thing I went to day care. I think that you learn a lot of social skills that are important.

Of course, not everyone concurred with Daniel and Kristen. When mothers hit a dead end on the job or got little support at home, concern and appreciation coexisted. Children noticed when their mothers seemed unfairly burdened with domestic work or unfairly treated in their paid jobs. Chrystal's father worked intermittently at a series of ill-fated ventures, while her mother was "the one who's always worked full-time," holding a series of jobs at a public social service agency. Although her mother seemed resigned and even moderately satisfied being the family's mainstay, Chrystal resented her father for not doing his share:

> My father's financial contribution has always been sporadic. He's more of a hustler, where if there's an easier way to do something, he's gonna find it. My mother's been the breadwinner. So it's unfair that my father never did the cooking or cleaning or anything like that. It didn't seem to bother them, but I think it should have been more equal. It makes no sense having one person do everything.

Children also felt shortchanged when excessive and inflexible work demands fell on mothers or fathers. Justin understood that his parents, Chinese second-generation Americans who struggled to establish an economic toehold in their adopted nation, had little choice but to put in long hours running their family-owned restaurant, but he still wished his father had been able to work less and spend more time with him:

> I'm proud of both my parents. They worked really hard, and they're great people. But I was disappointed that I could not see my father more. I understood, but I know that if I have a kid, I don't want to work that many hours.

With a single parent, Michael greatly admired his mother's dedication to her job as a college administrator, but he also resented her treatment by an indifferent employer:

> Work was her whole world, but her circumstances were really terrible. She worked there for seventeen years, and instead of getting a promotion, she was forced into retirement.

Women and men paid attention to the supports and obstacles their employed mothers—and fathers—had faced. Were they bolstered by well-rewarded, flexible work, opportunities to advance, supportive partners, and good child care? Or were they, instead, left with dead-end jobs and the lion's share of caretaking? While children embraced the work ethic for their mothers no less than for their fathers, they cared about whether the nature and conditions of their parents' jobs made it easier or harder to reconcile paid work with the rest of life.[11]

As they look back on their parents' work strategies, young adult children have far more intricate and refined views than whether they were better off with a stay-at-home or working mother. Having a home-centered mother seems to have been the best option when she appeared satisfied and the family could count on a father's financial contributions; the wisdom of this strategy appears suspect when a mother seemed ill suited for domesticity or a father proved unable or unwilling to be a reliable breadwinner. While some endorse a mother's domesticity, others view this path as too costly.

Although children with work-committed mothers are more likely to conclude this was the best option, they also hold nuanced views. Far from feeling neglected or put in second place, most appreciate their mothers' efforts. Employed mothers' incomes contributed to their families' standard of living, sometimes shoring up a shaky financial base or preventing a fall into poverty and more often providing opportunities that would not have been available. Paid work also provided mothers, no less than fathers, with a crucial source of self-esteem and personal gratification.[12] Yet even though most take pride in having a work-committed mother, many also worry that their mothers—and fathers—felt pressured and overwhelmed trying to "do it all."

In the end, whether or not a mother held a paid job matters far less than whether or not mothers and fathers were satisfied with their lives and with the life they were able to provide for their children. Rather than pitting working and stay-at-home mothers against each other, children consider the *meaning* and *context* of their parents' work experiences. As Kayla explained about her upwardly mobile, dual-earning African-American parents, both of whom had flexible schedules as college teachers, "If they're happy, I'm happy."

Parents Together and Apart

As in the larger society, slightly more than a third of my interviewees were reared in a home with some form of lasting parental breakup. Yet their experiences do not bear out the presumption that children always—or even usually—prefer any kind of marriage to seeing parents separate. While a slight majority of those who lived in a single-parent home wish their biological parents had stayed together, almost half believe parental separation was the better course of action. More surprising, two-fifths of those whose parents stayed together feel their parents might have been better off apart.

STAYING TOGETHER, FOR BETTER AND WORSE

All things being equal, it is surely better to grow up with two parents who remain strongly committed to each other. Yet all things are rarely equal.[13] Marriages take many forms, and my informants care more about how their parents' relationships developed than whether they stuck it out. Children are grateful when their parents seemed satisfied and happy with each other, but for many others, troubled marriages took a toll on everyone.

What made the difference? Marriages embodying an ethic of equitable sharing, mutual respect, and strong commitment balanced with individual autonomy appeared successful and satisfying. Growing up in a middle-class, predominantly African-American suburb, Tasha watched her parents forge a committed partnership that still left room for her mother to build a successful career as a physical therapist and for her father to rise to the vice presidency of a small bank. Asked to describe her parents' marriage, she pointed to an absence of domination:

> [They've been] very happy [for] twenty-three years. They always seem to have a really open relationship. My father never tried to dominate. Neither did my mother. So they get along well with each other.

Angel's parents struggled to make ends meet in an inner-city Latino neighborhood, while Brandon enjoyed the affluence provided by a father who rose to be an Episcopal archdeacon and a mother who worked as a hospital administrator, but they both used the metaphor of sharing "fifty-fifty" to explain the secret of their parents' lasting relationship:

> They've been together over thirty years. Through thick and thin, they always find a way together because it was a fifty-fifty relationship. (Angel)

> They would argue at the dinner table, but over politics, not over anything personal. It's fifty-fifty. I think that's wonderful. (Brandon)

Children drew different conclusions, however, when they believed their parents' marriages were either unfairly unequal or skewed too far in the direction of either too much closeness or too much separation. Leila resented how her physician father relied on her mother, who worked full-time as a nurse, to perform almost all of the domestic tasks:

> Their relationship—having the wife have to do everything, like the household chores and all that stuff—I wouldn't want that.

Alicia and Dolores considered even deeper inequalities and parental estrangements. Alicia wondered how her mother managed to endure her father's obsessive gambling, while Dolores asked the same question about her mother's acceptance of her father's not-so-secret infidelity:

> Even though my dad gambles, she's not really a type to fight. But I wouldn't put up with that. (Alicia)

> My father had a "woman thing," to say it nicely. She put up with it. I could never be like that. You just have to be a certain person. I'm not that person. I tell my husband every day, "Never!" (Dolores)

These women vowed they would not repeat the same pattern, but they acknowledged the strength of their parents' bond and did not question their mother's decision to stay rather than leave. Yet others reached a different conclusion. These children came to harbor serious doubts about whether it was best for their parents to have stayed together.

In traditional marriages, children worried their parents had, paradoxically, been both too dependent on each other *and* too separate. Megan viewed her parents' unexamined decision to stay together—despite their ongoing battles over her mother's displeasure with the size of her father's paycheck— as a sign of unhealthy attachment:

> As a young kid, I guess I thought that they were happy together, but now I see they just don't like to be separated. They fight, but they spend all their time together. They're very tied to each other—not necessarily in a positive way. A kind of crazy symbiosis.

Ken reached a similar conclusion about his parents' decision to stay together, despite a brief separation triggered by his father's "extramarital goings-on." The chasm between his father's life as the owner of a small aluminum siding business and his mother's domestic duties created a divide that left his parents living in different worlds under the same roof:

> They had typical male-female differences—two separate lives— and didn't really communicate or have a lot in common. My mom didn't have a lot of interests outside of the home, and my father, because he had his own business, was very much a workaholic. So there were disadvantages on both sides. My dad felt very much tied down and couldn't do what he enjoyed because my mother would make him feel guilty, and my mother wasn't happy because she felt neglected and still does. So there were no winners in any of that situation.

Yet traditional marriages held no monopoly on parental estrangement. When problems arose in two-earner marriages, they were more likely to center on disagreements about whether and how to share. These marital struggles took a different form but were no less difficult to endure. When Michelle's father, a successful architect from a traditional Filipino family, opposed her mother's pursuit of an MBA and finance career, their clash of wills created bitter and protracted battles that left her feeling they would have been better off apart:

> My mom was a very independent person. My father was more traditional. It was a recipe for disaster. My parents really didn't get along, so I think they stayed together for the sake of my brother and me. They tried not to fight in front of us, but inevitably a fight would break out and there would be screaming and yelling. I would get scared; my brother would get scared. It kind of ruined their lives.

Unresolved marital mismatches—whether they arose in traditional or two-earner contexts—left children questioning the status quo as the best course of action. As they watched conflict escalate, many began to wonder if their parents had remained married for the wrong reasons. When Suzanne's father moved from the passive resistance of refusing to help at home to the active use of verbal and physical intimidation, she wanted her mother to assert more independence and control:

> My dad would continuously badger and sometimes hit my mom. That's something that I can't forgive in any way, shape, or form. She hasn't gotten treated fairly through the course of their marriage. I would have wished, or do wish, for my mom to have more control over the situation and over herself.

Watching his parents' stay in their rocky marriage, Ken believed his mother's reluctance to leave represented a fear of emotional and financial insecurity, rather than an affirmation of her own or her children's best interest:

> For my mother, it was security of having the money from my father. And maybe she had a low self-esteem and didn't know she would ever meet anyone else. I've always wondered, "Would it have been better for them to divorce?" There's been times that made me think divorce would have been the best option.

Patricia did more than wonder if her parents should part. Frustrated by her father's refusal to do his fair share despite her mother's demanding career and equally plentiful financial contributions, she openly counseled her mother to leave:

My mom works full-time and takes care of all the bills and cooks every night. My dad doesn't do anything. My dad is not a horrible person, but we've had a lot of problems. I get very angry. I've told her, "Divorce him."

When their parents' marital troubles seemed intractable, my informants are convinced they, too, might have been better off had their parents chosen a different path. Regardless of the family structure, staying together "for the sake of the kids" seems ill founded, at best, when parental estrangement and conflict create a tension-filled home. Jennifer believed her parents' decision to remain in an unhappy alliance, with both parents locked in narrow roles, had not served their children well:

> There were plenty of times that they should have gotten a divorce. I know that. My dad knows it. My mother knows it but denies it. They were staying together because they thought that my sister and I needed them to be together when actually it was doing us no good. Being together when you're not working out didn't benefit us in any way.

And even though Chrystal's mother worked steadily, her parents also remained stuck in rigid domestic patterns, with her father silently refusing to share the load and her mother exhausted but unwilling to ask for help. The unacknowledged turmoil beneath their outwardly stable union left Chrystal convinced that living in a two-parent home offered scant advantages:

> We were close to the traditional definition of a family, but we didn't act that way. I didn't feel we were the Cleavers. I felt we were most of the time a mess. So I think it was more stressful than if we'd been in a single-parent household.

Looking back over the course of their parents' marriages, children are more concerned with the quality of the bond their parents forged than whether or not their parents stayed together. When a lasting commitment nourished each parent's sense of self, children came to see the marriage as embodying shared and interdependent lives, allowing parents and children alike to thrive. But when unequal or rigid patterns undermined the partnership, children questioned the wisdom of staying together "no matter what."

While these conclusions may appear naive and speculative, a number of studies attest to their validity. Researchers, too, have found a crucial distinction between high- and low-conflict marriages. Although children in low-conflict marriages may not be better off when their parents part, those in high-conflict marriages do not benefit when their parents stay together. Examining the relationship between parents' marital quality and children's psychological well-being, Paul Amato and Alan Booth conclude that "if parents' marital quality is high and stable, youth benefit; if it is of consistently low quality or unstable in quality, youth are adversely affected."[14] Children agree with these findings, judging their family paths according to the quality of their parents' relationship and not their marital status.

THE AMBIGUITIES OF PARENTAL BREAKUPS

Like their peers who lived in homes with lasting marriages, the children of divorced and single parents do not question the advantages of being reared by two happily married parents. But they also understand the obvious: happy marriages do not break apart, and their own parents were not happily married. Viewing their parents' actions through a different, more ambivalent, lens, they do not compare their families to some hypothetical ideal. Instead, they weigh the gains and losses of single parenthood and parental separation against more realistic, if less than ideal, alternatives.

Of course, the children of single and divorced parents acknowledge the obvious costs of parental breakups. Those old enough to comprehend the news reacted with a mixture of anger, dismay, and self-blame. Even though Tiffany now understands her father had serious personal difficulties and eventually had to be hospitalized for emotional distress, at the age of six, when she learned her father was leaving, she held herself responsible:

> Being twenty-five and looking back, I understand, but being a child who wants her father, I felt that it was wrong, and I tried to get them back together. I figured since I didn't understand, it must be me.

Those too young to remember the breakup had a delayed but similarly strong response. Although Richard's parents divorced when he was two, his anger only emerged as he grew older and decided fate had given him a raw deal:

> I hated the fact that my mother left my father, and I remember feeling miserable for a while. All of a sudden, I was in touch with how I was so angry and bothered. It was just so unlucky, I felt.

Yet over time, many reached a different conclusion about the folly or wisdom of their parents' actions. What prompted a change of outlook? Their long-term assessment depended on how the breakup influenced their parents' ability—and willingness—to support and care for their families. When fathers had been uninvolved or, in some cases, were hardly present, their departure was barely missed, especially if children could count on mothers and others for support and care. Shauna gave little thought to the fact that she never knew her father, because her mother, a model of self-reliance, made her feel secure:

> I obviously knew that my biological father wasn't there, but my mom never gave me any type of thoughts that I needed a man to take care of me. She was able to do it on her own, and she wanted to make sure that her children would be able to, too.

Even though Phil's father left much later, as he approached his teens, it also seemed a minor shift. Since there had never been a strong bond, his father's departure seemed to confirm rather than change their distant and tenuous relationship:

> Ever since I was a little boy, I was raised, basically, in a one-parent household. Even when my parents were married, my father wasn't there. He never came out to play or teach me how to ride a bike or anything a father usually does, so I didn't feel like I'd lost anything when he left.

Others found change more apparent, but not necessarily more upsetting. When parents in traditional marriages felt alienated by ill-fitting roles or parents in dual-earner marriages were caught in an interminable struggle of wills, a separation could offer relief along with sadness. In contrast to those who watched as their parents continued to endure similar circumstances, these children saw intransigent and destructive struggles give way to a separate peace. Even though Erica faced the prospect of downsizing from her large home in an affluent, leafy suburb, she was glad to see the end of "acting out roles" that seemed inauthentic:

> I was relieved. I never really sensed that they belonged together, so it was kind of a moot point. They were sort of acting out the roles rather than being involved. So by the time they got divorced, it was perfectly natural to me.

In contrast to the quiet estrangement in what Erica described as her "white-suburban" home, Anita's more emotive Latino parents fought constantly. As her father's drinking increased along with his opposition to having an employed wife, she was glad to escape the constant battles over her mother's need and desire to work:

I always knew this is the right thing because mommy and daddy weren't happy, and the way they were together was scary to me. It was very sad, but I remember feeling a sense of relief that the tension, the stress, the fighting, the fear of what was going on with my parents was over.

Although the causes of the breakups differed, the long-run consequences framed everyone's views. Did mothers, especially domestic mothers, get back on their feet or not? Did fathers become more involved in their children's lives or less? If less, did the loss of a father's—or, in some cases, a mother's—involvement seem to increase a family's difficulties or reduce them? The aftermath ultimately shaped the child's view. When caretakers did poorly on their own, children suffered. When they did well, it greatly diminished the costs. In the wake of his parents' separation when he was eight, Alex drew inspiration from seeing his mother grow stronger and more self-reliant as she shifted from working as a part-time waitress to supporting her family as a writer:

> In retrospect, I was pretty happy seeing my mother on her own take care of our family. That always made me feel like she was strong, which made me feel good because she was able to do it. My mother is one of the stronger people I know, and I think part of that has to do with [the fact that] she went through something that was really difficult and was able to handle it.

Observing her parents move from a contentious two-earner marriage, both as naval officers, to a far more friendly joint-custody arrangement, Danisha agreed their decision to part had been the right one:

> You miss your parents being together, but some people are better off being friends. They have strong personalities, a clash of wills, so I think that I got the best of both of them. After they broke up, they had a good relationship with each other and with me. That's why I think I'm well adjusted.

LOOKING BEYOND MARITAL STATUS

Because neither lasting marriages nor parental breakups are static events, making a simple contrast between the two prevents us from seeing how apparently discrete decisions about whether to stay together or break up are just one part of a longer process. To the children who watched this process unfold, the direction of their family trajectories matters more than any one distinct choice. Seemingly similar choices could evoke different reactions depending on their aftermaths. While most lasting marriages sparked admiration, marriages that remained mired in conflict or disaffection called forth less sanguine responses. Those who experienced a parental breakup had similarly diverse reactions; some could find no silver lining, but most felt a mix of emotions.

Whether their parents stayed together or separated, children focused on *why* they made the decision and *what consequences* it held for all. Traditional *and* dual-earning marriages appeared worthwhile when they seemed beneficial to both parents, but each arrangement had a less worthy cast if either parent suffered appreciably. Too much dependency and too much separation can both seem problematic in breadwinner-homemaker marriages, while two-paycheck marriages can stalemate over struggles about "who should be doing what." In the case of single-parent homes, some children marked their parents' breakup as the beginning of a downward spiral for those left behind, but others saw it as a chance for their families to escape difficulties and pursue new, more uplifting possibilities. Making dichotomous distinctions between "intact" and "broken" homes cannot capture these subtle shadings or explain how children derive lessons for building their own lives.[15]

Families as Diverging Pathways

Children are the most important recipients of their parents' wisdom or folly, and parental decisions can reverberate in unpredictable ways. No matter how carefully considered, parental choices can and often do have unexpected consequences. My informants learned lessons their parents had not intended to convey. Any specific parental decision, whether it involved changing their work, marital, and child-rearing arrangements or staying the course, could evoke very different reactions. Seemingly similar actions took place in different contexts and held different consequences for both the parents and their children. While some described their families as having fairly fixed arrangements, many more experienced transitions—sometimes abrupt and sometimes gradual—from one family environment to another. From common starting points, families' divergent pathways confound our conventional stereotypes about the differences between "traditional" and "nontraditional" homes.

BREADWINNER-HOMEMAKER FAMILIES
WITH CONTRASTING FATES

Alex and Joel both describe homes that shared a consistently "traditional" form, but their families moved in quite different directions as they grew to adulthood.

> At twenty-seven, Alex looks back on what appears to be a remarkably stable childhood, especially compared to those of his friends. He grew up in a small Midwestern city, where his mother stayed home until he and his sister began school and then worked part-time as a volunteer school assistant and substitute teacher. In Alex's words, she "worked for fulfillment, not money." Although she occasionally spoke about how her youthful dream of joining the Foreign Service came to an end when, upon submitting her application, she was told "women need not apply," the satisfaction she found in marriage and motherhood seemed to offset this disappointment.
>
> If Alex's mother hit a glass ceiling long before he was born, his father enjoyed a trip up the corporate ladder. After law school, he joined a small company and gradually rose to a vice presidency. As the undisputed breadwinner, his father devoted long hours to the office, but this effort paid off when a flourishing career provided growing financial support for everyone. In the end, Alex believes "they both benefitted [from] clear roles," although he also wonders how each might have felt if his father's career had not been so successful. As he put it, "I've kind of wondered what they could have achieved if things had been different, and I'm sure mom has the same question."
>
> Now a young adult, Alex is single, working in a small investment firm, and applying to business school. Well past the age when his parents married and began building their life together, Alex has no regrets about his slower pace. Although he respects his parents' arrangement, he has little desire to replicate it. "That was my parents' decision about the distribution of tasks, but I don't expect to do the same." Instead, he "wants a more equal relationship than my parents." But given today's fast-paced, time-demanding workplace, he worries about having to make sacrifices, either at home or work, that his father never faced.

A set of increasingly rare economic and social circumstances insulated Alex's family from the changes taking place in other children's lives. His father met few roadblocks on an upwardly mobile career, with its attendant financial benefits, and his mother enjoyed—and rarely complained about—her more domestic path. In the context of a stable marriage, where both partners found contentment, this clear delineation of different tasks and responsibilities seemed to work, even though Alex does not wish it for himself.

Joel's parents also chose to divide home and work according to a traditional gender calculus, but he has a very different perspective on his family pathway.

Joel lived in a white, working-class suburb with the feel of a small town, where two-parent families and stay-at-home moms were the norm, even in what he knew to be changing times. Like Alex, he lived with his parents and two brothers, including a twin born six minutes after his arrival. On the surface, little change took place over the years. Joel's father had held the same job selling medical equipment for a small company for as long as he could remember. His mother took odd jobs from time to time, and occasionally expressed a wish to return to the teaching career she relinquished when the twins were born. When his younger brother arrived, however, she felt a responsibility to focus her attention full-time on her home and children. Even now, with Joel and his twin gone and his younger brother away at college, her daily routine of housecleaning and cooking has remained largely unchanged.

Joel had a stable childhood, but not a happy home. As the years passed, his parents remained committed to their respective roles, but they also became increasingly disheartened in their separate lives and distant as a couple. His mother rarely strayed far from home, while his father spent long hours at the office, yet neither seemed inspired by their pursuits. To the contrary, Joel gradually came to suspect his father's time at work, which hardly signified a love of his job, was actually a way to avoid being home. Even worse, his father had mounting concerns about layoffs that might leave him jobless and his family without "a roof over our heads." Meanwhile, Joel's mother remained dedicated to her home and children, but grew increasingly unhappy in her marriage and her domestic world.

To Joel's eyes, his parents were stuck "in a rut" that grew deeper and took a growing toll as time passed. As he put it, "they've grown into their routine and just accept daily life and let life go on as it always will, but I don't think they're happy." At twenty-two, Joel worries his parents will never escape the confines of their seemingly self-imposed roles. He feels distant from his father, who recently had to downshift when his company hit tough economic times and seems "defeated" in his career. His mother's disappointments have left him feeling vaguely "guilty" and even a bit "selfish."

Looking forward, Joel wonders how his parents will cope when his younger brother leaves home and no longer fills the spaces created by an estranged and unhappy partnership. As for his own future, Joel has no desire to re-create a similar pattern, saying "I don't think I'd model my life after my parents, because happiness is more important." But he worries about his chances of pursuing other options. As a good student with an artistic bent, he hopes to avoid the track of a "mainstream" job, which he now believes offers few intrinsic satisfactions and only illusory security. Concluding that his father was betrayed by an employer who did not deliver on the promise of lifetime loyalty, he plans to become a designer who can rely on skills no one can take away. When it comes to relationships, he is hopeful, but in no hurry. It will take time, he reasons, to find the right partner and build the more balanced, mutual give-and-take his parents were unable to create.

Joel's story shows how parents who try to avoid the risks of change may face even greater risks. Since even stable marriages face unexpected challenges, the effort to remain steadfastly committed to earlier patterns can bring its own unavoidable but unfortunate consequences. Joel believed his parents' marriage became entangled in patterns that ultimately did not work for either. Looking back, he wonders about the road not taken. Would his mother have been happier had she not felt so responsible at home? Would his father have been able to find a more satisfying job—and become a more involved parent as well—if he had not felt it was his duty to bring home the only paycheck? Would a separation, with all its difficulties, have offered both a chance to consider more satisfying ways of living—either together or apart? He'll never know the answers to these questions, but he believes such an unknown journey, whatever the outcome, would have been worth the effort because it represented an active choice rather than two lives lived by default.

Although Alex's and Joel's homes had similar—and apparently unchanging—forms, this resemblance is misleading. In fact, they followed dramatically different paths, with contrasting meanings and consequences. Alex believes his parents' early decisions about "separate roles" proved to be satisfying and efficacious; but Joel thinks his stay-at-home mother became demoralized at home, his breadwinning father became frustrated at work, and they both became estranged from each other. While Alex's home lived up its stable image, the apparent stability of Joel's family masked a downward track that left him feeling uneasy and disheartened. Yet despite his family's more satisfying trajectory, Alex agrees with Joel about his own aspirations. Both hope their lives will strike a more equal balance between home and work than their parents achieved.

DIVERGENT PATHS AFTER PARENTAL BREAKUPS

Nina and Mariela also reached different conclusions about a shared experience, but in their case, it involves a parental breakup, not a stable marriage.

A child of international ancestry, Nina's father, a Mexican-American, met her Japanese mother when he was stationed in Japan during his years as an Army officer. The details of their courtship are sketchy, but by the time Nina and her older sister were born, her mother had joined her father in the United States, where they married and settled down in a small apartment in a mid-sized Eastern city.

In those early years, Nina lived in a quiet, if overly strict, home reflecting her father's fondness for military discipline and, in her words, "an order of command with him at the top." While her father launched a budding career as an entrepreneur, her mother struggled to learn English and adjust to her adopted home. Though her mother remained uneasy about venturing into public places, she loved taking care of her children and tending to her home.

At seven, however, Nina's father abruptly disappeared, dissolving the predictable order of her early years and undoing her financial security. Over the years, she learned her father had left her mother for another woman, but her first memories are of her mother's distress and her family's descent into poverty. Nina's father refused to offer any economic support, and her mother, unsure of herself and with no work experience, shied away from seeking a paid job. Within months, they were evicted from Nina's childhood home and went on public assistance.

Over the years, matters barely improved. Nina's mother remained fearful of joining the workplace, and her occasional forays into the labor market never produced much. Though her mother never managed to get on her feet, her father moved across the country and "struck it rich," but refused to share his good fortune with the family he left behind. He had never been close to his daughters, and they lost all contact for many years.

Despite these difficulties, Nina could always count on her mother's devotion and kindness. Determined to make her mother proud, she excelled at school and made her way through college by working full-time and taking out loans. Today, she is on the management track at a large bank, where she hopes to qualify for a program that will finance her MBA. She lives with her long-time boyfriend, who, unlike her father, does all the cooking and is "amazingly nurturing." Determined to avoid the decisions that left her mother so unprepared, she insists on separate bank accounts and makes certain to pay all the bills. Her love and respect for her mother remains undiminished, but she has no desire to repeat her "mistakes." She has also rebuffed all of her father's recent attempts to get back in touch.

Mariela's parents also broke up, but she does not share Nina's concerns about a downward spiral in its aftermath. Instead, looking back, she sees their separation as a turning point that marked the beginning of changes offering relief in the short run and a happier and more supportive home in the long run.

Life did not begin auspiciously for Mariela. She spent her preschool years in a housing project in a poor Latino neighborhood, where she shared a small apartment with her parents and two older brothers. Her most vivid memories, however, are not of the economic privation or crowded conditions, but the escalating conflict between her parents and her mother's outbursts of rage, followed by absences for days and sometimes weeks at a time. As the years passed, the departures grew longer and the returns briefer and more rancorous.

By Mariela's sixth birthday, her mother's appearances had grown so infrequent and unpredictable that, for all practical purposes, she had dropped out of her daughter's life. Mariela later learned her mother had moved in with another man, but this detail hardly mattered at the time. What did matter was having her father to lean on. Always a devoted and gentle presence amid the cacophony of her mother's tirades, he assumed sole care of Mariela and her two older brothers long before her mother departed. With his earnings as a worker in a local box factory, he also supported their steady, if modest, standard of living.

A calm seemed to settle over Mariela's household after her mother left for good. She missed her mother, but was relieved to see her father relax. He became an even more dedicated parent, who rushed home every evening to cook the family meals and tuck her in at night. Her parents' breakup also set the stage for better things to come. Several years later, her father brought a "friend" home to meet the family, but Mariela sensed this woman was much more than that. When her father announced plans to marry, Mariela's first reaction was fear she would lose her treasured place as "daddy's little girl." But it did not take long for her doubts to fade. Mariela's stepmother took her shopping for clothes, helped with her homework, and generally became a warm and reassuring family member. She became, in Mariela's words, "my real mother."

Mariela's new mother continued to pursue a promising career at a large insurance firm. As she ascended the managerial ladder, her rising income changed the family's economic fortunes. They moved out of their small apartment and into a spacious house in a quiet neighborhood with backyards and tree-lined streets. In these expanded quarters, Mariela welcomed new twin brothers, an occasion which prompted her father to stay home for several years while her stepmother temporarily assumed the job of sole breadwinner.

More than a decade later, Mariela still draws on the support of a warm, bustling "blended" family. Her estranged mother contacts her from time to time, usually with expressions of regret, but Mariela prefers to keep a polite distance. Their occasional meetings only heighten her appreciation for the family she gained after her parents parted. Now enrolled in a community college program offering real-world experience in a variety of job settings, she is taking classes, working as an intern in a financial services company, and preparing to move on to a four-year college. After college, she hopes to work full-time for as long as it takes to establish a foothold in some not yet determined career, with marriage and children to follow only when she gains enough experience to feel confident about her economic prospects and her ability to choose the right partner. Mariela harbors few misgivings about her parents' breakup. The end of her parents' marriage not only brought relief to a household mired in conflict, but it also allowed her father to create a better life for himself and his children. In the aftermath of her parents' separation, her fortunes improved beyond all reasonable expectation.

The accounts of Nina and Mariela, like those of Alex and Eric, illustrate how children can draw very different lessons from apparently similar experiences. In this case, family breakups, not stable marriages, had different consequences and held different meanings. While Nina's home seemed stable, if rule-laden, before her father's departure, Mariela's was suffused with hostility. While Nina's father left without warning, Mariela was not surprised when her mother moved out for good. Most important, Nina's father left his family economically bereft, and her mother was ill prepared to step into this unexpected breach. Mariela's father, in contrast, continued to be a devoted caretaker and breadwinner and was also able to create a new marriage with far more emotional and economic stability. In short, Nina's family never recovered from her father's economic and emotional abandonment, while the departure of Mariela's mother set the stage for new—and better—possibilities.

DIFFERENT TRAJECTORIES FOR DUAL-EARNER HOMES

In contrast to Nina and Mariela, Justin and Serena were reared in homes with two parents who stayed married. Unlike Alex and Eric, they both had parents who shared responsibility for breadwinning. Yet Justin and Serena also had quite different reactions to ostensibly similar homes. Justin looked back on his parents' two-income arrangement with decided ambivalence, while Serena felt nothing but enthusiasm.

> With a name seemingly drawn from an Irish novel, Justin is Chinese-American. Many decades ago, his grandparents left Taiwan in search of better opportunities and settled in California, where his parents met and married. Although they lived in what Justin described as a "Chinese enclave," he and his brother attended public schools, played Little League, and "generally became American."
>
> As far back as Justin can remember, his parents focused on achieving "the American dream" of affluence. They bought, managed, and sold a series of small restaurants in search of this elusive goal. Justin did his homework in a restaurant kitchen or at a dining table until his mother shifted to doing the bookkeeping, which allowed her to stay home in the evenings. Justin's father, in contrast, always left the house early in the morning and usually returned long after his sons had gone to bed.
>
> Despite their dedication, his parents' efforts at work never seemed to pay off as they had hoped. Their restaurants wavered between "just getting by" and "failing," and the tensions of working so many hours just to make ends meet took their toll. Justin never worried about losing his home or not being able to go to college, but he did worry about the pressures on his mother, whose single-

handed efforts to carry the load at home left her weary and demoralized, and on his father, whose limited rewards for his long work days left him distant and moody. As Justin put it, "I was slightly upset that I could not see my father more—because I understood, but also because it depends on the mood he's in. And it got worse as work [went] downhill."

At twenty-eight, Justin is married and working at an investment bank, where his employers demand as many hours as any of his parents' restaurants. He hopes to make enough money to help his parents in retirement and then find a less time-intensive job, perhaps as a teacher, so he can be a different kind of husband and father. As he puts it, "I can't model my relationship on my parents. My mother wasn't very happy. There was a lot of strain on her, and so I'm trying to change that." But Justin worries that this hope of reducing his work effort may be just as fanciful as his parents' dream of financial plenty. "If I could, I would work a few days a week, and Caroline would work the other days, and we would share equally. I would be extremely happy, and she would be extremely happy, but the chances are a lot less than fifty percent. I'm talking about Godzilla coming to New York City . . . that kind of chance."

Justin's dual-earner home was marked by intractable difficulties, but Serena tells a different story, even though both her parents worked as steadily as Justin's. While the combination of boundless work pressures and mounting financial uncertainty left Justin's mother doing double duty, his father feeling defeated, and his parents distracted and disengaged, Serena's parents achieved a different balance in their lives and relationship. Her parents found enough success and flexibility at work and gave enough support to each other at home to build an emotionally supportive and economically secure household.

Serena grew up in a predominantly African-American neighborhood on the edge of suburbia, where most families managed to avoid poverty, but only by "just getting by." With both parents steadily employed, Serena and her siblings, an older sister and younger brother, never experienced the insecurity haunting many of her friends. Although she now understands that her family enjoyed a modest standard of living, her parents owned their home and planned for all the children to go to college. Compared to many of her friends, she felt economically privileged, even upper-class.

Serena's parents shared the work of earning a living and running the household, seemingly with little rancor and generous amounts of goodwill. Her mother worked as an administrator in a large social service agency, and Serena took pride in her mother's rise from the secretarial ranks to a position of influence. Her father never went to college, but his unionized job driving a truck brought secure employment, a decent wage with good benefits, and enough flexibility to shepherd his children between school, dance lessons, and soccer practices. While neither parent commanded a huge income, their joint earnings enabled Serena and her siblings to attend a nearby parochial school and to aim for some distant colleges largely out of reach to her friends.

At twenty-six, Serena is now a college graduate juggling work as a counselor in the corrections department of a large city with graduate classes in psychology. Although she never doubted her parents' devotion to their children or each other, she looks back on her childhood with even more appreciation. Even though her mother's work meant she couldn't always be around, Serena never gave it much thought and certainly does not question the wisdom of this choice. She knows her mother's work ethic gave her a rich life beyond motherhood and, like her father's work commitment, provided critical contributions to the family's well-being. She also values the time her father took to care for his children and feather their shared family nest. As she surveys the difficulties facing so many of her childhood friends, she is grateful for the support she took for granted. Her parents' commitment to their children, their jobs, and each other provides an example of what she hopes to create in the years ahead. She declares that "I actually use my parents as a model for my relationships."

Serena sees nothing to criticize in her parents' arrangement. Far from feeling shortchanged, she takes pride in her mother's work accomplishments and the opportunities two incomes made possible. In the context of her mother's full-time work, her father's flexible job, egalitarian spirit, and enthusiasm for involvement in his children's lives allowed everyone to avoid the pitfalls and enjoy the advantages of a dual-earner home.

While Serena believes her parents were able to build a sharing partnership that nurtured a close relationship with each other and their three children, Justin wishes he had had more time with his parents and there had been less conflict between them. Unable to rely on jobs with steady incomes and clear time boundaries, his parents both seemed overburdened, albeit in different ways. His father spent too much time and energy chasing elusive monetary riches, while his mother strained under the weight of juggling her job and caring for two sons. Justin's parents lacked the flexibility that enabled Serena's two-worker arrangement to thrive.

Family Paths, Gender Boundaries, and Work-Family Strategies

These narratives show how families can take divergent pathways even when they appear to share a similar form. Although static concepts such as "homemaker-breadwinner," "dual-earner," and "single-parent" tend to dominate the debate about family and gender change, children can have different experiences and different responses to growing up in families with apparently similar "structures." Over time, similar "types" of households can follow different paths, and children reared in different types of homes can share a similar outlook on how well or poorly their families fared. Children take account of the context in which family relationships unfold, and the lessons they ultimately draw from their experiences depend on the longer-term consequences of their parents' and others' choices. In the long run, children view their families as pathways, not as static types.

Family paths can, and usually do, head in unexpected directions. Alex and Serena both had families that followed stable trajectories offering consistent support, even though Alex lived in a traditional home and Serena's had a more equal division of breadwinning and caretaking. Most young people, however, now grow up in families that undergo significant change and take unpredictable turns. Among my interviewees, change could be gradual or abrupt, and it could involve the erosion of support or its expansion. Eric perceived increasing difficulty, even though his parents' traditional arrangement seemed stable, while Justin had the same reaction to his parents' two-income household. The sudden and unexpected breakup of Nina's parents triggered a downward shift from which her home was never able to recover. Yet similar events marked a more positive turning point for Mariela, whose home life seemed to improve steadily after her parents parted.

Rather than focusing on their family's form, the young adults who shared their lives with me care about whether and how their homes either came to provide stability and support or, alternatively, failed to do so. As Figure 2.2 shows, about a third recounted consistently stable and supportive homes, while a quarter described families who grew more supportive as

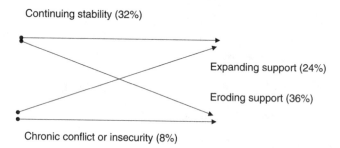

FIGURE 2.2 Perception of family pathways.

time passed. Taken together, slightly more than half believe their homes remained or became generally harmonious, supportive, and secure over time.

For slightly less than half, however, family life did not remain stable or improve. Just under one in ten had a home where chronic problems, such as high parental conflict, low parental morale, or abiding economic insecurity, never seemed to subside, while another third felt their family support eroding as they grew. These family paths either remained riven with difficulty or moved in this direction. In the long run, what matters is whether a child experienced high or increasing support or, in contrast, enduring or rising troubles.

These diverse experiences also show how the direction of a family path is not clearly linked to a family's type. As Figure 2.3 shows, those reared in homes that became "traditional" are almost equally divided about whether this arrangement helped to expand or erode their security. Children in homes that ultimately depended on a single parent are also divided in their outlooks. About 56 percent recounted an eroding family path, but the remaining 44 percent recalled how domestic life got better after a parental breakup. Most children raised in homes that remained or became dual-earner agree that this arrangement offered stable or rising support, but close to a quarter do not. Across all of these family types, children focused on whether or not their families provided emotional and economic support, mutually respectful relationships, and caring bonds.

If family form provides such limited clues about how children view their family experiences, what does? Across different family forms, the *work-family strategies* of parents (and other caretakers) are central to shaping the direction of their family pathway.[16] Most families faced unanticipated events that undermined rigidly divided ways of organizing breadwinning and caretaking. *Gender flexibility* gave all types of families a wider array of options and

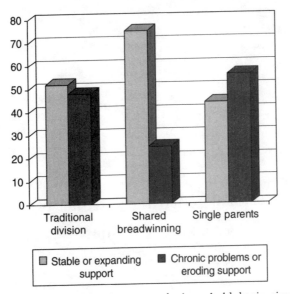

FIGURE 2.3 Perceptions of family support, by household destination.

resources to respond to these challenges. The ability and willingness to cross and blur the boundaries between earning a living and caring for others provides the key to understanding why some homes became more supportive and others less so.

As we will see, parental strategies for apportioning domestic and paid work shaped the paths families took. When parents and other caretakers transgressed gender boundaries, they were able to develop innovative ways to support their children. When parents clung to strictly drawn distinctions between women's and men's capacities and responsibilities, they were less able to respond to men's eroding place as the family's main breadwinner and women's declining ability and desire to be home-centered caretakers.

CHAPTER THREE | The Rising Fortunes of
Flexible Families

E VEN WHEN FAMILY LIFE gets off to a bumpy start, as it did for many of
my interviewees, it can take a turn for the better. For about two-fifths,
family life began with serious difficulties, ranging from economic distress to
severe parental depression and conflict. But among this group, two-thirds
(or a quarter of all those interviewed) believe their homes ultimately became
supportive and secure. Dwayne's family hit "rock bottom" when his father
left and the household descended into poverty:

Whether it was two parents or one, I just thought life was a struggle.
We were at rock bottom, so it could only get better.

Early domestic difficulties can take many forms, from a clearly unhappy
parent to pervasive marital discord to severe economic uncertainty to neglect,
abandonment, and mistreatment. Among those with improving family fortunes, most experienced some combination of these domestic woes early on.
By the time they reached adulthood, however, all of these young people had
a far more optimistic outlook. When Dwayne was twenty-four, his family
seemed "on top of the world, maybe with little minor setbacks, but still on
top of the world," and Josh (whose experiences were introduced earlier) saw
his household shift from one saturated with parental hostility and estrangement to a close-knit, supportive home:

[Things got] happier, simple as that. It got better as it went along.
Now it's very, very good. It's good that the good part came last.

Why did these children develop more positive outlooks on their family's support system and their own life chances? By developing more flexible ways of working and providing care, custodial parents, whether married or single, overcame a variety of domestic crises and created more economically stable and emotionally supportive homes.

Domestic Impasses

Like Tolstoy's unhappy families who are all unhappy in different ways, the homes of those with severe family difficulties in their early years varied in composition, class position, and the problems they faced. A fifth had single mothers, but the rest lived with two parents. Close to 55 percent had an employed mother, but the remaining 45 percent started out with mothers who did not hold a steady job. Almost two-thirds lived in working-class homes, many of which faced severe economic insecurity and skirted the edge of poverty, but more than a third had access to middle-class economic and social resources.

Some families faced breadwinning crises as fathers found themselves unable or unwilling to provide needed economic support. Others faced caretaking conundrums as mothers became unhappy at home and unsuited to full-time motherhood. Still others coped with a conflict-saturated home or an uncaring parent who could be distant, neglectful, even abusive. All these domestic difficulties involved some kind of impasse that undermined the ability of fathers to be "good providers" or nurturers and home-centered mothers to provide needed financial and emotional support.

NOT-SO-GOOD PROVIDERS

Although being a "good provider" remains central to cultural definitions of what it means to be a responsible, successful father, it has become increasingly difficult to live up to its tenets.[1] When a father could not or would not comply, families who relied solely or primarily on a male earner were pushed into difficult waters. Growing up in Texas, Miranda found her father's enduring employment woes painful to watch, especially because his liabilities as an entrepreneur stood in contrast to his devotion as a parent. Despite his love of his family, his failed efforts to build a business and his refusal to give up on "impossible dreams" left her and her mother coping with what seemed like impending calamity:

> My dad was one of those followers of dreams—he wanted to have his own business, didn't want to be anyone's employee—but things did

not turn out the way he expected. He is totally lovable, but he was a mess financially. Things would look okay and then all of a sudden my mother would find out we were seven months behind on the mortgage. It felt like every time you made a step forward, you end up getting hit with something else. The most obvious thing was the economic instability, but it created so much instability in the family 'cause we were so busy just trying to survive each day.

A father's resistance to acknowledging his limitations or to sharing the responsibility for providing income compounded these economic woes. Anita sensed her mother's frustration with a husband who was unable to work steadily but nevertheless opposed her desire to take a job:

He was a very stubborn man, very macho and controlling, so he objected to my mother going to work. [He said] there's no way she's going to emasculate him. But with the drinking and just his lack of responsibility, he was jumping around from job to job. So she finally had to put her foot down and got a waitressing job.

If having a father at home provided little guarantee of economic security, having a father who departed the household left children far more vulnerable. In these cases, a parental breakup precipitated an acute financial crisis. When Donna was still a preschooler, her father's abrupt departure left her mother with no job and three children to support:

My father was into hanging out, and my mother was home with three kids. He put my mother down for everything. One day he brought her to a lawyer's office and said "I want a divorce." And he was gone just like that [snaps fingers]. We had to go on welfare for, like, two years.

Louise was too young when her father left to remember his presence, but years later she learned that her family's early precarious finances stemmed from his refusal to provide child support:

My mother used to say, "I wish I could, but I can't get you what you want." I found out later that child support was awarded and never received.

Still others faced a different set of problems. When a father's occupational success demanded too much time, economic security and material affluence came with a price. As a lawyer for a major corporation, Paul's father rose quickly up the ranks and supported his family in style, but his long days at the office left Paul feeling he had a parent who was "missing in action":

The biggest problem was Dad working all the time. The work really was a big drain on his time. Typically, he wouldn't get home until nine o'clock or later, and then he'd be out the door before we were up to go to school.

Some families could not rely on a father's job to keep them financially afloat, while others had problems when his work demanded too much. Too much reliance on a father's paycheck created vulnerabilities for everyone.

NOT-SO-HAPPY HOMEMAKERS

Like fathers who found it hard to live up to the "good provider" standard, some of my interviewees had mothers who were unhappy at home and frustrated by the pressures of "intensive mothering."[2] Even when fathers were capable providers, mothers could languish under the responsibilities of domestic work, especially if they felt isolated at home and lacked access to an independent income. Though they sought fulfillment in domesticity, they found limited pleasure and even less security in full-time parenting. When Ken's mother had an obvious emotional breakdown around his sixth birthday, he concluded that staying home left her feeling personally insecure and clinically depressed:

> When she was at home raising the children, going through the nervous breakdown, those were very hard years. My mother didn't know what she wanted to do with her life; she didn't have a chance to develop her own interests. My dad had tons to talk about, and my mom didn't have anything, so she wasn't happy.

Children also worried when a stay-at-home mother lacked the personal autonomy an independent income could provide. Connie felt her mother was "stuck at home," but was even more concerned about her mother's reluctance to take a stand against a distant, uncaring husband. As Connie watched this helplessness grow, she began to feel a mixture of sympathy and anger:

> My father was just something that sat in the corner and once in a while got angry at us, but [my mom] was dependent. I don't know if it was him or just the money, but she didn't stand up for herself as much as I think she should. As I got older, I started realizing, "There's all these strong women out there, so why are you taking this?" I was very angry at her for not being independent enough to leave.

In extreme cases, a mother's dissatisfaction could produce neglect and abandonment. By the time Tamika was six, years of maternal disregard left her feeling disregarded and unloved:

The worst was definitely when my mother was living here. She was neglecting me. She'd hang out all day, all night. She never hit me, but she'd just be mean!

For Mariela, her mother's lack of concern took the form of unmet promises followed by increasingly frequent and lengthening disappearances:

She would dress me really nice to go out, but by the time I got to the door, she was gone. She would storm out of the house. I would be really disappointed.

For these children, mothers appeared to languish, and sometimes break, under expectations they could not meet. The pressures to be a devoted caretaker seemed to backfire on their mothers, leaving their children to feel cast off rather than cared for.

ESTRANGED AND OVERBURDENED DUAL EARNERS

Parental discontent is not the exclusive province of breadwinning fathers and home-centered mothers. When parents in two-earner families could not reconcile the demands of paid jobs with the needs of the household, the stresses of work-family conflict also took a toll. Ray's parents fought openly over his father's resistance to helping out, which in turn drove him further away from the family fold:

When I was younger, they argued constantly, and when [my father] was angry, he'd go upstairs. We knew he was our father, 'cause he was there, but we distanced ourselves—like not having conversations and, if he came downstairs, we would go upstairs.

Children reared in these circumstances concluded their parents were mismatched in basic, potentially irresolvable ways. Steve grew up in a small Southern town, where social norms discouraged the explicit expression of anger or conflict. Despite the veneer of civility between his mother, a high school math teacher, and his father, an insurance salesman, he recalled his early years in a home where marital discontent was evident:

I don't think they were happy together. I never really knew what my father was thinking or doing, but things were always more tense when he came home.

Considering her parents' separate lives, which included sleeping in different bedrooms, Erica echoed this feeling:

I could tell they weren't getting along. It wasn't that they were fighting all the time, but you could feel the tension. I don't have any memory of doing something with both of them together and really feeling comfortable.

Dual-earner families are not immune from crises, even if they take a different form than those in more traditional households. Family troubles can take many shapes, but these troubles shared a common ingredient. From fathers who buckled under the pressures of the good provider ethic to mothers who could not meet the demands of intensive mothering to dual-earner couples caught in a web of work-family conflicts and marital mismatches, an impasse between parents left children facing surging difficulties, including parental conflict and strained marital bonds, low parental morale, economic uncertainty, and, for some, neglect and desertion. While households varied in the types of problems they faced, all of them strained under the weight of increasingly unworkable expectations about who should be responsible for providing income and who for providing care.

Becoming a More Flexible Family

These diverse family difficulties framed my informants' views on their early childhood. For those with an improving pathway, early problems established a baseline for assessing future turning points when homes became more secure and supportive. Though not always obvious at the outset, paths of family change could range from subtle transformations within marriages to obvious and often tumultuous events like breakups or remarriages. These events could create concern and fear, but the ultimate destinations made the journey seem worthwhile.

RESOLVING MARITAL STALEMATES

While few modern marriages remain sheltered from some kind of crisis, improving family paths highlight how events inside and outside the home can prompt parents to find new ways of sharing. Dissatisfied stay-at-home mothers went to work, while employed mothers demanded and received more support from their partners at home. Distant fathers became more involved, while employed wives provided unhappy fathers with the economic support they needed to improve their employment prospects. Whatever the trigger, these changes reverberated throughout the household, setting the family on a course to a more flexible marriage and a happier home.

For some traditional marriages, the key to change involved a mother's decision to take a job, especially if she felt discontented at home. Faced with a spiraling loss of confidence, Ken's mother resolved to escape her mounting feeling of confinement by launching a business career. This more independent life not only boosted her morale, but also helped both parents shift to a more balanced and closer relationship:

> Now that she found a job, she's happy. She has her own friends from work. She's become more of an individual with her own interests. They're both more independent, and they have more to talk about. So they're both happier now. It seems like they've grown up. It brought a lot more love into the family. And that makes me happy, so I have a better attitude, too.

Josh found that his mother's return to work—even in the modest position of office manager—gave her the courage to seek profound changes at home. Fed up with her husband's reliance on drugs and alcohol, which left him surly and uninvolved, she relied on her new income, and the self-assurance it gave her, to demand he leave and not come back unless he could be a better partner and father:

> My parents fought almost constantly. That's all I was used to. Then my mom got a job. They separated about eight, nine, ten months. Even though I was upset, I thought it was for the best. That's when [my dad] got into some kind of program and got clean, and my mom took him back.

While some watched their mothers become more self-confident and empowered by moving into the world of work, others saw a dual-earner partnership become more equitable. As a young girl, Dolores was concerned her father "didn't have one stable thing." Not only did he move from job to job, leaving her mother to act as the family's economic mainstay, but he also "liked to spend money" and "hang out with other women." As matters worsened, Dolores's mother (much like Josh's) confronted her father with a choice to change or leave:

> At one point, for my mother, it was, "This is it. You get it together or get out." They went through a change, both my father and my mother. He got stable. They got more happy together. And he got a job as a porter, and he's been happy there for years.

Through a variety of routes, a dual-earner arrangement produced a more collaborative partnership where husbands thrived along with wives.

Employed wives did more than make demands; they also enabled fathers to seek new options if their work circumstances deteriorated. When Chris's father became frustrated with a dead-end, alienating job, his mother's higher earnings as an intensive care nurse made a critical difference. This financial cushion, along with her willingness to be the primary breadwinner, allowed his father to shift to a more satisfying career when he fell on hard times:

> Between seventh and eighth grade, my dad had a business which didn't work and then worked as a printer for six months. It was a dead-end thing, and he came home frustrated, so my mom got him to go to school as an X-ray technologist. It was hard financially, but it was a good time because he was actually enjoying what he was doing. He really flourished.

Aware that his mother's career made his father's mobility possible, Chris sensed no drawbacks to living in a home where his mother brought in the bigger paycheck:

> My mother's salary is about two times more, but it was not a big deal. A lot of people say, "Wow, your mom is the breadwinner, and that's strange." It's not. She never says, "This is my money. I can do with it what I want." It's a very joint thing.

In the best circumstances, fathers became more engaged caretakers, just as mothers became more committed earners. Chris saw a change for the better when his father found work he loved:

> He was prone to coming home grumpy as a printer, because it's a monotonous job of just sitting there with the machine, but when he started going to school, he loved coming home and talking about working with patients. He's still tired, but he's not grumpy.

Despite early difficulties, all these families reached turning points where parents created more cohesive and gratifying ways of sharing. The key to this positive change rested with the ability of parents—whether they began with a traditional or a dual-earning arrangement—to resolve interpersonal and financial crises by creating more flexible, egalitarian partnerships.

RESILIENT SINGLE PARENTS

Though many children watched their parents resolve marital impasses by developing more collaborative ways of sharing paid and domestic work, a parental breakup provided others with a second chance. Like those whose parents found ways to resolve their marital impasses, a parental breakup set a similar process in motion for these children. Amid the undeniable losses, these separations created the time and space for a custodial parent to resolve domestic standoffs. When single mothers became successful breadwinners and single fathers became involved caretakers, they provided children with greater emotional and, in some cases, financial support than would have been possible if their parents had stayed together. These single parents, like their married counterparts, responded to unexpected crises by transgressing gender boundaries in search of more flexible ways to support and care for their children.

Work-Committed Single Mothers

Conventional wisdom sees becoming a single mother as the beginning of an inexorable downward slide for their children, yet many of my informants disagreed. For them, family life became more—not less—secure when a mother strengthened her ties to paid work and separated from a partner who provided neither money nor love. Some of these mothers took jobs that enabled them to leave a marriage mired in conflict and financial uncertainty. Others joined the workplace and became capable breadwinners after a spouse abandoned the household and left them to fend for themselves. Despite the odds, these changes ultimately brought children more security and support.

Miranda's father refused to let her mother take a job, even though a series of ill-conceived business efforts left him unable to support anyone. After years of economic uncertainty, her mother ended this standoff—and her own extended hiatus from work—when she took a sales job in a clothing store. Miranda rejoiced, even though she knew her father disapproved:

> We were getting to the edge and didn't see where the next dollar was coming from. So one day we went to the mall, and [my mom] was hired in two minutes when they saw the experience she had. I was so excited about her going back to work, but my dad wasn't happy. I think it was a blow to his pride—like we can't trust you anymore. I remember him telling me, "I'm sure you're glad that she's back at work." He was definitely *not* glad, and he knew I trusted her more than him.

When Connie's mother took a job after years of depending on a husband who routinely came home hostile and inebriated, her defiance of his wishes and newfound independence transformed the marriage. Despite her father's opposition, this decision relieved the family's financial strains, enabled her mother to stand up to a distant, controlling husband, and gave Connie a renewed optimism:

The biggest change was when my mother went back to work when I was about ten. She started part-time but eventually went full-time. We were always financially in trouble, so that tension eased, and that's also around the time she stopped buying him beer and making separate dinners for him. I think the job led to independence, because she felt worth something again, by herself, away from her family. Once she got that sense of independence, the tension between my mother and father got worse, but the results weren't bad. I wish she had done it sooner.

When the marriage seemed oppressive, a mother's growing financial independence led children to accept—and even hope for—more fundamental changes. As Connie's father's angry outbursts and domineering style continued unabated, she felt relieved to see her mother gaining the strength to protect herself and her children:

The tension with my dad never eased, and my mom had gotten so sick, we took her to the emergency room with multiple bleeding ulcers. That was her real turning point. It was building inside of her to leave, 'cause she'd got herself a job and started to realize she had her own money. So once she saw that, what was she was waiting for?

Observing a similar situation, Anita also celebrated her mother's decision to leave:

[My dad] was the manager of this bar, but his drinking and lack of responsibility got in the way, and we fell on hard times. They separated when I was seven for six months and then we moved back for another year. But that was it. She just knew that this wasn't going to work, and from what she tells me, he didn't really fight her when she finally decided to leave. He was probably relieved because the responsibility wasn't as immediate anymore.

In all of these cases, children interpreted their single mother's growing work commitment as a clear indication of their caring, not their neglect. Even when the job seemed modest, it could make a crucial difference. Samantha's mother was able to pull the family out of poverty by putting herself through school and getting a job:

My mom went on public assistance, but she got her GED when I was about four or five, and she was working by the time I was seven. It was clerical work, but we had better clothes and better food. A lot of things changed. I got to go to the circus and stuff like that. I remember her telling me she wanted to be able to give me something better after everything we had been through. She always said she lived her life for me. Always.

The benefits were even greater when, often against substantial odds, a single mother broke out of a female labor ghetto of low-wage work and moved ahead. Far from sapping attention from their children, such accomplishments enhanced a single mother's ability to care for and inspire her children. Recall the case of Isabella, who took pride in her mother's unexpected accomplishments and felt no loss of love or attention:

> I don't know what position she started as, but she was promoted and now she's an executive treasurer at the bank. I'm so proud of my mother.

And these reactions are not confined to women. Considering his mother's move from "a classic housewife" to a "practicing architect and loving it," Todd felt the same way:

> What she's achieved, where she's gotten in fourteen years is amazing. And she is very caring and always there. So I hope she feels successful. Because it's really good for her to be feeling her self-worth.

Whether single mothers achieved unexpected heights or simply managed to summon the strength and determination to do it all, facing—and overcoming—these daunting challenges inspired their children and provided lessons for their own lives. Paul perceived personal benefits from watching his mother learn to stand up for herself:

> She's a lot more self-assured now that she's on her own and not having to rely on somebody. She's doing well, which is good for her self-confidence and good for me.

And so did Steve, who also watched his mother's self-confidence grow when she separated from his unfaithful father:

> Getting away from my father really helped my mother. If my parents had stayed married, she might not have continued working. This way, she was able to do things and began to be able to talk to him and say, "This is ridiculous." She stood up to him.

This process reverberated in unexpected directions. Rather than losing attention, children often gained a more responsible, involved caretaker. After Connie's mother discovered pleasure and self-esteem in her newfound autonomy, her rising morale nourished Connie as well:

My mother became a much happier person. And because she was better, I was better. I had a weight taken off of me. I think we all would
have been better off if she left sooner, but the fact she's done it at all is
something. I'm very proud of her. She's come a real long way.

Whether these mothers launched promising careers or secured more modest but still steady work, their persistence and dedication provided inspiration
for both daughters and sons. Even though Anita's mother never graduated
from college or rose higher than an administrative assistant at a local college,
her efforts to combine work with raising her children offered Anita a blueprint for how she too could navigate life's obstacles:

> To have supported a family, raised her children, gotten a college degree
> all by herself—I think she's amazing. She doesn't want to be a model
> because she feels she's underachieving, but she's a model because she
> did this all by herself. I have an incredible amount of respect. She's
> proud of the way we turned out, and I hope she's proud of having done
> what she did.

Shauna drew the same lesson from her mother's work commitment, even
though a string of secretarial jobs did not seem to do justice to her mother's
talents:

> My mom's just such a smart woman, and she went to night school to
> get her Associate's college degree. Even though she never verbalized
> it, I knew she wanted more for herself. I sometimes wonder what she
> would have accomplished if she didn't have me at such an early age,
> but she didn't shun her responsibility.

All of these children saw their mothers' efforts as the strongest kind of
love, which opened doors for them that would have remained closed. Antonio
appreciated how his mother's banking career placed a good education within
his reach and gave him a vision of a better future:

> My mom's first priority was family, but you couldn't take care of the
> family if you weren't working. She seen that we were poor, and she
> wanted to be mother and father, and she has [been]. She even paid for
> private school. I read somewhere about upward social mobility. That's
> exactly how I explain it. She branched off to do this, and now she's
> teaching me.

Whether these single mothers found a job that helped them escape an
unworkable marriage or they adjusted to a partner's desertion by building a

career of their own, they all enlarged their children's support by enlarging the boundaries of their own lives. In these cases, a mother's pursuit of personal autonomy did not conflict with her "selfless" dedication to the family. To the contrary, as Miranda noted, these equally worthy goals seemed inseparable:

> My mother has always been very selfless and fully responsible for me financially. She has completely and entirely dedicated herself to me in the true sense.

Involved Single Fathers

While parental breakups mostly produce custodial single mothers, an increasing share of parents are single fathers. The percentage of single-parent homes headed by a father, while still low, is one of the "fastest growing demographic groups."[3] It may not be typical for a mother to leave, but when this happens, it can prompt a father to become more involved and, in the process, create a more stable home. Indeed, when mothers are not present, single and custodial fathers, as well as gay couples, routinely nurture and care for their children in all the ways we associate with mothering.[4] Mariela and Tamika felt hurt and abandoned when their mothers moved out, but they did not wish for a different outcome. Since their mothers' frustration and anger pervaded their early childhood, tensions eased and home life improved in myriad ways after they left. Mariela compared the incessant hostility prior to her mother's departure to the calm, affectionate atmosphere following it:

> My father was like, "This can't keep on; the kids can't be in this environment. If you want, you can stay with them." But she didn't want to, so he stayed with us. It made things a lot better. If they [had] stayed together, it would have been the biggest dysfunctional family because she was looking for an argument all the time.

For Tamika, a similar sense of relief eventually followed the initial shock and pain:

> One day I came home, and my mom wrote with lipstick on a mirror that she was leaving. I could read the whole thing. I was miserable at the way she left, but I was happy that she did leave. It was calmer. My dad wasn't stressed, had nobody nagging at him. The way that she did it was bad, but it's better that she left.

When Erica's parents divorced, she felt estranged from her mother, even though she was readily available. Resisting the pressure to make the "socially appropriate" choice, Erica took the opportunity to live with her father, who made her feel more cherished even though he had not been her primary caretaker:

> Initially they had decided that it was best that my sister and I stay with my mother, but I wanted to live with my father. I wanted to surround myself with people I felt comfortable with and that I felt really cared about me. What was important was getting the attention that I needed, not the right clothes or whatever.

Fathers who became involved, attentive caretakers provided a key to surviving—and thriving—when children became disaffected from their mothers. Erica's decision to live with her father sparked a "turning point" that led him to reassess his priorities, reduce his preoccupation with work, and focus on being both "mother" and "father" for his two growing daughters:

> The divorce was really a turning point. Before, [my father] had been traveling so much that we were not that close. After, he became much more involved. There were a lot of bigger issues going on than work. The responsibility was truly on his shoulders. So it made my father closer. He played both roles, if there is such a thing as a role.

A mother's departure, however difficult, could have a silver lining by opening the space and providing the spark for fathers to develop parenting skills and share activities they never imagined they could or would enjoy. Tamika's father became a careful, concerned parent who learned the intricacies of cooking, cleaning, and hair braiding after her mother left the household:

> Me and my father were closer. We used to go everywhere. He learned how to do all the things he had to do, like making dinner and getting my hair done. He paid my tuition by himself. My dad was more of a mother than my mom, so I feel lucky.

As custodial fathers eased the impact of other losses, all of these children renewed their optimism about the possibility of creating spiritually closer family ties. In the aftermath of a breakup, these once divided families became happier and more cohesive, even—as Erica explained—if others viewed their homes as less than "ideal":

> Living with my dad, my sister, and me, we really established a strong relationship for having gone through this. It didn't matter that there wasn't a mother figure. It felt better, stronger. So this was my idea of what a family should be—that they can really talk to each other, get along under any circumstances, no matter how small the apartment.

Mariela agreed:

> It was hard, because my father would struggle. But I had a lot of fun.
> I felt loved. My father did everything, and me and my brothers got
> really close. We all got closer.

Still Parents, If Not Partners

Parental breakups, like parental efforts to transform their marriages, have
continuing, but unknown consequences. In the short run, they usually evoke
fear and resistance. A happy ending is never guaranteed. But a breakup does
not always initiate or continue a downward drift. Some breakups bring more
than just a sense of relief.[5] They also create contexts where children can experience tangible gains. In these instances, children believe one or both parents
acted courageously to give them a better life.

Those who view a parental breakup as a change for the better also experienced a shift to more expansive forms of caretaking and breadwinning. Mothers became more work-centered and self-sufficient, while fathers became more
dedicated and family-centered. By embracing more flexible parenting strategies, these single parents provided relief from marital impasses and intractable
domestic conflict. Without discounting the unavoidable difficulties and losses
a separation brings, these children also perceive significant gains. Far from
believing parents should always stay together for the sake of the children, they
think it was better to face the inevitable than to postpone or deny it. Aware
that, in Miranda's words, "it was just the lesser of two evils," they feel fortunate to have not endured the greater one. Despite the undeniable pain of her
mother's departure, in Tamika's eyes, it spared her far worse consequences:

> I think they would have broken up eventually anyway. I probably
> would have hated my mother even more. 'Cause then I would have
> had to live with her. I was better off without my mother being here,
> being more miserable.

And Isabella reached the same conclusion about her father:

> It wouldn't have worked, and [my father's] existence has proven
> that. He's really irresponsible. He can't handle having a job; he can't
> handle having a wife and children; he can't handle anything. So my
> mom wouldn't have been happy at all with someone like that. And
> I wouldn't have either.

Since parental breakups only occur when one or both partners are no longer prepared to work through their difficulties, we tend to equate separation

with conflict and recrimination. Yet, by changing this context, separation can also provide an opportunity for parents to face and resolve their conflicts in a more collaborative way. Some separations initiated such beneficial changes. Relieved to know her parents were happier apart than they had been together, Danisha felt lucky to remain close to both:

> My parents really tried to make me feel comfortable. It wasn't an easy thing but it wasn't screaming and crying, either. Sometimes you know that your personalities just won't make a compatible union anymore. Some people are better off being friends, so their relationship got better. And I saw my dad so often, he didn't disappoint me.

These new partnerships helped parents become more engaged caretakers. Sharing custody seemed to spark more involvement from both of Todd's parents:

> It improved it quite a lot with both of them. [There was] more attention from both sides because now both parents are fighting for our attention.

When a breakup eased conflict and sparked sharing, children felt closer to both parents than they had when everyone lived together warily under the same roof. These children noticed—and appreciated—the irony that physical separation had allowed more emotional closeness.[6] Grateful her parents had relieved her of the responsibility to "save" their marriage, Erica was able to focus on the bonds she had with each:

> Their emphasis was on us, so we wouldn't feel like it was our fault. And it shouldn't change individually how we feel about each other. I really got to know my father, and my mother as well. It did not affect my school; it did not affect my grades. It made us all closer.

By undermining the strict division between women's "mothering" and men's "fathering," beneficial breakups created both the need and the opportunity to transgress gender boundaries.[7] When single parents were able to take on responsibilities they once deemed out of bounds, they were in a better position to meet their children's needs. In the best of circumstances, separated parents also developed a respectful postmarriage relationship that fostered a sharing of work and care.

REMARRIAGES, NEW AND IMPROVED

Parental separations can do more than provide relief from domestic conflict and malaise. They also create an opportunity for custodial parents to forge new, more satisfying partnerships. In fact, more than 40 percent of all marriages are remarriages, and about one-third of remarriages involve children. About 17 percent of U.S. children live in stepfamilies (and in such families, stepfathers outnumber stepmothers five to one). When a remarriage brings a nurturing, committed caretaker, a stepparent can feel, as Mariela declared, like a "new parent." Several years after Mariela's mother left, her father's new marriage gave her a sense that having a family could mean sharing rather than fighting:

> After about a year and a half, Sonia and my dad got married. Things were a lot better than when I was with my mother. This was so different. This is like, what's hers is everybody's, what's his is everybody's. Instant family! I was so lucky to have her. She *is* my mom.

Remarriages do not guarantee domestic improvements, and many do not create them. The quality of remarriages and blended families, like the quality of first marriages, varies greatly.[8] Yet despite the common concern that most stepparents are not good parents, studies show that in about 25 percent of cases where an adolescent lives with a stepfather, children have a close relationship with both their stepfather and their father, while another 35 percent have a closer relationship with their stepfather.[9] Shauna exemplifies this process. Born to a single mother, she experienced a dramatic change at five, when her mother married. Although she worried that her new stepfather would drain away her mother's time and attention, his evident warmth and excitement melted her skepticism. When her mother explained that he wanted to be her "real father," she realized she was not losing a mother but gaining another committed caretaker:

> At first, I was feeling it was a bad change because I wanted my mom to myself. Then my mom said, "Why don't you call him daddy?" The next thing I was just saying "Daddy!" He picked me up, and I remember the look on his face and his laughing and saying "She called me daddy!" I was so happy, like it's good now. After that, he's always been my dad, and there's never been any question about it.

These new partnerships appeared to work because they were collaborative, flexible, and egalitarian. Shauna believed her parents' commitment to sharing the load at home and work was the key to their success:

> Money was always an issue, but making sure that the family was taken care of was their number one priority. The way my dad did that was to work and be home, and the same thing for my mother. Both of them did everything. My dad would get home before my mom, so

he would cook the dinner and clean. My dad spoiled me for any other man because this is the model I had.

Mariela agreed:

They take turns, and they share. She works and does everything, and so does he. We're all grateful. Of course, they have a little problem here and there, but they seem so happy compared with my mother.

By adding a new parent who contributed emotional, practical, and financial support that had once seemed elusive, a successful remarriage—whether it brought a new father or mother—marked a turn for the better.

Stepparents as Earners and Nurturers

Stepmothers and stepfathers could become both trusted caretakers and crucial financial contributors. Tamika's new "mother," who worked as a supervisor at the post office, provided both parental guidance and much appreciated economic resources:

My little sister and I have a stepmother who's better than my own mother. My first boyfriend, my first whatever—we talk about everything. And financially, it made a big difference. I went to a private school, and we're about to move into our house, and that's 'cause of my stepmother.

After watching his single mother struggle, Phil rejoiced about finally having a father to confide in and to share his mother's financial load:

When Charles came into the picture, it was like a godsend. My dad never paid child support, so he became a breadwinner. And when I had a problem, I could go to him. Charles was more of a father than my father ever was.

When remarriages brought stepparents who, as Mariela said, did "everything," these newly constructed families also provided children with reassuring images of family life. In contrast to the parental stalemates preceding them, these new partnerships offered lessons in how to build a satisfying relationship. When Erica's father brought home his soon-to-be new wife, she found it gratifying to finally see him giving and receiving affection:

With her there, I got to see my father really happy. It was a big chance for me. Finally, he's smiling! He was holding her hand, and that was just unheard of with my mom.

Collaborative remarriages also offered children new models about how to love and work. Donna drew life lessons by watching her stepfather persevere at work:

My stepfather worked two jobs and never complained about it. When he wanted something, he did it. That's how I am—very determined. He taught [me] not to give up. You do what you gotta do, and you'll survive. He is a hero to me.

After watching her mother's mistreatment by men, Samantha gained renewed hope about the prospects of finding a worthy partner by observing her stepfather's kindness:

He's very loving to my mom. I learned a lot from him about how men are supposed to be with a woman and with his children.

Even though gaining a "new" parent was not always a smooth process, in these cases, it ultimately enlarged a child's emotional and practical support, expanded their notion of kinship, and provided a more uplifting vision of what a family could be.[10] These remarriages show how the "case for marriage," to use Maggie Gallagher's and Linda Waite's phrase, really depends on which marriage. Like families, we need to look beyond the fact of a remarriage to its quality. For children who benefited from remarriages, the breakup of an unhappy, destructive relationship provided an opportunity for parents to create a new, more cooperative and cohesive one.[11]

IT TAKES A VILLAGE

While some argue it takes a marriage—and only a marriage—to raise a child, many children are certain it helped to have a village as well.[12] Support from real and fictive kin expanded their material and emotional resources. In the short run, care networks provided a safety net amid rough times. In the longer run, they offered sustained contributions of time and money. At moments of crises in the relationships or economic fortunes of parents, these additional breadwinners and caretakers became not only critical, but visible.

Additional Earners and Caretakers

Though American culture extols the self-sufficient nuclear family, children often relied on both financial and caretaking contributions from extended kin and friends. Like remarriages that brought earning and nurturing stepparents, these extended networks enlarged a child's practical and emotional support, especially when parents could not make ends meet on their own.

Relying on others could mean the difference between falling into poverty and retaining a comfortable standard of living.[13] When Ray's father was laid off, his grandparents bolstered his mother's modest earnings, kept the household afloat, and allowed his brother and him to remain in parochial school:

> We knew there was something wrong 'cause I remember being taken out of class, but that was only for a couple of hours. With the grandparents, when you have one deficiency, somebody always stepped in and provided for the other.

Extended kin were especially important when single-parent homes experienced economic crises.[14] When they stepped in, a crisis could even become an opportunity. Like the 8 percent of U.S. children who live in a household containing a grandparent, Antonio relied on his co-residing grandparents as much as his single mother.[15] In his eyes, they were a team who worked together to make certain he got what he needed:

> My mom and grandparents were the type of people that even if we didn't have money, we was gonna get it. Their ideal is, "I want to give you all the things that I couldn't have when I was young." My grandparents and my mother thought like that, so no matter how much in poverty we were living, I was getting everything I wanted. They've raised me right, so I can't be a screw-up.

Children also relied on the caretaking of extended kin. For some, relatives filled the gap when parents went to work. Although Dolores lived with both parents, her grandparents were equally involved:

> My mom was there for us when she got home, and [being with] my grandmother was just like time with my mom. Whatever my mom didn't give me, she was gonna give me, and I knew that (laugh).

Still others counted on a wider group. When Anita returned to the old neighborhood after her mother separated from her father, she gained a close-knit web of relatives:

> We moved four blocks away from my grandparents and my aunt, and they were all very involved. My grandmother passed away not too long after, but my grandfather was always there, and we were a very tight unit. The six of us were all very connected.

Children from middle-class homes also relied on other caretakers, although they were more likely to be paid workers.[16] When these arrangements fostered close, reciprocal relationships, they were as important as the support of kin.[17] Even before Todd's parents broke up, he cherished his babysitter's presence:

> We were really lucky to have Margie, someone who took care of us and instilled good morals. She definitely was a member of the family. And the good thing about it is that in the last several years, when Margie couldn't really work, my mom took care of her.

Whether children relied on grandparents, other relatives, or fictive kin and paid caretakers, these financial and care networks helped parents meet their own obligations, provided added support for children, and softened the impact of unforeseen crises.[18]

Standing in for Parents

By providing sustained emotional and material sustenance, a child's care network could augment and even stand in for parents. Daily support from his grandparents made them seem like "real parents" to Steve long before his mother and father parted:

> Even before my parents broke up, I spent every weekend with my mother's parents, and every day, we would go over to my grandparents' house after school. They would drive me to school every morning, and my grandfather would sometimes bring my lunch to school. In a lot of ways, they were more like parents.

Nonparental caretakers made a crucial difference during temporary crises and longer periods alike. Ray's track coach took over and got him through when his father became lost in a haze of beer and wine:

> During that time my father was drinking, my track coach took us out and kept us busy. He was kind of a father figure. He was only seven years older, but he really helped when I needed something important. So in my life, when someone dropped out, somebody else always stepped in.

When Isabella's father stopped visiting her after years of becoming increasingly distant, she looked to her grandfather, on whom she had already come to count on for love and attention:

> It's not like I didn't have a father, because my grandfather was always there. He was always there to take me to my after-school clubs and pick me up and then take me wherever I needed to go. I was still sheltered—he had to take me to the library, wait till I finished all my

work, take me home. I call him dad. Nobody could do better. I never missed out on having a father.

Stan, too, was filled with appreciation for his grandparents, who provided more unconditional love and support than either his father, who never gave him much attention, or his mother, who was always around but seemed less concerned about his happiness than her own:

> They were just always so good. When I would go on a trip, my mother was like, "I want you to bring me this, this, this," but my grandparents would say "Just enjoy yourself!" They wanted me to be happy and live for myself.

The support of these parental figures helped children cope with the short-term crises and prolonged difficulties besetting their households. Rather than feeling deprived of a "normal" home, they felt fortunate to receive care and attention from people who loved them genuinely and generously. Since contemporary nuclear families increasingly experience unpredictable (and unavoidable) economic and caretaking squeezes, they are not—and cannot be—self-sufficient entities. When all goes well for families, the wider supports on which they depend may be invisible; but when families encounter economic, practical, and interpersonal difficulties, the crucial contributions from those who dwell just outside this small circle become more apparent. The children who experienced improving family pathways treasured the help given by real and fictive extended kin. It made little difference if care came from grandparents, other relatives, or paid helpers. What mattered is that these "villages" cushioned the blows of unexpected change, provided children with a sense of stability in uncertain times, and helped families overcome the crises parents could not resolve on their own.[19]

GENDER FLEXIBILITY AND FAMILY SUPPORT

Families with rising fortunes were able to overcome domestic difficulties by transgressing gender boundaries and developing more flexible strategies for supporting and caring for children. Some children watched their parents create a more collaborative marriage when a mother went to work and a father became more involved in child rearing. Others saw a single mother get on her feet economically or a single father take on caretaking duties in the wake of a parental breakup. Some also gained more plentiful financial and psychological support when a custodial parent remarried. Finally, many children enjoyed expanded support when others joined in the caretaking and breadwinning work of family life.

All these strategies helped families create more economically secure and emotionally cohesive homes. They nourished parental morale, increased a home's financial security, and provided inspiring models of adult resilience. While children acknowledged the difficulties accompanying tumultuous family changes, they valued the opportunity these changes provided to develop more flexible and effective family strategies.

All's Well That Ends Well

When families moved from difficult beginnings to reasonably happy, if not perfect, endings, children concluded "all's well that end's well." Looking back, Eric is convinced his parents' separation ultimately led to a better destination:

> Some might argue, but I'm pretty happy with the way things turned out. I'm a firm believer it doesn't matter how the road is. We've gotten there, and we have good relationships, and everyone is decently happy. I truly believe they did the best they could, and I have no one to blame for my own mistakes.

Samantha reached the same conclusion about her single mother's journey toward a successful career and happy marriage:

> [My mom] was able to come from so low and bring herself up high. Even though we went through everything, she was able to pick herself up, move on, and just make sure I had everything that I needed. We had our thick and thin moments, but we managed to get through 'em, and now it's just great. I guess you could say we triumphed.

Yet childhoods that took a turn for the better are, by definition, marked by periods of substantial difficulty. As children weigh their improving fortunes against the struggles they endured, the journey to a better destination offered valued lessons along the way.

THE ROAD NOT TAKEN

Improving family paths leave children to ponder how stressful experiences can nevertheless lead to a far better destination than "what might have been." Without denying the losses, Miranda harbored no doubts about her family's transformation from a debt-ridden two-parent home to a more stable existence with her single mother. As she explained, when the ideal is not an option, people must search for the most responsible choice among the remaining alternatives:

> In the end, though I would have liked for things to work for my dad, of all the options that were out there, this is definitely the best way it could have worked out. The things that we can do now, the freedom and independence we enjoyed—it's such a contrast to that time when the future looked so unpredictable. You have that weight off your shoulders, so this is that much sweeter.

Mariela agreed. Rather than dwelling on her mother's absence, she was grateful that her father and stepmother were there to protect her from what could have been a far worse fate:

> Considering the way it turned out, I'm happy. It could have been a lot worse. I saw how a lot of the girls I went to school with ended up pregnant or with guys who hurt them. They probably didn't have parents like mine. They probably had parents like my [biological] mother. And it just made me feel so good because I didn't end up like that.

Even though Josh's parents managed to create a more loving partnership, he also believed it would have been far worse to live amid "constant fighting" than to see them part:

> It always seemed like a war on each other. So if things hadn't gotten better, I would have wanted them to be divorced. Even though I knew initially it would have been painful, it would have been best. Divorce definitely is better than some marriages, [where] two people living together can be detrimental to the children. My parents didn't stay together for the kids. They stayed together for themselves.

Surveying the sweep of childhood, all these young women and men took pride in knowing their families found ways to overcome, however tumultuous the trip. This knowledge softened the memories of hard times and left them feeling fortunate.

HIDDEN LESSONS

Rising family fortunes also offered hidden benefits. The experience of prevailing over difficulty, these children reasoned, offered lessons not available when families traveled smoother paths. Looking back on his parents' efforts to weave an egalitarian balance at home and at work, Chris was inspired by their ability to tackle conflicts he knew he would face:

It made me realize that there's a certain dynamic between work and a family and it can be done. It's not an impossible thing. And to hear things like, "Both parents working isn't going to be successful, the kids are gonna get shortchanged or something," I really can't see that. If there's love, and that love is apparent, it's just something that can be felt. It's not about the time, the gifts, things like that. Love can only come through a certain way.

Keisha was inspired by watching her mother journey from single motherhood and public assistance to a good job and a committed marriage. Her mother's early "mistakes" provided a cautionary tale about what to avoid in her own life, while her mother's determination to prevail gave Keisha hope that she could also overcome life's unforeseen difficulties as well:

My mom's independence and her pushing, her succeeding has pushed me to want to achieve my goals. She's my hero. Looking at it now, I know I don't have to make the same mistakes because I've seen it with my own eyes, I've lived it, I know what it's like. Knowing that no matter how low you are, you can bring yourself up. And you can say that you've been through it, so it's not just an abstract thing.

In addition to providing lessons about how to cope with a rapidly changing age, these "happy endings" make the struggles seem worthwhile. Josh believed his family's path helped him become stronger, more grateful, and better prepared to face adulthood:

I wouldn't change it. Just to undergo such things at a younger age, I think I'm more appreciative, more aware of things, more emotionally tougher. I definitely appreciate the life I have now 'cause I knew how it was to not have those things.

A MATTER OF LUCK?

As children compared their improving circumstances with others less fortunate, "luck" appeared to play a large role. Despite his family's struggles, Paul felt "lucky" to receive so much support and avoid the troubles befalling others:

I really had a sort of tragedy-free childhood, so it's interesting to meet people who had horrible stuff happen to them. It just taught me how lucky I was. If the worst thing that happened was my parents' divorce, that wasn't even that bad, so it really kind of made me appreciate things a lot more.

Todd concurred:

I was just so lucky in so many ways. I've had so many great people around me, so I think I have less faults. And I think it's because they were all so wonderful in so many different ways. My cheering crowd is big.

Whether they benefited from a transformed marriage, a resilient single parent, a more collaborative remarriage, or an expanded care network, most felt luck had spared them from a bleaker fate. Yet rising family fortunes did not depend on luck, but rather on how new social conditions allowed parents and other caretakers to reorganize their households in more flexible ways. By blurring the boundaries between breadwinning and caretaking, mothers could seek an economic base at work, fathers could become more involved in caring for their children, and partners could establish more independent lives and more sharing, equitable relationships.

The option to reconsider the terms of a deteriorating marriage gave some parents an exit strategy and others the courage to ask for and receive needed changes. The option for women to seek committed work outside the home allowed mothers to provide a more secure economic base and allowed fathers to pursue new work options when earlier ones dead-ended. The option to create new marriages, with more respectful and sharing partnerships, allowed children to gain more stable and cohesive reconstructed families. The option to rely on a wider network of real and fictive kin allowed vulnerable children and overburdened parents to call on a safety net in good times and in times of sustained stress. In all these ways, new options for women *and* men to organize earning and caring gave families second and even third chances to develop new, more flexible ways of meeting their needs.

New opportunities to cross gender boundaries and develop more flexible patterns of breadwinning and caretaking help families meet the inevitable but unpredictable challenges of contemporary life. Yet improving family paths are always hard-won, and these reasonably happy endings are never guaranteed. Families often lack the social and personal resources to develop flexible responses, and many homes are ill equipped to acknowledge, much less overcome, the obstacles they face.

| Domestic Deadlocks and
Declining Fortunes

Though many experienced improving family fortunes, even more saw their family fortunes decline. Most of my interviewees—about 68 percent—recalled an early family life full of promise, but for about half of this group, childhood sooner or later took a significant turn for the worse. Across the full range of family forms and domestic circumstances, including once seemingly idyllic homes, these families faced challenges that cascaded into domestic deadlocks and declining fortunes. Some changes in family fortunes were subtle and difficult for a child to discern, while others were impossible to ignore. Isaiah could easily contrast his "first" home, where he lived comfortably with both parents in a growing African-American suburb, to his "second" home, where he lived on the edge of poverty with a single mother:

> The first, you could say, was ideal. It was a good arrangement. And the second wasn't. So I was pretty angry. [My father] continued to make the effort, but I didn't want to deal with him [because] he's the one who decided to leave. My trust was betrayed.

For others, stability itself slowly but inexorably became a problem. Growing up in a traditional home, Rosa only gradually realized her family had fractured despite its outward appearance. From the vantage of her early twenties, Rosa clearly saw the growing distance among the once close-knit members of her large Latino household:

> I would say, when I was eight or nine, it was an ideal family. Now, it's not even close to ideal. We're not close. We don't communicate with

each other. We have no trust with each other anymore. We argue. We didn't realize it, but we're all broken up.

Whether family change involved dramatic events, such as a marital breakup or job loss, or more gradual troubles brought on by parental estrangement and disappointment, the pace of change mattered less than the losses it entailed. As Isaiah put it, "it's probably harder to have the ideal and lose it than never to have it at all."

Why did these young women and men conclude that their family life took a turn for the worse? How did their situations differ from those who received stable or growing support? Families from both groups faced similar challenges, from parental separations to stressed two-parent homes. All families face hardship sooner or later, and a mother's decision to take a job, a father's growing involvement at home, and even a parental breakup can trigger beneficial adjustments. But when families were unable to adapt to such unforeseen difficulties as divorce, employment insecurity, or parental malaise by crafting new, more flexible strategies for earning and caring, their fortunes declined and their children's support eroded.

Off to a Good Start

Children need both economic security and attentive, reliable caretakers, but they can receive these supports in a range of ways. Among the slightly more than two-thirds who started off with stable and secure early family experiences, more than half were born into a traditional family with clear gender divisions between breadwinning and caretaking, while about a third had dual-earning parents, and the rest lived with single parents.

Barbara, Hank, and Rosa have different ethnic and class backgrounds, but all had early homes anchored by parents who seemed happy in their separate spheres. Barbara was raised by white, working-class parents in the country, where:

> The stability lasted up until I was eight. We were a very picturesque family. Nice house, and we lived in the country, and it was just picture-perfect. And everyone got along in their roles, the way they were supposed to.

Hank lived with his parents and sister in a newly forming predominantly white, middle-class suburban tract:

It was the suburban house with the yard. We moved in there when I was three. It was great for a kid—trees and the whole Ozzie and Harriet routine. We didn't need malls. Not at that age.

And Rosa lived in a modest apartment with her parents and siblings in an inner-city Latino neighborhood:

Me and my sisters and father and mother, we used to have great fun. We used to spend lots of time together and go out all the time as a whole family.

All three lived in stable, warm, and very traditional homes, but less traditional families could prompt similar reactions. Children in dual-earner homes, where parents blurred the gender boundaries between working and parenting, also shared a sense of promising beginnings. Growing up in an upper-middle-class suburb, William relished the idea of living in a home where his mother, a bank vice president, and his father, an engineer, shared the work of earning a living and caring for the children:

If anything, my dad did more than my mom. He always did the cooking. They sort of split the cleaning, and there were four of us kids, so they managed to get us to do a little bit of work. It seemed great! I was very conscious of women's lib and stuff like that, so I thought it was great that I lived in this backwards family.

Recalling her mother's job as an office manager for the Board of Education and her father's work on the night shift as a bus driver, Jasmine valued her parents' commitment to sharing domestic duties and providing economic security by combining the resources from two modest but secure occupations:

It seemed like I had everything I wanted. My mom worked at a good paying job and was doing great. My dad worked at night, so he was around when I'd get home from school. He cooked and everything, 'cause he went to culinary school, so he liked to cook. I just thought of it as the way it was supposed to be, and I still think that's the way it should be.

Being born into a single-parent home might evoke less enthusiasm, yet many of these children originally felt cared for and financially secure. Even though he lived in the suburbs, where two parents were the norm, Richard looked back fondly on early life with his single mother. With his neighbors' acceptance, he "never had a problem saying my parents are divorced. I never got nasty looks or got treated like an outsider." He noticed the difference but did not feel stigmatized or deprived:

From the beginning, it was just me and my mom. My mother was everything—the provider and a super-involved mother. Everyone else on the block had the mom and the dad, so I realized that there was a definite difference, but the relationship I had with my mother, I felt like I was the luckiest guy in the world. My mother is so great, nothing could beat that, and I didn't want anything else.

An extended network of relatives and friends helped offset the drawbacks of single parenthood and even offered some advantages. For Richard, regular visits with his father and a close relationship with his mother's boyfriend created a web of support:

My father was always up for weekends, plus Neil was like a substitute dad. He took the place of a father, even though they weren't married. He always had time for me, and it seemed like he always had me in mind. As far as I was concerned, this was normal. I really didn't feel like I was missing out on anything.

For Lucius, living in a large house with his grandparents, aunts, uncles, and cousins more than compensated for his father's absence:

Most people have a nuclear family, but I lived in an extended family. Your grandparents are around, your uncles, your cousins. The only disadvantage was being in the situation where I wasn't raised with my father. But I think, on the whole, there was more of an advantage—a bigger support group, having a lot of people around.

All kinds of families—from two-parent homes with one or two earners to single-parent homes embedded in an extended network—were able to provide a wealth of supports. Despite outward differences, these families contained attentive, financially secure, and seemingly satisfied caretakers. Children looked back on homes they deemed both "normal" and happy. Yet this early stability did not last. Gabriel's "perfect" suburban family proved to be an illusion:

I thought we were very lucky, that we had a great family. We had a house in a decent neighborhood; I always knew I could go to either parent; we did a lot of stuff together. I was too young to really appreciate it, but I felt happy and satisfied. I had no idea what was going on behind the scenes.

Nina found it was easier to ignore the problems lurking in her parents' relationship all along:

Would I say there was a lot of love? Probably not, but I never paid attention to it. It was just like that was your mom and dad, and they were always there.

Just as many types of events can mark a turning point when a problem-plagued family begins to chart a more hopeful course, a range of unexpected challenges—from a deepening marital stalemate to a destructive breakup to a shrinking care network—can knock a family off a once promising path.

Taking a Turn for the Worse

Almost half of those with promising family beginnings enjoyed stable support throughout childhood, but the rest lived in families that took a turn for the worse. While it might be tempting to focus solely on how a parental breakup or a mother's job can precipitate a downward turn, children in all kinds of families reached this conclusion, including those whose parents stayed together and those with mothers who stayed home.[1] Neither an enduring marriage nor a domestically centered mother could insulate a child from a downward drifting path. Just as some lasting marriages brought beneficial changes, others deteriorated. Just as some mothers found gratification in domesticity, others became demoralized and depressed. Just as a parental breakup could bring better conditions for some children, it worsened life for others. And even though shared breadwinning created more collaborative and financially secure homes for most, it brought more conflict and exhaustion to others.

In the long run, a family's response to the challenges it faced matters more than its particular form. When a parent's morale languished in a traditional marriage or unresolved work-family conflicts deepened in a dual-earning partnership, family life suffered. When a father abandoned a mother who could not cope, single-parent homes followed a similar path. And when vulnerable families lost economic and practical contributions from extended and fictive kin, children also lost much-needed emotional and practical resources. In short, children in all types of families lost support if their household could not resolve the crises it faced.

DEEPENING MARITAL STALEMATES

Lasting marriages could not shelter children if parents could not overcome the difficulties they encountered. Some saw parents become disheartened and estranged when mothers withdrew from work to focus on domestic duties. For others, their parents' inability to solve the dilemmas and stresses of combining breadwinning and caretaking took a similar toll. In both situations, a couple's failure to find satisfying work and caretaking strategies reverberated in children's lives.

Reluctantly Opting for Separate Spheres

Those reared by a home-centered mother and a breadwinning father are divided in their outlooks. If both parents were satisfied with their separate spheres, children support the arrangement. But if mothers or fathers seemed dissatisfied or regretful, children noticed. When parents conveyed ambivalence or doubt about moving toward 1950s-style traditionalism, their children focused on how cultural pressures or social obstacles led their parents to make unfulfilling choices, even if they did so with the best of intentions.

Some stay-at-home mothers made fateful decisions long before their children's birth. Internalizing the injunction to place marriage and family before work and career could exact heavy costs in the longer run. Hannah grew up hearing her mother tell stories about lost opportunities and roads not taken:

> She always told the story [of how] she gave up a scholarship to marry my father, which would have made her life go in a totally different direction. She looks back now and blames him, but she felt she had to stay home [even though] she preferred working and being out in the world.

As Lauren's mother grew increasingly frustrated by limited work options, she also became haunted by an early decision not to pursue a career in publishing:

> When she graduated from college, her first job was in the publishing industry, but then she met my father and got married and that was the end of it. She liked having kids, but when she was older, she resented it more—she wanted something more than the secretarial jobs.

Others had mothers who developed a satisfying career and then relinquished it when child-rearing pressures mounted.[2] At the age of six, Sarah watched her mother struggle with an unplanned pregnancy and, faced with the arrival of another child, give up a teaching career. While Sarah's mother acted on a strong conviction that this decision would benefit her children, she also could not hide her disappointment and resentment. Despite the best motives, her conception of responsible mothering backfired, since Sarah came to see her mother's choice as a dismaying turning point:

> When my sister was born, that was a tumultuous event. [My mom's] job had started up, career-wise, so she wasn't too happy. It wasn't so intense that she would have terminated the pregnancy, but she felt she had to be home. Eventually she went back part-time, but never really worked full-time again. She lost her place, and it never was the same.

She always had a lot of conflicts about work and home and opted to be really committed to family stuff, but also resented it.

In addition to cultural pressures, practical exigencies led some mothers reluctantly and ambivalently toward domesticity. After her younger sister arrived when Jennifer was eight, her parents grudgingly adopted a more traditional arrangement that upset the delicate balance constructed when they were caring for only one child:

It was basically equal until my sister was born. It was about who can make it to a school function and who couldn't. When Amy was born, those things weren't happening anymore. Before my mother had a full-time job, but then my father basically was the money-maker, so that caused a conflict. My mom went crazy, 'cause she didn't want to be tied up in the house.

Finally, some children believed obstacles at work, not internalized guilt, prompted a mother's reluctant move toward domesticity. When her mother faced discrimination and then lost her job, Ashley worried that this turn of events took an emotional and financial toll on both parents:

My mom was a mortgage specialist, but people were getting ahead of her. She took on more responsibilities but never had a real title or anything, probably because she's a woman and Black. So a few years ago, when they were downsizing, she lost her job. Since then, it just hasn't worked out. So she's been at home feeling really down, and dad's been upset and angry.

Regardless of the source or timing of a family's turn toward traditionalism, it reflected a largely unquestioned assumption that, when work and family demands conflict, mothers are responsible for the home and fathers are duty-bound to support their wives and children. Whether couples took a dissatisfying turn before they became parents or in response to conflicts and pressures after children arrived, they did what they believed to be the right thing. Yet children could see how these well-intentioned actions often clashed with other, often unacknowledged, desires. When career-oriented mothers chose home instead, or when fathers found themselves doing all of the breadwinning despite a preference for sharing, their ambivalence spilled into daily domestic life.

Mothers who reluctantly adopted separate spheres lost economic autonomy, personal control, and a sense of purpose beyond the home. When Jennifer's mother left the workplace after her second child arrived, conflict over money signaled a shifting balance of power in the family. Jennifer felt her mother's loss of a separate income left her father with too much power in the relationship:

> My father basically became the money-maker, so that caused a conflict. If he would get mad, he would use a control method and say, "I'm not gonna pay the insurance for your car," or something like that. So there was tension over how much power bringing in the money meant. 'Cause it was the same thing with me. "You don't bring in any money, so you don't have a say."

Eduardo had similar worries, speculating that his father's control of the purse strings contributed to his infidelity as well as his mother's fear of abandonment:

> It got worse. They're not as close as they were. My mom worries when he wants to take a vacation because she thinks he might stay away. I wouldn't doubt that he has other women. He's got a lot of control.

Even when fathers seemed fair and caring, some children were troubled by their mothers' withering morale. Sarah saw her mother become increasingly depressed and "overinvolved" after leaving a gratifying career:

> She was the supermom, but she just seemed really unhappy and depressed a lot of time. I wish my mom would have worked so that she would be happier.

For Stephanie, her mother's material advantages could not make up for the mounting discontent:

> My father got the better deal. He could go out and do his job and come home and have a hot meal on the table. My mother got things that maybe she wouldn't have gotten, like financial stability, but she was lacking more. So I think she was dissatisfied.

Other children believed the costs of unwelcome traditionalism fell more heavily on their fathers. Being the sole support of a family on limited earnings exacted a heavy price. Eduardo watched his father grow distant as he struggled to support four children on the modest earnings of a "maintenance worker" who cleaned offices even after better-paid employees went home:

> My father showed little things, like saying what if he wouldn't be here. 'Cause he's always been working, and he was tired of things and wanted to take it easy, enjoy life more. He said it himself, he's been doing a lot!

Ashley watched her father grow angry and distant when her mother lost her job, even though he continued to count on a steady job at a bank:

He sits behind a desk. I don't know what he's doing, but he's making his money. And I think that's what attributes to the chip on his shoulder, because he's like, "I'm working, you're not. I'm making money, you're not." He sees her as being lazy and not going out there to look, but he hasn't been there for us either. Even though he's been there, he's been very distant from everybody.

As mothers languished and fathers became disheartened, unwelcome or ambivalent traditionalism spilt over into children's lives. Some felt their mothers became *too* involved. Sarah strained under the weighty expectations of a mom who was "overly responsible":

She would make these beautiful toys and throw these incredible birthday parties, but all along [it came] with an edge to it—"in return, I want you to be devoted to me." If we did something separate from her, that was a major problem. She didn't want us to grow up. I was overly cherished, if that's possible. So I was making distance because I felt I had to protect myself from this invasion.

Karen also believed too much time at home, with too little else to do, prompted her mother to make inappropriate demands for undivided loyalty:

My mom seemed unhappy, and as I grew up, she started getting really weird. She felt competitive with my friends, feeling like I liked them more than I liked her. She was overprotective and got a little crazy at times, telling me not to repeat the same mistakes that she made. I didn't feel comfortable inviting friends over, and having dinner at my kitchen table was tense.

The same dynamic contributing to overinvolvement among mothers could leave fathers estranged and insufficiently involved. For Lauren, the move toward traditionalism left her father spending too much time at the office and much less time with her:

It changed over the years. When I was younger, we would do a lot of stuff together, and then it separated along gender lines. We were about as traditional as they come. My father spent more time at work. He was like an absent father.

Carlos, too, noticed a change as his father began adding trips to a local bar onto already long days as a supervisor for the transit authority:

My father started to work a lot of nights and overtime, so there were times I would only see him like five minutes a day. Then he used to leave work, go to the bar. My mom's worried; it's four o'clock in the morning, and he should have come home already. He'd rather be drinking instead of being with us.

When circumstances pulled parents reluctantly and ambivalently toward traditionalism, the result—whether it involved a mother's declining morale, a father's estrangement, or rising marital strains—eroded family cohesion. Claudia wistfully recalled an earlier time when her mother enjoyed working at a bakery, her father spent time around the house, and she attended a neighbor's day care center. Her mother's decision to stay home when her father faced longer working days as a radio executive became a disruption to their family rhythm despite everyone's wish:

> I always liked it better when they both worked. It just seems like the sort of thing adults should do. Everybody else had both their parents working, and I had fun at the babysitters, 'cause I got to play with a bunch of other kids. Before we would do things together. Now we're not as close because my father works twelve hours a day and has very peculiar hours, which he hates.

These rising tensions and conflicts left young women and men feeling torn between the assumed benefits and hidden costs of their parents' strategies. Despite the injunction to be an intensive parent, Sarah had decidedly mixed feelings about her mother's choice to do just that:

> I think she thought she was doing something good for us, to change her life and sacrifice for us. It might have been slightly less secure, but it would have been better if my mother was happier working.

Karen also concluded there should—and could—have been a better way:

> I'm grateful that I had someone watching over me twenty-four hours a day, but I wish she had done something to enhance herself. I wish she had been more examining of herself and what she wanted to do, more secure and confident, because she could have done anything. My brother and I would have been fine.

In the long run, reluctant traditionalism held unforeseen consequences for parents and their children. Though few doubted their parents tried to do the right thing, they witnessed the ways good intentions can backfire when they conflict with more deeply felt but unacknowledged wishes. When mothers were pushed or pulled away from the workplace despite their desires, and fathers were pressured to work too much, the result could be declining parental morale, rising domestic strains, and eroding family cohesion.

STRUGGLES IN DUAL-EARNER MARRIAGES

Children in homes where both parents established strong, lasting commitments to paid jobs are not immune from difficulties. A mismatch in the outlooks, opportunities, and practices of dual-earning parents can produce difficulties as intractable as those in more traditional homes.[3] Most children growing up in this setting had stable, supportive family paths, but about one in five experienced eroding parental morale and rising family conflict. These dual-earner homes faced different dilemmas than their traditional counterparts, but their failure to find satisfying resolutions had similar consequences. If a two-income couple could not find a flexible, equitable, and mutually acceptable way to apportion caretaking and paid work, the growing mismatch brought tension and conflict.

Some observed a clash between mothers who sought equality and fathers who wished to be in control. Though Michelle was reared in a middle-class suburb and Theresa lived in an inner-city neighborhood, both observed an escalating "power struggle" when fathers opposed their wives' efforts to build a career and get more support at home. Michelle's father resisted her mother's determination to work:

> My mom was very independent, very strong-willed, very get-up-and-go. My father was more traditional. His mother was the typical obedient wife, and he expected the same from my mom. She definitely wanted to make something of herself—which was for the better, but it was a recipe for disaster.

Theresa also saw an escalating power struggle, which centered on her mother's refusal to cater to her father's wishes:

> My father was demanding. For example, he wanted his food done, so my mother's like, "Get it yourself." My mother wasn't really happy in the relationship, and she used to let us know this and this is going on.

Unequal opportunities, not differing worldviews, could also contribute to rising domestic tensions. Especially when fathers faced limited job options, conflicts could emerge even when a couple preferred a more egalitarian arrangement. Shawn's father never recovered from losing a promising job when he needed to take the children to school:

Mom had to be at work, so [my dad] took us to school, but they wouldn't let him arrive late, so he had to quit. Since then, he's worked for some messenger service and things like that, but it just wasn't the same anymore. It wasn't his fault, but ever since, any time he's out of a job, he'll start drinking. I wish I could have took my brother to school so he still had that job.

A stressful, dead-end job prompted a similar reaction from Jermaine's father, who gradually withdrew from family life:

They were both working, and they both took care of the financial situation together, but he wished to have a better job. He came home mad a lot, and some evenings he did not come home. He went out to the bar, and if we needed him, we had to go and get him.

When employed mothers took on a disproportionate load either at home or at work, children, especially daughters, sensed the buildup of marital injustices, even when their parents were reluctant to acknowledge or address this dynamic. Patricia grew up in an affluent, predominantly white neighborhood with two professional parents, while Chrystal lived in a much poorer African-American community, but both believed their fathers had not performed a fair share of the housework. Patricia wondered why her father's "laziness" did not provoke her mother's anger:

For a long time, I've had a feeling it was really my mom who was pulling all the weight. Even though she works full-time, dad doesn't do anything. He can't cook for himself; he doesn't know how to do his own laundry. It makes me really upset, because he still doesn't see it, but it also bothers me immensely that she lets herself be put in that position.

Chrystal agreed, noting it was fine for her mother to be the main breadwinner, but not for her father to resist taking up the slack at home:

My mother's been the one who's always worked full-time. My father's contribution has been sporadic. As we got older, we started resenting him, 'cause she's been the one who's been doing everything, and he's always found a way to make it seem as if he was the one holding it all together.

A clash of worldviews, constricted workplace and child care support, or simple resistance to sharing domestic tasks could all produce a dual-earning mismatch. Whatever the cause, these couples became locked in a cycle of unresolved conflict, personal frustration, and seeming injustice. Unable to find mutually supportive ways to share caring and earning, unacknowledged struggles over who should do what often produced growing concern among the children who observed these battles. Like those reared in traditional homes, these young people wished their parents could have created more flexible and equitable ways to apportion family tasks. But they did not necessarily blame their parents for these troubles. Like Chrystal, children often recognized the social constraints their parents faced and wished they had enjoyed more options:

> I think if my mother had more choices, and my father, too, then she wouldn't have had to work as hard as she had to—not just at her job but also at home.

Unhappily Ever After

Traditional marriages could leave some mothers unhappy and some fathers ill equipped to support the family, while dual-earner marriages could leave some wives feeling overburdened and some husbands chafing at the loss of control. These disparate arrangements had different dynamics, but shared a parental reluctance—or inability—to adopt more flexible, egalitarian strategies for sharing breadwinning and caretaking. When this happened, children had mixed reactions. Most, like Sarah, wished their parents had been able to break away from frustrating and conflicting patterns:

> They had the same conflicts over and over that never resolved themselves—about how much to let go of the kids, about parenting stuff. My father would have rather had my mother work if she were happier, but she insulated herself.

But some wondered if a separation might have been the better course. When children no longer provided a small buffer zone or a reason for staying together, the fragile bonds holding together a troubled marriage could break. Several years after Michelle's younger brother left for college, her parents announced they were parting:

> There were threats all along, when I was growing up—we're gonna divorce soon, and that sort of thing. I was very uneasy about it, but every time they threatened to divorce and ended up staying together, it was a false sense of relief, really. Once both kids were out of the house, they realized they couldn't live just the two of them by themselves.

Aware of their parents' disappointments, everyone wanted to avoid these conundrums in their own futures. Giving up hope that her parents would ever find a way to settle their differences, Patricia resolved instead to learn from her parents' mistakes and avoid the "trap" into which they had fallen:

> I think they're both lost causes. They just deserve each other. My mom has actually said stuff to me like, "Don't marry someone like your father; don't fall into this trap." And I won't.

As children looked back on the downward turn in their family paths, they wondered if the fear of change had been more destructive than change itself.[4] Joel wished his parents had summoned the nerve to take a risk and try more flexible strategies:

> I guess they became accepting of their relationship, just like other things. It's a lot of "what ifs." They never found out what the alternatives are. You have to explore the options. At least you tried, but not trying kills you.

Change is not always for the better, however. When a marital breakup left children without a committed breadwinner or a satisfied caretaker, this shift seemed no better to the children in these situations than did staying the course.

"WORST CASE" BREAKUPS

Though some children were relieved when a parental separation ended protracted conflict, others were distressed to find their parents' seemingly happy marriages fall apart. When the news of an impending breakup came as a surprise, a presumption of stability became the first casualty. With two seemingly content professional parents, Gabriel greeted the news of their divorce as he turned thirteen with astonishment and grief:

> I thought we were living a very good life, and everyone was happy. I had no idea my parents weren't getting along. So when my mother came into my room and said, "Your dad and I don't get along anymore, and we're gonna get a divorce," it came straight out of left field. It was just culture shock, like someone splashing cold water on my face.

Though parental breakups brought relief from adversity and set the stage for expanding support for the children in the previous chapter, life took a turn for the worse in other families. Like those who lived amid ongoing but deteriorating marriages, the children who endured destructive parental breakups focused on their parents' inability to renegotiate more flexible arrangements for breadwinning and caretaking. When children felt let down by fathers who fled or mothers who could not step into the breach, they lost a once taken for granted sense of emotional and economic security.

Flight, not Flexibility

Harmful breakups typically involved the loss of a once responsible and caring parent, most often a father who fled the family rather than accept a more flexible gender strategy. A parent's abandonment could take place slowly or abruptly, but it took a heavier toll on those who were taken by surprise. When Barbara was eight, her father had a "midlife crisis" and gradually withdrew from her life:

> My father got it in his head to give up his job, sell the house, load the family in a Winnebago, and head to California. He got despondent, started drinking more, got weird. The transition period we went through across the country, he pulled away emotionally, and so the physical part was just an extension of that.

Hank felt even less prepared when his father, without warning or explanation, failed to return from a trip to the local drugstore:

> I thought he was the perfect father, so when he left, it was a total surprise. I remember him saying, "Be back in five minutes," and I didn't see him again for five years.

Even when children understood what drove their parents to part, they did not understand why it should also mean severing their parental tie. Looking back, Hank could sympathize with his father's desire to separate from an alcoholic partner, but could not forgive him for cutting the connection to him and his sister:

> My mother was drinking a lot, and I'm sure he gave a lot of hints that he was not happy. I think her drinking gave him an excuse to finally say, "All right, let me get out of here." You can understand why he didn't want to be with her, but why didn't he want to be with his kids anymore?

Others saw their departing fathers as victims, rather than culprits, whose social disadvantages and personal demons left them unable to sustain the "good provider" ethic. Lucius lamented his father's decline, but tried not to place too much blame:

He was a computer programmer, but drugs caught up to him, and he skated downhill. If he didn't have those problems, I would have been better off. My father's intelligent. He can earn money. He's not lazy. He wanted to help. It's just the drugs and the problems he faced.

A variety of reasons prompted these fathers to leave, but all of them left children without needed financial and personal support. While a parental breakup brought some families relief from economic difficulty, most experienced a sharp erosion of their economic security.[5] As Barbara noted, her father's contributions dropped precipitously even before he left for good:

> But it was a constant test to figure out how we were gonna survive, and it got worse and worse. When my mom finally took over the finances, my father was like, "Well, okay, I really don't need to be around."

Losing a family breadwinner could also mean losing a once involved caretaker, and if this happened, it magnified the costs. When Jasmine's father left to live with a new girlfriend, she mourned the loss of his daily support as the household's chief cook and afterschool sitter—a loss deepened by knowing that his new partner's children were now eating his food and receiving his attention:

> I was used to him always being there, cooking dinner for us. He was the housewife during the day because my mother didn't cook and didn't get home till 5:30. So after he moved out and then moved in with another woman and her children, it made me feel worse 'cause I felt that he was leaving me to be with other kids. I miss him, and I know he misses me.

When Catherine was five, her mother asked her father to leave despite his participation as a "kind and gentle" parent. Although he took seemingly heroic steps to remained involved with his two daughters, Catherine mourned her father's departure and blamed her mother for his exile from the household:

> I hated my mother because she broke up with my father, and I still have a lot of resentment. I really cried for him. He used to sneak into the window when we were eating breakfast, and whenever he heard my mother coming, he'd go out the window. In hindsight, they were not meant to be together, but I was very, very sad for my father.

Whether a father left willingly or found himself exiled, the loss of his involvement and support could clearly mark a downward turn in children's lives. These "lost fathers" did not—and often *could* not—fulfill traditional breadwinning responsibilities, but they were also unable or unwilling to develop new ways of providing care.

Unprepared to "Do It All"

Wrenching in itself, a father's departure compounded children's difficulties when it left mothers unprepared. In traditional households, mothers often lacked the experience, skills, and desire to become the main breadwinner. If they could not adjust to this new and unexpected challenge, it produced a drastic decline in children's economic fortunes and daily care. When Hank's father left, he realized how his mother's reliance on her husband's paycheck had left them vulnerable. In addition to his ire toward his father, Hank felt angry at his mother for placing her own and her children's security in the hands of a man who deserted them all:

> Every time we paid for something, my father took out his wallet. My mom never worked, so she didn't have a job, nothing. She ended up taking welfare, which I could not stand. We would have been better off if she didn't listen to my father, went to college, and at least had something she could fall back on if this happens, which she never expected.

A father's desertion combined with a mother's economic vulnerability to leave some families living in poverty.[6] When Nina's father left with little warning, no forwarding address, and no support for his wife and two daughters, Nina watched her stay-at-home mother "give up her pride" and go on welfare because she could not figure out how to build a life outside the home. Her mother's reluctance to adjust to her father's disappearance triggered a descent from the middle class to barely getting by:

> My mother ended up going on welfare. We went from a nice place to living in a really cruddy building. And she's still in the same apartment. To this day, my sister will not speak to my father because of what he's done to us.

While the costs of a father's desertion fell heaviest on families with mothers who did not have a job or the experience, training, and self-confidence to find one, having an employed mother did not ensure economic safety, especially if she faced limited work opportunities and inadequate child care. All seemed well in Jamal's preschool years, despite his father's absence, because his mother had a seemingly secure career with the city's transit system. When she could not find care for her children and then lost her job, his family fortunes took an ominous turn:

Till [I was] five or six, things were going real well. She was working as a token clerk, and finances was great. But she got fired because she had three kids, and she couldn't work and do it all. So she went to waitressing, and spotty jobs which weren't a decent salary, and then it just got harder. So she was on public assistance by when I was ten or so.

Of course, single mothers faced many other challenges even when they did not suffer a precipitous financial slide. An inability to get help from others could prompt declining morale and rising stress among both home-making and employed single moms. Stay-at-home mothers were more likely to become isolated and depressed, while working mothers could feel overwhelmed by the intensified pressures of juggling work and home. Although Hank's mother was home, her worsening morale left him feeling alone and neglected nonetheless:

It was really hard living with my mother and sister, sometimes neither of them home, sometimes my mother home, but upstairs, yelling and crying. The dog was my best friend. My mom really didn't do much. Once in a while she'd clean up, but she'd watch TV pretty much. When I finally told her, "You weren't exactly the ideal mother," she said, "At least I was there for you." No! You weren't. You were there because you had no choice, you had no job, you had to stay in that house. I'm sure if you had a choice you wouldn't have been there either.

And though Catherine's hard-working mother was clearly attentive, her attention became obsessive and hostile—a shift Catherine attributed to fatigue brought on by juggling long working hours with caring for two daughters on her own:

We were not neglected; she had her eye on us. But if you so much as stepped too loudly across the kitchen, you'd better run. It was because she had to work twelve, sixteen-hour days and would constantly become exhausted. When she came home, you had to be very careful. She was always in a bad mood, and we just knew she was worn.

In the worst cases, the unexpected loss of a partner left mothers so debilitated they also lost confidence in their abilities as a worker and parent. When Jasmine's father departed to live with another woman, her mother became despondent and bedridden. Accustomed to being proud of a mother who had "moved up to the second to highest job you can have" in her office,

Jasmine watched her withdraw into a "private shell" and surrender her hard-won accomplishments:

> For ten years, she moved up, and I used to tell my friends, "She's office manager of such and such." But she had pretty much of a nervous breakdown and took off of work. She hasn't really gotten herself back together the way she used to. That's what makes me angry. She used to dress up, go to work every day. To see every morning with her still in the bed, it seemed like I'm taking care of her.

When a parental breakup left a mother unprepared and overwhelmed, children watched them wilt under the crushing weight of new expectations. Though a father's abandonment triggered this decline, these mothers also lacked workplace and neighborhood supports to help them create new ways to provide love, care, and economic support. These circumstances added insult to the injury of a father's rejection. Watching her mother struggle alone and unprepared, Nina blamed her mother's limited opportunities, not her heart or desire:

> I know she was frustrated that she couldn't give us more. I truly believe that if she had the opportunity to work, she would have. She would have never been on public assistance if somebody gave her the opportunity. So I knew, just watching my mother, I never wanted to depend on a man, because she really depended on my father's salary.

In contrast to breakups that brought relief from domestic conflict and financial insecurity, these were marked by a breadwinner's abandonment and the consequent financial and emotional descent of a once "good enough" care-taker. When neither parent was able (or willing) to develop a more expansive gender strategy, the fracturing of a traditional marital bargain left children on shaky ground.

FROM THE FRYING PAN INTO THE FIRE

A parental breakup sometimes had its worst consequences when a new marriage supplanted an earlier one. In contrast to the children who gained support and happier homes when a parent remarried, these children lost support and family cohesion. In some cases, they watched an independent mother cede power; in others, they became estranged from a once involved father; in still others, a new stepparent pushed them aside. All these remarriages brought family shifts in which mothers and fathers took on more stereotypical "roles."

Richard had not worried about his parents' divorce until his mother remarried. Though his parents lived apart, they shared responsibility for rearing him. During the week, he lived with his mother, who enjoyed her career at an investment firm; he spent every weekend with his father, and felt lucky to have a close relationship with both. When he was twelve, however, his mother acquiesced to her new husband's wish for her to stay home:

It was fine till my mom got married, and that's when the problems started. Harry wanted a pet and was very serious about her not working, so she tried to be a house woman. But she was frustrated and began to feel really bad about herself. When she left work, she felt very weak, very dependent, and I felt like, "Wow, what are you doing with yourself?"

As Richard watched his mother give up her job—and, in his view, her "self"—she grew distant and unhappy, prompting a sense of loss he had not felt before. He began to resent his mother for giving up her identity and his father for leaving him in the home of an uncaring stranger:

When my mom got married again, that's when I realized it was a very messed-up situation. [My stepfather] was very jealous and wanted me out of the way, and I could sense it. It made me look back on my life and say, "What went wrong?" All of a sudden, my parents weren't super people. Mom, how could you do this? And dad, where are you? I felt I got dealt a bad hand.

William and Noah were disappointed and disillusioned when their involved and seemingly admirable fathers chose a new partner they could not accept or understand. For most of William's childhood, he took pride in his parents' dual-career partnership. His mother thrived in her banking career, while his father, a lawyer, did more than his share of child care. As he entered his teens, however, he discovered his father had become involved with a woman almost twenty years younger. Reluctantly and painfully, he lost respect for someone who had once seemed "a dashing young man" and "the family's core":

When I was a kid, my dad would read to me every night. He read me the whole *Lord of the Rings* series, which took like a couple of years. He was very, very involved, a big solid family man, but then he had an affair. If [the marriage] had ended under different circumstances, he would probably be the nucleus of the new family, but because he went off with another woman who was so young and unappealing, I felt disgusted.

At age sixteen, Noah also had to redefine what once looked like a stable, happy past. His father seemed content as a lawyer, father, and husband until his mother, a high school teacher, discovered him having an affair and asked him to leave. At that moment, Noah "found out that nothing was what it seemed":

> Up until the point they split up, I thought we had the perfect family. It was a very dull, white-bread suburb, and we just figured they wanted this life. I thought my father was happy and that turned out to be absolutely the opposite. [It was] a total shock.

Richard, Gabriel, and Noah all felt disillusioned by a parent who opted for a more stereotypically traditional relationship. Some felt doubly disappointed. When Gabriel's parents both remarried, each crumpled under the demands of a new partner. His previously caring, custodial father acquiesced to his new wife, who asked Gabriel, then an admittedly "rebellious" teenager, to leave. When he turned to his mother for help, she, too, placed her new partner's wishes above his needs. At seventeen, Gabriel found himself living with his girlfriend's family and wondering what happened to parents who once were so attentive:

> When I was having a hard time with my dad's new wife, I called my mother and asked to stay there. But after a couple of weeks, the guy she was with, who was domineering, told me that your mother doesn't want you here anymore. She's sorry now, but there's absolutely no excuse. You never can apologize enough. Blood should be thicker than water, but I didn't have many advocates then.

These new partnerships involved stereotypic gender strategies, not a flexible sharing of earning and caretaking. Mothers ceded their independence, fathers became less involved, and stepparents failed to contribute practical or psychological support, leaving children to feel let down and left behind.

DISAPPEARING VILLAGES

Those with eroding family paths also lost the safety net of surrogate parents who could supplement or substitute for biological mothers and fathers. Jasmine viewed her grandmother as a third parent, who gave her time, attention, and money even before her father left:

> My grandmother was very important. I was pretty much over there all the time. I would spend weekends with her and go to church with her.

And all the money she made, she gave to us. She had no other grand-kids, just me and my brother. So it was anything I ever wanted.

Brianna moved in with her grandparents when her single mother felt too overwhelmed to care for a toddler:

When I talk to people who had that quote unquote idyllic childhood, the time in the South with my grandparents is the only time in my life I can think of. That was the happiest time of my life.

Yet unanticipated circumstances could shatter this support. When Jasmine's grandmother died as she entered middle school, it left her feeling even more bereft than her father's departure:

It was so great when my parents were together and my grandmother was alive, so when she died, it was really hard. I lost the money, and I lost her just being there. We were going through a real trauma in my whole family, so when [my father] left, it was like another death. I don't think it would have been any better if they'd stayed together, but my grandmother being alive would have been much more of a difference.

A similar turning point came when Brianna's mother remarried and asked her to leave a secure and happy life with her grandparents—"the best parents I ever had"—to return to a household that never seemed like a home:

I didn't want to leave the South. I was moving back up North because my mom had just given birth to my little sister, and she wanted me back. The father was a man I'd never even heard of, and my mom was just never meant to be a parent, so getting back with her was totally counterproductive.

Even when a care network remained nearby, it did not guarantee secu-rity or stability. Lucius's life worsened when his grandparents "made a bad decision, financially." Their economic crisis reverberated through his three-generation household, leaving all of them on the brink of poverty:

One bad decision by my grandparents slowed my family down. They lost money, lost time, almost lost the roof over our heads, stuff like that. It was scary; it got hard. I guess that's life.

Sarah's family life also spiraled downward when her nearby grandparents became an emotional drain. Far from helping out, they added to her mother's caretaking burdens and undermined her parents' relationship:

My grandparents were right next door, but they got more and more crazy, so it wasn't a good thing. My grandfather's mentally ill, and my grandmother was always depressed, and they were miserable together. They made things harder for my mother, and treated my father badly, so it became a detriment.

These children either lost parental surrogates who had once provided essential support or found that extended kin added to their parents' burdens rather than lessening them. The loss of a supportive safety net deepened the difficulties brought on by a father's abandonment, a mother's declining morale, or a couple's deteriorating marriage.

WHAT MIGHT HAVE BEEN

When a family path took a downward turn, children from all kinds of families experienced cascading and compounding losses. For some, traditional arrangements left stay-at-home mothers and breadwinning fathers chafing under the strictures of fixed gender boundaries. For others, dual-earning parents could not develop satisfying ways of sharing. Still others suffered when their fathers left and their mothers struggled to adjust. And finally, some homes lost an additional earner or caregiver who had provided an emotional, practical, and financial safety net. Lurking beneath these apparent differences, families with declining fortunes shared some similarities. Lauren felt her parents' estranged marriage closely resembled the single-parent homes she knew:

> Later in high school, I met more people who didn't have that same traditional family. I have one very close friend whose parents weren't together, and she lives with her mother, and it reminded me a lot of my mother. Even though my parents weren't divorced, it was a similar situation.

Many also recognized how social conditions, and especially a lack of other alternatives, constrained their parents' choices. Chrystal rued her mother's limited options:

> I wish my mother had stood up for herself more, but she did the best she could under the circumstances. I just wish the circumstances were better.

A set of diverse events created unexpected challenges to families with established gender boundaries. When parents could not develop more flexible ways to apportion paid and domestic work, rising difficulties propelled families on a downward track. Stay-at-home mothers and single-earner fathers could not escape a cycle of declining morale; dual-earning couples could not renegotiate their division of responsibility; divorced parents could not find new ways to share earning and caring; and neither mothers nor fathers were able to draw on the help of others to meet children's needs. These impasses and breakups left children with far less to count on than they had once taken for granted.

When All Does Not End Well

When home life followed a downward slope, all did not end well. In contrast to their peers with improving family fortunes, these children had no second chances. They nevertheless searched for silver linings in their difficult experiences, using the sense of trauma and loss to formulate ideas about how to live a better life. Most agreed with Isaiah, who believed adversity can be "a good teacher," and Gabriel, who declared "you could say it was a good experience 'cause it taught me a lot." They drew lessons from their parents' missteps about what *not* to do in their own lives.[7]

SILVER LININGS

Living through family change, even unfortunate change, left most feeling better prepared to face the challenges ahead of them. Although Noah felt constricted growing up in "conformist suburbia," his parents' troubled marriage gave him insights about how to live his own life differently:

> We could have been pretty one-dimensional, but we're real deep. I would never say, "I'm glad this happened because now I've got deeper insight into humankind," but that just happened to be the way it turned out.

William, too, believed his parents' breakup left him sympathetic to a wider range of experiences and family situations:

> As a kid, I had a pretty Beaver Cleaver type experience, and it was only later it broke down. I think it's given me a deeper, richer experience. I can relate to somebody who comes from a nuclear family and to somebody from a less traditional background. I feel more experienced.

Though few would have willingly chosen such a difficult path, most felt stronger because they survived the bumps and bruises. Barbara and her mother both learned self-reliance when her father left:

We had to learn how to depend on ourselves. It gave me a whole battery of skills very early in my life. At age ten, I got to figure out how you run the house, how you move into a new place. I'd probably still be learning those skills.

Not wanting to be seen as victims or simple stereotypes, most used their experiences as a motivation for doing better. Now a young manager at a large corporation, Nina wanted to make her still struggling, single mother proud:

I see a silver lining, because looking at my sister and my brother and me—we always had such high expectations for ourselves and we really pushed to really do well. We were not going to become one of these statistics; we had to make something of ourselves. It helped prove a point to my father that "we didn't really need you, and we did this because mother helped us do it all."

CAUTIONARY TALES

Whether they represent social disadvantages, parental failings, or simply bad luck, family difficulties offered cautionary tales. Children view used their parents' missteps as a guide to avoid the same traps. As Jennifer put it, "It's about all the bad stuff, what not to do." Men and women both drew lessons about the perils of clinging to strict breadwinning and caretaking boundaries, but they viewed these lessons through the lens of gender. Men focused on the burdens of sole breadwinning, while women worried more about the dangers of domesticity and the difficulties of doing it all.

Sons hoped to avoid the fate of fathers who chafed under the pressure to keep food on their families' table. Though Noah's father was a successful lawyer, this model of conventional manhood appeared too costly and insincere:

Even though he was working hard, he wasn't enjoying it. And he always seemed to be thinking about something else. I never said "Oh, my dad's pretending to be a father," but looking back on it, I knew he wasn't genuine. You've got to be true to yourself.

Eduardo sympathized with his father's struggles to support the family on a janitor's earnings, but he also had little desire to follow in his footsteps:

My father's been through a lot. He's worked all his lifetime. If there comes a time for me to get married, it's gonna be way different, way better. It's gonna have to be fifty-fifty so I won't have to worry about working all the time and have nothing to show for it.

Men also vowed to reject the example of fathers who abandoned their families. Lucius used his father's decline into drug addiction as a spur to work hard and postpone parenthood:

> It just made me more serious and know what to avoid. I'm gonna finish school, be a successful man. I'm not gonna settle for less than that. I'm gonna reach for the stars.

Luis drew on his father's example by pledging to give his children what he had not received:

> Anybody can be a better father [than my father]. I think I'll be better because of what happened. Because I experienced it, and I know what not to do.

Unhappy breadwinners and deadbeat single fathers represent two extremes, but both left sons searching for a more balanced, rewarding, and responsible alternative. Women drew similar lessons about their mothers. Neither frustrated married mothers nor vulnerable single mothers offered their daughters appealing options. Rosa was determined to chart a different course than her home-centered mother:

> You're supposed to follow in your parents' footsteps, but I don't want to be in my mother's situation, and I don't want a husband like my father. My mom says she's weaker than I am, that I have more will-power. So I'm more positive. I want to have a career and keep my own money. I don't want to depend on a man.

Patricia also planned to pursue a career, but she rejected her mother's willingness to work full-time "without any help" at home:

> I'm just happy that I've come out of it enough to see that's not what I want. I'm going out with someone now, and I'm just thinking, "I will not let this happen."

Women from all types of families focused on the perils of looking to someone else for personal happiness or economic security. As Jennifer explained, they hope to protect themselves by rejecting strategies that left their mothers at risk:

> I learned not to get married early, 'cause the other person can still fall out of love with you, can still cheat on you. All those bad things can still happen. Just because you have that piece of paper, it's a false security. It doesn't really promise you anything that can't happen anyway.

Parents' stumbles can provide vivid cautionary tales, but they do not offer a road map for finding a better way. Sarah had a clear sense that she does not want her parents' "traditional" marriage, but she is less confident about how to get what she does want:

> In nontraditional families, people make more of what they want, whereas [in] traditional families there's a mold and it forces you into it. I have a lot of conflicts now, work versus home and all that stuff, and having such a standard model hasn't helped. But I want to be independent and career-oriented, so I am.

Without a blueprint to follow, they hope to resist the pressures, overcome the obstacles, and exert the control their parents lacked. Hoping is not the same as doing, but at least, as Joel put it, they are aware of the pressures and will face them squarely:

> I can't see things from my father's point of view. He doesn't want to face the mistakes that he made. He's in a situation he doesn't like, and his way of dealing with it is not facing it.

There but for Fortune

As they grow to adulthood, contemporary children are likely to encounter unavoidable and unpredictable family change. While some young women and men experienced turning points from early difficulties toward more promising destinations, others lived through a cascading series of destabilizing events that shattered an earlier sense of security. Yet pathways of both expanding *and* eroding support unfolded in all family contexts, whether they began as a homemaker-breadwinner, two-earner, or single-parent home. The type of challenge may differ by class and household type, but all families face some kind of risk as they go about the daily, monthly, and yearly tasks of rearing children from infancy to adult independence. Over the course of this two-decade journey, family life develops in unforeseen ways. Growing up amid deep-seated work and family change, young women and men saw their families undergo too many twists and turns to view them as snapshots frozen in time. Instead, like a film whose ending cannot be known at the outset, their families traveled unfolding pathways, where fortunes sometimes improved and sometimes eroded.

What explains why some families prevailed and others did not? While it may be tempting to attribute the course of divergent family paths to the idiosyncratic strengths or shortcomings of individual parents, they actually reflect how a mix of expanding opportunities and new insecurities shape the social contexts confronting parents and other caretakers. As marriages have become more voluntary, parents have new options to demand change or to leave. These second chances in relationships can prompt some households to change for the better and others to suffer painful losses. Similarly, the rising fluidity of jobs and careers expands opportunities for some but imposes new insecurities on others. And while the gender revolution makes it possible to achieve a more egalitarian balance between home and work, demanding workplaces and lagging child care supports leave many parents overwhelmed and stressed on both fronts. In all of these ways, social shifts have created both new opportunities for gender flexibility and new conflicts between breadwinning and caretaking.

These shifts also make flexibility in paid work and care work not only desirable but essential. The erosion of single-earner paychecks, the rising expectations for modern marriages, and the expanding options for and pressures on working women all require partners to invent new ways of combining caretaking and breadwinning. In this irrevocably changed social context, flexible approaches to work and parenting help all types of families overcome economic uncertainties and interpersonal tensions. On the other hand, inflexibility in the face of new social realities leaves all sorts of families ill prepared to cope.

The direction of a family's pathway reflects how well—or poorly—parents and other caretakers were able to develop flexible gender strategies to cope with unexpected but increasingly pervasive changes in relationships, jobs, and child rearing. By creating more harmonious and egalitarian bonds, a more satisfying balance between work and home, or an expanded network of care, parents and other caretakers enhanced a child's sense of support. When caretakers held onto fixed gender arrangements that no longer provided personal satisfaction, marital cohesion, or sufficient economic resources, a child's support eroded.

Recognizing that family life is a process, not a static structure, also draws attention to the social contexts that help some families do well and leave others vulnerable. Parents with job opportunities and child care supports were better able to develop the flexible gender strategies that helped them cope. Building on these lessons, young women and men from all family backgrounds are searching for new, more flexible ways to combine love and work. But mindful of the obstacles that block this path, they are also preparing for a bumpy journey with no preordained destination.

PART TWO | Facing the Future

| High Hopes, Lurking Fears

THE CHILDREN OF THE gender revolution face the same fateful choices as previous generations, but they must grapple with new circumstances their parents could scarcely perceive. Since marriage has become just one among many options, they must decide not only what kind of lasting intimate bond to create but whether they want one at all. Since work and family life both demand more time, they must decide how to balance earning a living with caring for others. And since gender boundaries are no longer clear, they must decide how to apportion work and family tasks. No matter what the lessons of childhood may have been, contemporary young women and men have entered uncharted territory.

Amid these uncertainties, two opposing perspectives have emerged about how young people will negotiate the future. One view sees family decline and worries that the prevalence of single parents and working mothers creates self-absorbed individualists wary of commitment and disinclined to sacrifice for others. Neoconservatives concerned about family decline share this perspective with more liberal "communitarians," who are also concerned that modern America suffers from rising individualism and a decline of community that is draining civic participation and social cohesion.[1] Another view, in contrast, sees a stalled movement toward women's rights and a return to traditional families anchored by a new generation of stay-at-home mothers. From this perspective, the young women who were reared in harried, time-deprived homes are giving up on trying to "do it all" and choosing to "opt out."

A small kernel of truth exists in both of these apparently contradictory visions of the future. Young adults are increasingly likely to postpone marriage, live alone, cohabit, and enter temporary partnerships. Indeed, they are more likely than earlier generations to see living independently and supporting oneself, rather than getting married and having children, as the most salient markers of adulthood.[2] Their growing inclination to postpone marriage to focus first on establishing independent lives, combined with their stress on the quality of a relationship, suggests that permanent marriage is not likely to return as the only acceptable—or even the most prevalent—option.

Yet the recent, albeit slight, decline among employed married mothers also points to a halt—and potential reversal—in women's long emerging movement into the workplace. Inflexible jobs, a dearth of child care, and resistant partners continue to place roadblocks on the path to blending motherhood with a time-demanding career.[3]

While each of these views seems to signal bad news, my interviewees suggest that concerns about declining values and low aspirations are exaggerated on both sides. Images of young adults as either self-absorbed individualists or backward-looking traditionalists are too one-dimensional to capture the hopes and plans of a generation facing such multifaceted and contradictory options and cultural messages. Most strongly hope to create a lasting relationship *and* to balance home and work. Whether reared in a single-parent, dual-earner, or more traditional home, the vast majority want a permanent bond, but they do not wish for that bond to be defined by rigid gender distinctions. Instead, they seek a third path that combines aspects of the past, such as respect for lifelong commitment to an intimate partner, with arrangements that better fit modern contingencies, such as flexibility and gender equality. They want to create enduring *and* egalitarian partnerships that allow them to strike a personal balance between earning and caregiving.

Aspirations, however, provide only half the story. The roadblocks young women and men will likely face lead them to soberly assess their options. Amid time-demanding workplaces, pressures to parent intensively, and rising standards for a fulfilling relationship, they harbor considerable doubts about the chances of achieving their ideals. Aware of these obstacles, they know they must prepare to cope with less-than-ideal realities and to pursue "second-best" options that will help them survive in an imperfect world. In fashioning these fallback strategies, women and men alike must weigh their highest hopes against their greatest fears.[4]

The gender revolution has nourished a multifaceted set of *ideals* and *fears*. It is often easier to hold values than to live up to them, and young adults face a gap between what they want and what they think they can actually get. This conflict produces enacted compromises between ideals and real-world options. The higher rates of divorce and out-of-wedlock pregnancy in the "red states," where so-called values voters predominate, provides a vivid example of this process. It is thus necessary to distinguish between aspirations and practices, taking both seriously but never assuming they are the same.[5]

Although young women and men share the ideals of lasting commitment, gender flexibility, and work-family balance, they harbor some different fears about what might happen if these aspirations remain beyond their grasp. Women stress the dangers of depending on someone else for their identity or financial well-being; men focus on the costs of failing at work. These contrasting concerns point toward a gender divide lurking beneath the surface of shared ideals. They pit "self-reliant" women, who see personal autonomy as essential for their survival, against "neotraditional" men, who see work success as a key to self-respect.

Different Experiences, Similar Ideals

Young women and men face three intertwined questions about their futures. Do they wish to create a permanent bond with one intimate partner or retain the option to switch partners or remain on their own? What kind of balance would they like to strike between paid work and family life? And how would they like to share the challenges of earning a living and rearing children with a partner or others? Taken together, the answers coalesce into three distinct outlooks. A self-reliant outlook stresses the importance of personal independence, even if that means forgoing a lifelong partner. A traditional outlook stresses permanent marriage and clearly defined gender boundaries. And an egalitarian outlook stresses lasting commitment and combines it with a preference for balancing and sharing work and family tasks.

Each of these outlooks represents an ideal type, but they do not reflect equally desirable options.[6] While public debate has focused on the growth of self-reliant and traditional outlooks, most of my informants do not aspire to either of these options. Indeed, as Figure 5.1 shows, only 5 percent of women *or* men see self-reliance as an ideal option. Almost everyone wishes to create an enduring intimate partnership, though there is less agreement about what form this bond should take. Fewer than 30 percent of the men want a relationship with strict gender boundaries, and only about 15 percent of women do. Overall, the traditional and self-reliant groups together remain a minority. Four out of five women and almost seven out of ten men prefer a committed but egalitarian relationship with flexible gender boundaries that allow both partners to balance family and work rather than specialize in one or the other.

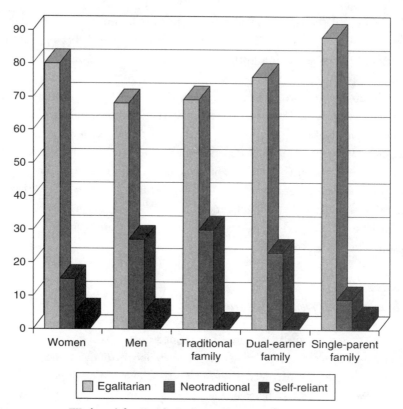

FIGURE 5.1 Work and family ideals, by gender and parents' family destination.

In addition to these small gender differences, family background has only a weak link to current ideals. Despite worries about neglected children and time-stressed homes, three-quarters of those who grew up with two working parents hope to share work and parenting with their partners. Concerns that children from divorced and single-parent families will eschew marriage seem overblown, since close to nine out of ten of them hope to get married, stay married, and share work and caretaking. Perhaps most surprising, almost seven out of ten people reared in traditional homes want egalitarian partnerships for themselves. Finally, children from all class and ethnic backgrounds also generally share egalitarian ideals, as Figure 5.2 shows. Middle-class children are only slightly more likely to favor equality at home and work, and African-Americans only slightly more likely than others.

Of course, "equality" is a vague and elusive concept, whose centrality as an ideal often clashes with the difficulty of achieving or even measuring it in practice. For my interviewees, "egalitarian" does not mean a rigidly organized division of everything all the time. It refers instead to a long-term

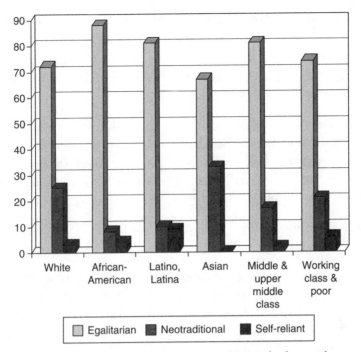

FIGURE 5.2 Work and family ideals, by class and ethnic background.

commitment to equitable, flexible, and mutual support in domestic tasks and workplace ties.[7] Defined this way, the majority of children from all kinds of families hope to find a lifelong partner, to balance work and family, and to share breadwinning and caretaking. Their diverse experiences with parents, friends, and other adults and peers led most to this shared conclusion.

SEEKING A LIFELONG COMMITMENT

The overwhelming majority of young adults hope to forge a lifelong commitment with a single partner. In fact, a recent survey found that "even though a decreasing percentage of the adult population is married, most unmarried adults say they want to marry."[8] For most, this means getting and staying married, but everyone who identified as gay or lesbian also hoped to create a "marriage-like" relationship.[9] Children with happily married parents hope for this outcome, but so do children with parents who were dissatisfied together, divorced, or never married. Serena's parents' egalitarian partnership provided a template for friendships as well as intimate bonds:

My peers saw shouting matches, [but] I never experienced any of that. It taught me to not throw in the towel with a friend or a guy. It taught me that if it's worth your being there, it's worth your going through disagreements. It's actually a role model for how I treat my relationships.

Even those who lived with unhappily married parents seek a long-term commitment. Troubled marriages provide clues about what missteps to avoid in a relationship, but they do not necessarily lead children to reject marriage altogether. Reflecting on his parents' emotional estrangement, Jermaine hoped to create a closer bond:

I hope [my marriage] would be different—different in the sense that I'm an affectionate guy. My father was never that type of person.

Divorces also provide lessons about what to avoid. Like a photograph's negative, Jasmine vowed to create the unbreakable bond that had eluded her parents. She preferred to affirm the values her parents stressed rather than the choices they made:

I really want "till death do you part"...Just take what they did and flip it around, the opposite. The only thing I wouldn't change [is] what they instilled in me. What they did really didn't influence me as much as what they told me to do.

The experience of divorce can actually strengthen the desire to marry and stay married. Contrary to the view that the children of divorce want to avoid commitment, most of my interviewees responded to watching their parents break up by developing an appreciation for making marriage work. Alex's father's departure helped him realize how much he valued binding commitment:

I don't think that it was good that he left, but in some ways it could have been good for me. It definitely makes things harder, but I also feel strongly that it taught me that family is important, and I think that is because I've seen it from the other side.

In a similar way, William viewed his father's affair with a younger woman as a valuable lesson about how to prevent a "schizophrenic life":

I'm not going to do a freak-out like my dad. Now he's living out his adolescence with this younger woman.

Parents' troubled marriages also prompted children to search for more uplifting models. Some compared a failed first marriage to a more successful second one. The remarriage of Tamika's father provided an antidote to the prior conflict and tension:

> The ideal family would be my father and my stepmother. They don't let little arguments come between them. They took care of their kids. It is the opposite of my mother. I want my kids raised by both parents all the time.

More often, however, the children of unhappily married parents found inspiration from others in their social network who made long-lasting, satisfying relationships seem possible. Determined to avoid her own parents' fate, watching her boyfriend's parents changed Hannah's outlook:

> My first boyfriend's parents were so reasonable, so calm, and so human to each other. It was such a contrast to the way my parents existed that I made them into some sort of ideal couple, and I recognized that as the way I want to interact with someone I was married to.

Catherine also looked to other families and ultimately discovered that her own relationships did not have to follow the course of her parents' contentious marriage and subsequent divorce:

> As far as commitment goes, I've learned that it's very satisfying to work together with somebody, and even when you're struggling, the outcome can be great if you're both working on this. It's such a good sense of accomplishment that you're giving a part of yourself to somebody who appreciates it, especially when you get that back in return.

In short, young people with all kinds of family experiences hope to marry and stay married—or, especially in the case of gays and lesbians, create a lasting partnership. Some parents provided models to emulate, but even when they did not, children did not turn away from the ideal of commitment. Instead, they used these shortfalls as examples of mistakes to avoid and looked to others for inspiration.[10] Very few concluded it would be more appealing to go it alone, depend exclusively on a network of close friends, or move endlessly through a series of temporary partnerships.

Not content with just a commitment, those who hope to marry also set high standards for the ideal relationship. In addition to looking for the best context to bear and rear children, they seek commitments that offer intimacy, support, and lasting romantic attachment. While Dwayne's parents did not achieve these ideals, he still sought them for himself:

It's a bond that can't be broken. Once you make it, that's it. So I want to be able to say in twenty-five years, "I love you more than the day I met you. Would you spend the next twenty-five years with me?" That's something my parents didn't do.

Jonathan believed his parents came close to the ideal he sought, which left him even more determined to settle for nothing less:

I see my parents together, and I couldn't imagine getting married just 'cause you think, "If you get divorced, that's okay." I'm very much like, "The right one's out there." I'm fortunate for the way I was brought up, and I'd like to be able to have that.

While almost everybody values permanent commitment, it is not the only value that matters. In a world where remaining single or getting a divorce are abiding, if less appealing, options, the quality of a relationship matters as much as being in one. The desire for lasting love, rooted in mutual respect, support, and romance, has not diminished the desire to marry, but there is little reason to hurry.[11] Making a bad choice can be worse than not making any at all, especially with such high standards and fateful consequences. Bruce pointed out, "There are many people who I've seen crushed by either a bad marriage or not [being] married, so I have to make sure it's right."

SEEKING A PERSONAL BALANCE

Most women and men also hope to strike a relatively equal balance between paid work and the rest of life. Younger workers are more likely than members of the boomer generation to be family-centric or dual-centric (that is, to place their priorities on both career and family) rather than work-centric.[12] A few wish to follow in their parents' footsteps, but most want something better. Those raised in traditional homes generally seek to avoid the extremes of their parents. Suzanne believed her mother's domesticity had been unnecessary and counterproductive, prompting her to look for something more:

It just seems kind of unnatural to just stay home with kids. Work and child rearing would be of equal importance.

Rachel agreed:

Life is too short, and it shouldn't have to revolve around a household. I know I wouldn't want to do that. I'd feel trapped just being in a house all the time.

Ken wished to avoid the opposite problem. By spending less time at work, he hoped to find the balance that had eluded his father and left him feeling shortchanged:

> It represents me hoping to be less workaholic than my father. I want to be more active in the early years. I want to have a huge role—the overprotective father, and more caring towards my wife, too.

Joel concurred:

> I guess you realize more what you don't get. So the lack of attention [from my dad] played more of an influence in how I'd raise my child, ideally.

Living in a single-parent home also triggered a desire for balance, especially among men whose fathers were largely absent. Richard wished for far more than weekend parenting:

> Because my father was a weekend dad, I have to set a better example. I would like to be more like my mother and be very involved with the kids. Extremely, I want to be there. My father would be like, "That's terrible," but I think it's a much healthier way to live than to do the same thing every day for the rest of your life.

Hank remained angry and baffled by his father's desertion, but he hoped to emulate his grandfather's involvement:

> [An] ideal father [is] somebody who's willing to spend time with kids, to counsel, to teach as well as to provide. Because my dad left, because I experienced it, and I know what I don't want to do, and just from watching my grandfather, who did those things.

Dual-earner homes come closer to the ideal, but even these households left most children hoping for a better balance. While they want to "do it all," they do not want the hectic daily schedules that often left both parents having to do too much. Men are apt to focus on how work pressures crowded out family time. Watching his working-class parents struggle in a series of blue-collar and pink-collar jobs, Dwayne concluded that spending less time at work was the key:

> My parents wanted to spend more time [with us,] but their time was compromised with the nine to five grind. I want to take my kids to a park, to be able to call and [say] I'm taking my family on a vacation.

With parents who were busy therapists, Mark felt the same way:

My parents worked so much. I don't want to have that type of life. I want to be less stressed. I want to have more relaxed work so that I can be more relaxed at home. [My dad] would work nine to five at the hospital and do private practice in the evenings, so he was never home.

Women, in contrast, focus more on doing better at work. Kristen knew she could manage both, but hoped to escape the toll that home duties took on her mother's chances of moving out of the secretarial ranks:

My mom could handle family and work, and she did both well. She did a great job of raising me. But work, she could have done better. I want to do better in my work.

Isabella's mother became her model as she moved up the ladder to become an executive at a bank:

Like my mom, having children and having a successful career—a happy career—are both things that I want. So if I have one and not the other, I'm going to feel like I'm missing out on something.

While women and men alike want to avoid spending too much time at work or at home, the lens of gender slants their views in different directions. Women hope family obligations will not undermine their work prospects, while men hope work obligations will not unduly interfere with family time. Most, however, share the wish for a more equitable balance than their parents were able to achieve.

SEEKING AN EGALITARIAN PARTNERSHIP

A lasting commitment and a personal balance between work and family both require finding a partner with similar goals, and most seek such a relationship. Although women in particular desire equality, most men agree. In fact, a recent survey found "sharing household chores" now ranks third in importance on a list of items generally associated with successful marriages (with 62 percent saying sharing housework is very important to marital success, compared to 47 percent fifteen years ago), well ahead of adequate income (53 percent) and even having children (41 percent). Equally important, there are no significant differences in the views of men and women, whether single or married.[13] Young adults are especially likely to endorse this view. Another survey thus found that two-thirds of people under thirty-two strongly support gender equality at work and in the home, and 90 percent feel closer to that position than to the view that women's place is in the home.[14]

Those from traditional homes hope to overcome the boundaries of gender emphasized by their parents. Women want a partner who will do far more parenting and housekeeping than their fathers, while men find a work-committed partner more appealing than their mothers' domesticity. Melissa contrasted her preferences with those of her parents:

[My ideal] is kind of opposite. I never wanted to be my mom. Wouldn't it be great if it were as fifty-fifty as it could be? You each get to see how difficult everything is. Nobody would go unappreciated.

Jonathan reached the same conclusion about his father:

I definitely don't want what my father did. He wanted the traditional thing. I actually find it more exciting to meet a woman who has a career, a direction. Maybe deep down inside it's because my mom didn't, so I'm looking for someone who does.

Those reared by single parents drew more complex lessons. Watching one parent—usually a mother—struggle to care for her children and make ends meet made equal sharing seem a far better alternative. But these children also take solace from their parents' displays of strength in the face of adversity. Alex explained:

From living with my mother, I was exposed to people who are strong. That attracted me. So I would like to have an equal relationship.

In a case of "actions speak louder than words," Keisha found her custodial grandmother's autonomy contradicted the words she spoke:

My grandmother's like, "He's the man; he should give you money; he should support you." It's weird, but she does say that. But I want fifty-fifty, 'cause I think we're equal, we should help each other.

Dual-earner homes appeared, in Rosanna Hertz's words, "more equal than others," and some provided models of equitable, flexible, and fair sharing.[15] Mariela took inspiration from her father's relationship with her stepmother:

[My ideal's] the same thing. If I'm cooking, he can wash the dishes, and when the kids are there, he can do the homework, and I'll get them ready for bed. We would share fifty-fifty.

Mark shared this judgment:

My dad and my stepmother function well as a couple. He cooks; she cooks. If a woman feels comfortable being a housewife, I don't see the problem, but in terms of having a wife like that, that seems like a lot of pressure on me. I'd rather have a more equal partner.

Even in the best circumstances, however, people are careful to distinguish between what they wish to emulate and avoid in their parents' marriages. Women, especially, want to evade a disproportionate share of the housework. Michelle, for example, did not doubt she would follow her mother's path toward a career, but she hoped for a much more supportive partner than her father had been:

> I'd like to be like my mother, definitely not staying at home, but I want both parents to be equally involved in the kids' lives and maintaining the house. So I put a lot of responsibility on the father. The main quality I look for in a guy is being very willing to compromise and not be rigid, because that's what happened with my dad. You can't communicate with someone who is just unwilling to see your point of view.

Men and women view equality in different ways. Women are eager to find a partner to share caretaking, while men look forward to sharing the financial load. Yet the desire to transcend gender boundaries provides a common element to these aspirations. As William said of his mother and father:

> I was very proud of my mom for being so successful in banking, a pretty patriarchal industry. And my dad always did the cooking. Certainly, it gave me a strong sense of traditional masculine-feminine roles being bunk.

THE MINORITY VIEW

Though most wish to create a flexible, egalitarian relationship, a noteworthy minority hold outlooks harkening back to an earlier era. Close to a third of men and about 15 percent of women prefer to maintain clear gender boundaries between earning and caring, although here, too, their views do not directly reflect family background. Some are eager to follow in their parents' footsteps, while others hope to avoid the difficulties of living in less traditional homes. Traditionally inclined men want to retain the option to fully commit to work. With a father who did well as a self-employed home inspector, Sam saw his parents' strict division of labor as the only ideal:

> Ideally, like my parents, have my wife take care of the kids and me going out working, bringing home the money. Wrong is someone who

wouldn't care for the kids as much, wouldn't be there, who would expect me to come home from work to a filthy house and me do all the housework, something like that.

David, whose dad was a lawyer, agreed:

I am working my ass off. My father was very ambitious and cared a lot about being hugely successful, and I have the same thing.

Though fewer women hold traditional ideals, those who do also stress the benefits of a breadwinning man. After watching her mother struggle to support her family, Keisha wanted a partner who would bring home the bacon so that she could cook it:

Actually, with children, I think a man should do more than half the breadwinning. Because that's not the way I was raised, maybe that's why I think it's about due time somebody does it.

While homemaking mothers and breadwinning fathers may seem ideal to this group, they do not entirely reject the changes taking place around them. Women can hold paid jobs, they argue, and men should be involved family members, but only if these activities do not interfere with their primary obligations. For Hank, it is fine for women to work, but not for a mother to have a career:

I want someone who's willing to work, but not somebody who's more concerned about their career than their own kids' well-being, not somebody saying, "I could be so much more successful," when they sacrifice my children. Once there's kids, you're gonna be a mother— not a housewife, a mother.

Tiffany wants a partner who will help with child care, but also provide the bulk of the income:

I would like to be the primary caretaker, but I expect a lot from someone else. I want someone who supports us but also is thrilled to be with them and where that's a priority.

Mindful of the decline in 1950s-style families, even those with traditional ideals want to soften the edges of gender divisions. As Annie explained, complete domesticity brings too many dangers:

The ideal? Stay home. I'd like to raise my kids, and I'd like my husband to make enough money to be comfortable. But for your own mental sanity, I don't think it's healthy if you have a husband who's making all the money. So it involves a partner who's willing to carry his own weight and balance career with home.

If Wishes Were Horses, Beggars Would Ride

While a small minority of women and a larger minority of men would like to recapture the mid-twentieth-century world of Ozzie and Harriet, most hope to forge a different path through adulthood. Neither unbridled individualists nor nostalgic traditionalists, they seek a lifelong partner who will join them in integrating satisfying work with ample family time. This is not a selfish wish to have it all, but rather a shared desire for the best of both worlds.

If young people could count on achieving their ideals, the future would be easy to predict. But the terrain of twenty-first-century adulthood is far too uncertain for that. In the words of Frank Furstenberg and his colleagues, "growing up is harder to do."[16] Watching their parents' generation cope with marital uncertainty and work-family conflict has left them with doubts about finding the right partner and achieving economic security. Amid their own rising standards for personal fulfillment, they perceive a widening gap between their aspirations for equality and work-family balance and their ability to achieve them.[17] Their highest ideals are tempered with a heavy—and realistic—dose of skepticism.[18]

UNCERTAINTY IN RELATIONSHIPS

The tension between increasingly fragile relationships and rising standards for a partner leaves young people wondering whether they can find the right person or create a lasting bond if they do. Although divorce rates have stabilized and even declined slightly, they remain in the range of 40 to 50 percent of marriages.[19] The rise of cohabitation has also changed the demographic landscape, since many cohabiting couples break up without ever marrying, and about 70 percent of those who marry live together first.

The scope of these demographic shifts permeates young people's worldviews. In a national survey of American youth between the ages of eighteen and twenty-four, Anna Greenberg found that although most believe in the *ideal* of marriage, they are far more skeptical about the *institution* of marriage. Fifty-seven percent believe "the institution of marriage is dying in this country," while only 25 percent disagree, and those reared in traditional and nontraditional homes reached the same conclusion. Less than half (45 percent) disagree with the statement, "You see so few happy marriages today that you begin to question it as a way of life."[20] The children of intact as well as divorced families have concluded that love does not necessarily conquer all. Even though his own parents stayed together, Paul knew the best of intentions would not—and could not—guarantee permanence:

I hope I don't have to go through a divorce, but this is very unrealistic to say. Divorce shouldn't happen; you should marry somebody and make sure it's right the first time and make it work. It's easy to say that, but who knows what's gonna happen down the road.

Concern about the impermanence of relationships also fuels a focus on finding the right partner rather than just finding one. Now that commitment is both optional and unpredictable, the quality of a relationship takes center stage. In fact, a full 70 percent of eighteen- to twenty-nine-year-olds believe the main purpose of marriage is "mutual happiness and fulfillment."[21] In this sense, as Stephanie Coontz observes, love has "conquered" marriage.[22] Jeff feared being alone, but not as much as he feared being in a relationship that left him *feeling* alone:

I need love. I need intimacy. But I couldn't really set a goal saying, "I need to be married by this time," because you do that to yourself and all of a sudden you're marrying somebody you're not going to be happy with.

Even those raised by happily married parents are unsure about finding a suitable partner. Reflecting on her dual-earning parents' egalitarian give-and-take, Kayla worried that they set the bar too high for her to reach:

I just love to introduce my parents to people because I feel that people have a greater sense of respect for who I am through my parents, because I always hear positive things. If I didn't have that, if I had someone who didn't meet my standard, it would be hard.

While women and men agree it is difficult to find the right partner or sustain a worthwhile relationship, men worry that women will expect too much of them and women wonder if marriage will threaten their quest for personal autonomy. Hank felt that the rising tide of "modern women" who want to retain "control" would reduce the pool of acceptable partners:

A lot of women just hate men and have no respect for them. I don't know if it's because their fathers abused their mothers or they just thought their mothers were worth more, but there are so many women that just want to be in control, and they're probably better off by themselves.

Although Serena expressed no lack of respect for men, she did not want to build a relationship at the cost of giving up a separate self:

> It's not just equality; it's about being your own person. And it's hard to see how you can keep your independence and have a relationship. It's difficult.

Despite the popular images of domestically oriented women and independent-minded men, these reflections suggest young women are actually more fearful of traditional marriage.[23] Concern about the pitfalls of relationships mingles with anxiety about the fragility of intimate bonds, leaving everyone to wonder if it is possible to build a lasting relationship that is also fulfilling. As Serena put it:

> I want an equal partner, but I'm also confused because I find a lot of my male peers think the woman's inferior in the relationship. Or I find a lot of guys are intimidated by someone being educated and being able to pull their own weight. And it makes me wonder if I will find someone compatible that I also am attracted to.

In this bewildering context, finding the right match and sustaining this bond seems like finding the proverbial needle in a haystack. The understandable response is to postpone marriage, leaving almost three-quarters of twenty-something men and almost two-thirds of twenty-something women still single.[24]

WORKPLACE PRESSURES

The workplace is a "greedy institution," which has only grown greedier since Louis and Rose Coser coined this term over three decades ago.[25] While occupational success has long been tied to full-time, uninterrupted commitment, the definition of "full-time" has grown to include workweeks extending well beyond the once standard forty hours to fifty, sixty, seventy, and even eighty hours.[26] Whether or not they watched their own parents struggle to find family time, most worry that rising work demands put any semblance of balance beyond their reach.[27] While Nina grew up with a stay-at-home single mother, she feared that the relentless time pressures at work would make it impossible for her to stay sane while moving up:

> People [who] strive to be VPs, I see what they go through. Literally, it feels like twenty-four hours is not enough in a day. You're in at 7:30 in the morning, and it's back-to-back meetings all day. You don't have

time to run to the ladies' room. Sometimes you don't even eat lunch. And you work at home on the weekend.

Even though Mariela's father and stepmother did a good job of juggling two jobs, she still worried about the demands on today's workers:

These people where I work, sometimes they don't leave until eleven o'clock at night. And they have families of their own. That's what I don't want.

New uncertainties abound for young workers of all stripes in the changing American workplace. Lower-paying, nonunion service jobs have replaced the blue-collar jobs that once promised job security and a living wage for the less educated. Even middle-class professionals with advanced degrees and generous paychecks face more fluid and unpredictable job ladders. As a result, men are anxious about the demise of the secure, well-paying jobs their fathers counted on.[28] Manny wondered how—or if—he could re-create his father's success as a construction worker and the family breadwinner:

I always looked at my father taking care of his wife and children and felt it was my responsibility completely. My wife is the mother of my child and my responsibility. My job is to make money. But you have to worry about it. My thought right now is playing Lotto.

Though Adam's father brought home more money as a physician, he had the same concern:

My biggest fear is that I won't be as successful as my father. That's always in the back of my head, which may sound selfish but it makes it tough.

Some believe declining economic security is contributing to rising job pressures. Concerned about downsizing and retrenchment, Noah felt the need to concentrate on finding and keeping a good job rather than being an involved, attentive parent:

In terms of my values and goals, I would want to experience my children's childhood. But pursuing a career and raising a family at the same time are tough because a lot of places today, especially in business, want you to work weekends and around the clock, even though I really don't want to do that.

Women and men both see rising time pressures and economic insecurities as significant obstacles to balancing family involvement with a sustained career. More than ever, workplaces are greedy organizations with scant room for other loyalties. Andrew concluded he had little chance of achieving his "ideal balance":

> It would be best to make them both first priorities, although I'm not sure if that would be possible. It would be nice if they were all perfectly compatible, but I think if you have a career, then you generally have to maintain it.

Greg echoed these sentiments:

> I'd say the chances are very fifty-fifty, very "possibly yes" and "possibly no." Work situations are not very accepting of people who want to put kids in an equal priority with their job. Maybe I'm just not in a work environment that can accommodate kids.

PARENTING PRESSURES

The high demands of modern parenting also leave young people skeptical about achieving balance in their lives or equality in their relationships. In addition to expanding workweeks, young Americans also face rising standards of parenthood. Although some argue this trend is largely confined to the middle class, the working-class women and men I interviewed are just as likely to believe that children are better off having a parent at home, especially if they lack the resources to purchase high-quality child care.[29] Although the overwhelming majority support mothers' employment, most also remain convinced that children fare better when at least one parent is devoted to their care. Todd declared, "I don't want a nanny raising my child; I want my wife and myself to raise my child."

Though men and women agree on the problem, they have reached different conclusions about the solutions. Egalitarian language notwithstanding, men more often argue that women should bear the first responsibility for caretaking. Matthew argued that the ideal of equality conflicted with his own and his children's best interests:

> Financials aside, it's probably better for the children if the mother doesn't work. That's ignoring her interests and desires, too—just purely for the children.

And Adam worried that neither he nor his partner could have their cake and eat it too:

> I would like to share, and far be it for me to tell her not to work. But if we have a child, I don't know how I'd feel. I couldn't expect her to

give up her job, especially if it was important to her, but I wouldn't want to quit my job, so that's something I'd have to cross when the time comes.

Women more often feel caught between caring for children and bringing home a paycheck. Mothers continue to face pressure to be at home with their children even as they also face pressure to bring home an income. Brianna acknowledged her own view probably had more to do with social norms than a child's inherent needs:

Because society's created a place where mom is the one who's supposed to have the cookies when you come home from school, it's probably better when she stays home. But that's because of society.

These pressures heighten women's inner conflicts, but do not dictate a conforming response.[30] Often raised by working mothers, many are prepared to resist this cultural standard. Reflecting on her mother's example, Anita felt torn, but also defiant:

I suppose women take a different role [than men] in the family, but that obviously wasn't my mother. You can have a career, but maybe you can't. This is the most scary thing. I want to be able to do this, but really, I don't know.

Gender differences aside, women and men agree that the conflict between an "intensive parenting" standard, which requires the single-minded devotion of one parent, and an "ideal worker" model, which requires undivided commitment to a job, creates dilemmas for everyone. Karen concluded that rising demands at work *and* at home make it difficult to find—or be—an egalitarian partner:

Ideally, my husband would cook, split cleaning very evenly, definitely do more than my dad does. But now I understand what it's like to work all day and come home and do stuff. Now I see how it's hard.

Beyond Ideals

Workplace pressures, rising standards for parenting, and a limited pool of suitable mates creates skepticism about the chances of creating the lasting, flexible partnerships most desire. In response, women and men both acknowledge the need to prepare for real-world options that might—and probably will—fall significantly short of their ideals. Their strategies for adulthood emerge not only from their high hopes for a committed, egalitarian relationship and a balanced personal life but also from their realistic doubts about attaining these aspirations.

Faced with social and cultural obstacles that make it difficult to achieve equality and work-family balance, women and men seek protection against the potentially dangerous contingencies they anticipate. What should take the place of an enduring, egalitarian partnership if it proves elusive? Is it better to return to a more traditional pattern or venture forth on a more independent path? Everyone found a fallback plan not only attractive but necessary.[31] Yet since women and men perceive different dangers and envision different worst-case scenarios, they also develop different insurance strategies. In contrast to the popular belief that younger generations of women want to return home, Figure 5.3 shows that men, not women, are substantially more likely to prefer to fall back on a breadwinner-homemaker arrangement.

Although some women are prepared to place marriage before all else, almost three-fourths are not. They plan to pursue a strategy of self-reliance instead. Hoping to avoid being stuck in an unhappy marriage or deserted by

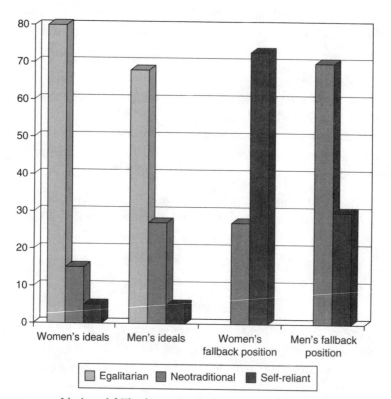

FIGURE 5.3 Ideals and fallback positions of young women and men.

an unfaithful spouse, these women see paid work as essential to their survival and to the well-being of any children they might bear. Women look to self-reliance and personal autonomy, within and outside the boundaries of marriage, to protect against economic dependence on a partner or personal malaise in domesticity.

Men's views reverse those of women. While a minority lean toward personal freedom, seven out of ten men favor a modified form of traditionalism if an egalitarian relationship proves unworkable or too costly. Worried about time-greedy workplaces and convinced that work remains at the core of manly success, they hope to avoid the sacrifices of equal sharing through a neotraditional arrangement in which they can continue to place a high priority on work while their partner provides more of the caregiving.

Beneath the surface of shared values lies a new gender divide. The fragility of modern relationships and the persistence of work-family conflicts prompt young women and men to craft not just different but conflicting fallback strategies. It is important to remember, however, that limited opportunities, not suspect motivations, drive this division. Whether women stress the need for self-reliance in a world of uncertain partnerships and devalued care work or men find traditional gender divisions attractive in a world where family involvement threatens work success, these strategies represent second-best adjustments to a social order that nurtures high hopes but offers limited chances for making them possible. And just as drivers and homeowners feel safer knowing they have insurance, these fallback positions provide reassurance even if they never prove necessary. Women's and men's contrasting survival strategies may portend a growing gender divide, but they do not reflect deeper aspirations.

| Women's Search for Self-Reliance

THE FRAGILITY OF MODERN relationships and the conflicting pressures of parenting and work leave young women with deep concerns. They know a marriage license does not come with a lifetime guarantee, and they might not be happy even if it did. Most want to be an attentive parent and a successful worker, but fear it might be easier to win the lottery than to find both good child care and a flexible job. Most want an egalitarian partnership, but finding a suitable, supportive companion hardly seems a foregone conclusion.

As they negotiate these uncertain waters, young women hope for the best, but are determined to avoid the worst. In the face of persistent obstacles to gender equality, about a quarter of the women I interviewed are prepared to stress the primacy of marriage and motherhood, even if this means forgoing a career. But three out of four seek a level of independence they cannot find in domesticity. Like a lifeboat in rough seas, strong workplace ties and a sphere of autonomy within their intimate relationships offer the separate base they want and are convinced they need. Even the minority inclined toward more traditional marital arrangements hope to fashion a modified form of traditionalism with some tie to paid work. Whether the fallback strategy focuses on self-reliance or domesticity, it represents young women's best efforts to cope with the obstacles to achieving their ideals.

If Not Equality, Then What?

Women from all backgrounds view the chances of "getting it all" as disappointingly low. Despite their disparate backgrounds and personal circumstances, Anita, Lauren, and Monique all agreed. With the help of a minority fellowship, Anita managed to earn a college degree from a selective school despite her modest economic background. Single at twenty-six and working full-time as an administrator for a large academic organization, she realized it would not be easy to find the perfect package of a good relationship, a satisfying career, and several children:

> I'm asking for a lot. I'd say [the chances are] 10 to 20 percent, if that good. I'm realizing that things are so impermanent and my expectations can only get me so far.

Also twenty-six, but married and employed at a public relations firm, Janet agreed that career and parenthood would be hard to combine:

> God only knows. Fate and destiny have to intervene to save me at this point. Can you arrange that?

A single mother at twenty-three, Monique faced the challenge of rearing two young sons on her own. Living on public assistance and searching for child care and a good job left her wondering how her earlier optimism had evaporated so quickly:

> I had very high hopes. I figured I'd do the kids and the husband thing and work on a career without stopping. But that didn't work out.

Women are counterbalancing their high hopes with contingency plans. Single at twenty-nine and working as a commodities broker, Maria found that searching for a satisfying, secure life means keeping one eye on her dream of combining a career with marriage and motherhood, while the other remains focused on more practical matters:

> I'm not pessimistic, but I'm realistic. As much as I would like to live in utopia, a lot of it is chance. So you have to set up insurance policies for yourself in life.

What form do these insurance policies take? If "having it all" is a matter of chance—and possibly a low chance at that—what options remain? For Letitia, her generation has more options than their mothers and grandmothers, but they must still choose between marriage and family, on one side, and personal independence, on the other:

> Women have their own choices now. They can choose to be dependent on a man and be home and be a housewife. Or they could choose to have an education, their own life, and make whatever they want of it themselves. I'll probably have to pick one or the other.

As Letitia implies, women's contingency plans take these two general forms. A minority accept, often after much soul-searching, that if push comes to shove, domestic commitments will come first, even if this means sacrificing a career they once anticipated. After seeing the relentless time demands and glass ceilings in her work as a television producer, Lauren reluctantly concluded that her career ambitions might need to take a back seat to parenthood:

> If you asked me a few years ago, I would have said I'd like to make work and child rearing equal. Now, if one has to take more importance, I would pick child rearing...Maybe I'm not meant to be this career woman that I thought I was going to be. I've changed my goals, and they're more attainable now.

At twenty-six, Stephanie, an accountant, grappled with a similar shift in her outlook:

> Family and children, that's the most important thing to me now. As far as a job goes, I don't know if I'll ever find the career or have the time to have the career that I actually wanted or am right for.

While these sentiments conform to stories of "opt-out" women who relinquish work to focus on marriage and motherhood, most women had different contingency plans. Chrystal and Miranda exemplify this different approach. As a twenty-six-year-old single mother and midlevel administrator in a publishing firm, Chrystal stressed the need to take care of her family all by herself:

> My philosophy is I'd rather think about it as if I have to do it all myself. And if someone else helps, it will be extra. But depending on someone else—that's when you set yourself up for disappointment and failure.

Single, without children, and working at a computer company at twenty-seven, Miranda focused on holding onto her hard-won and vigilantly guarded realm of personal control:

> I'm always conscious of trying to be responsible for myself. I fiercely fight for my independence. Any time I feel that someone's threatening that, my claws come out. I'm usually easy-going, but my independence is something I cannot have anyone overstep.

As Figures 6.1 and 6.2 show, fallback positions stressing self-reliance are much more prevalent than those stressing domestic pursuits. This view persists

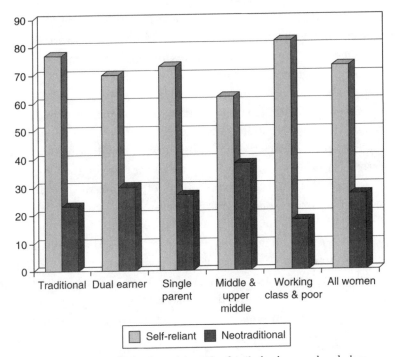

FIGURE 6.1 Women's fallback positions, by family background and class.

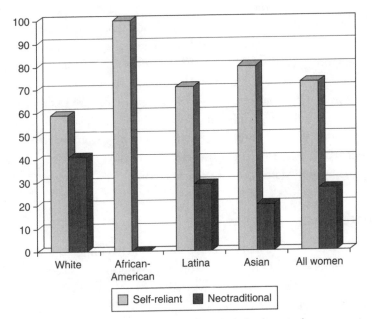

FIGURE 6.2 Women's fallback positions, by ethnic background.

across the boundaries of family experience, class, and ethnicity. Seven out of ten women from dual-earner homes, slightly less than three-quarters of those from single-parent homes, and more than three-quarters of those from traditional homes hold this view. While women's positions on this question differ slightly by class, it is not in the direction that might be expected given well-educated women's better job opportunities. Over 60 percent of middle-class women stress self-reliant strategies, and over 80 percent of working-class and poor women concur. Racial identity also shows some variation, from a high of nearly all African-American women to a low of three in five non-Hispanic white women stressing self-reliance.[1] In short, despite their diverse backgrounds, most young women emphasize self-reliance as a practical strategy for navigating the uncertainties of twenty-first-century life.

Why do so many young women seek self-reliance, and what distinguishes them from those who veer toward a more traditional pattern? Widespread and fundamental shifts in the structure of marriage, work, and child rearing are reshaping women's options and life chances. Few young women have been insulated from these shifts, but they have been touched in different ways and are prompted to craft a variety of responses.

Pushed and Pulled toward Self-Reliance

The lives of parents, other adults, and peers, as well as their own experiences in jobs and relationships, have provided lessons about the dangers of domesticity and the attractions of independence. These observations and encounters have convinced most women that their security and personal happiness are too important to leave to the vagaries of someone else's choices. Most have never been married, but some are divorced and others are in exclusive partnerships. Most are postponing childbearing, but some have become mothers. They grew up in different types of households and economic circumstances, but across all these differences, a combination of fear and hope has pushed and pulled young women toward self-reliance.

MOTHERS' MIXED MESSAGES

Even though mothers' lives provide an especially important template for their daughters, they do not provide unambiguous models to emulate. Young women see complexity in their maternal examples and distinguish between admirable features and ones they prefer to reject. They derive life lessons not simply from their mothers' options and choices but also by observing—and judging—their longer-run consequences. Whatever the model, young women see compelling reasons to seek independence in their own lives.

The Perils of Domesticity

Daughters feel appreciation and empathy for mothers who stressed domesticity, but most also see psychological, social, and economic risks in following a course that might leave them isolated, overburdened, or financially vulnerable. Some mothers explicitly pointed out "mistakes" they hoped their daughters would not make. Anita took to heart her mother's urging to hold onto the work aspirations she herself had surrendered:

> My mother's always saying she doesn't want me to repeat the same self-defeating mistakes she made and not live up to my potential. So I don't want to succumb to that kind of mind-set.

Some domestic mothers conveyed a veiled sense of regret, leaving the impression that too much devotion to caring for others, however important and satisfying, can hinder the development of an independent self. Lauren reflected on the cost her mother paid, even though she enjoyed a high standard of living as the wife of a successful stockbroker:

> My mother sort of gave everything she had to the family and now that we're grown up, she's taking care of my grandmother, so I fear that would take away from my "self."

Women are also concerned about the perils of being left alone or with too much housework. They vow not to cater to an absent or "lazy" husband.[2] Reflecting on her mother's responsibility to keep the home fires burning while her father worked late and traveled to faraway places, Rachel refused to risk the same fate:

> I'm not afraid of being alone, but I am afraid of being with somebody who's a jerk. I'm very much afraid of making a wrong decision and marrying somebody who's absent like my dad was.

And Patricia rejected her mother's example of doing everything at home while also pursuing a demanding career:

> My mother's such a leftover from the fifties and did everything for my father. I'm not planning to fall into that trap. I'm really not willing to take that from any guy at all.

When a mother's domesticity led to financial decline or ruin, it provided an especially powerful lesson. Nina never forgot how her family slid into poverty after her father abandoned them. Vowing to never find herself so unprotected and vulnerable, she refused to share economic control, though she had been living happily with her boyfriend for several years:

> 'Cause of what I've seen my mother go through, I'm a big control freak. All the bills are under my name because God forbid he doesn't pay something. He says, "You're too independent," and I say, "Would you rather me be dependent on you?" It's not that I don't trust him. I just don't want to see what happened to my mom happen to me, so I'm doing things to prevent that.

These experiences convinced women that even if domesticity may look appealing in the short run, their long-run happiness and survival depend on establishing an independent base in the world of work. Looking back on her mother's sense of betrayal, Angela knew she needed to prepare for the unknown:

> She trusted that her marriage would stay together and it wouldn't matter that she didn't work, wasn't marketable. When somebody makes all these vows, you should be able to trust that. It's a little tragic, but I would never put myself in that position, ever. I feel like I always have to be ready if my husband leaves me.

The Advantages of Self-Reliance

Mothers' efforts to achieve autonomy also proved inspirational. Barbara drew lessons not just from her mother's difficulties after her father left home but from her mother's subsequent efforts to get on her feet. This resilience convinced her to seek her own goals, with or without a partner:

> The implicit message coming from my mom was that there's no happily ever after with marriage and if you want a certain life, you have to support yourself. It taught me the ability to survive. That's a big thing I still carry with me—you can do it.

Women extracted the same message even when their parents stayed together. Danisha noticed her mother benefited not only from having a job but also from the identity and way of life it gave her:

> She taught me your marriage is not who you are. It's one thing to want to live with your husband and all that good stuff, but don't get to the point where you can't do things on your own. Because a lot of women, friends of hers, regret that life has passed them by and they're stuck.

Michelle took a similar message from her mother's struggle to break out of a deflating marital dynamic by building her own career:

> When I was younger, my mom was very dependent on my dad, and any unkind word he said to her, she would burst into tears. She had to get over that, and now she's at the point where she is a very independent person, very get-up-and-go.

Mothers also inspired daughters by using their resources to care for their children as well as themselves. Chrystal saw the strength of all women in her mother's hard work:

> It says a lot about her dedication to me and my sister, trying to make sure that we were taken care of. On a broader scale, it says a lot about women in general. No one's gonna do it for you; you have to go and do it yourself.

Beyond Mothers

Teachers, mentors, and bosses also provide models of independence that can underscore the rationale for self-reliance. Watching her mother languish with no job or husband, Nicole turned to her high school teachers for motivation and guidance:

> My mother was so fragile by the time I was coming of age that other women had an impact personally and in terms of career. Several teachers were very important because they were independent women, who I looked up to. I really grabbed on to them as role models.

Letitia struggled to figure out how to build a life different from her stay-at-home mother, who fell into poverty when her husband left. Looking to women who "are doing it for themselves," Letitia glimpsed the person she could become in her high school mentor, a young woman who directed an after-school program and took her "under her wing":

> Belinda was raised two blocks away from here, so I see me when I look at her. She's a single, beautiful, twenty-nine-year-old Puerto Rican female. She has a car, a condo, everything. She got her master's, and she did it all by herself. She takes no shortcuts.

Nina adopted a similar road map from her boss, who offered an uplifting example of occupational and financial achievement:

> My boss, she's phenomenal, truly a role model. She did the executive MBA program and got her degree in two years with the company.

The lessons young women drew from others accentuated the messages their mothers conveyed. They illustrated how self-reliance can nourish self-esteem and also provide insurance against such risks as being abandoned or stuck in an unworkable relationship.

Models to Emulate and Avoid

Most daughters distilled the same message from different examples: self-reliance has intrinsic value and offers protection in an uncertain world. A daughter might have qualms about making different choices than her mother, but such mixed feelings do not prevent her from following a different path, especially when she can draw on other, more attractive models. Angela compared her mother's domestic "choice" to her stepmother's "modern" stance:

> I respect my mother's choice, but my father left her, so I feel like I have to prove I can support an entire family on my own if I have to. I know my stepmom feels this way. She's more modern, so she would never put herself in a position to rely on her husband for a sense of security.

Most daughters considered the mix of attractions and pitfalls in their mothers' choices, weighing what to admire against what to question. They also found inspiration in other women's lives. All of these sources conveyed the message that they should hold onto a base in the world outside the home, whether or not they marry; maintain their own identity, even if they are responsible for the care of others; and preserve a realm of personal control, whether or not they are in an intimate relationship. These strategies offer a practical and hopeful alternative to the Hobson's choice of either being left unprepared or trapped in an unhappy marriage.[3]

EXPERIENCE AS THE TEACHER

The examples set by others are important, but they cannot substitute for lived experience. Even when mothers and other women provided appealing images of domesticity, most daughters nevertheless veered toward self-reliance. For Rosa, personal experiences reinforced the life lessons gleaned from parents and others:

> I've become who I am not only because of my parents, but also the situations I've been in. I learned from my mistakes. The bad situations have made me stronger and wiser. I am independent, and thankful for that.

Experiences with boyfriends and other partners reinforced a growing conviction that self-sufficiency provides the best insurance against the uncertainties of modern relationships.[4] At twenty-six, Anita gradually realized she had given up too much of herself in her early relationships:

> I would like to be in a relationship, but I haven't had such great experiences. I would tend to say "whatever," even though it's not really what I want, and look back on it later and see I ignored my needs until it became a real problem. So I'm realizing I don't need a man to be happy.

Serena, also twenty-six, felt regret about allowing a relationship to undermine her law school plans:

> In some ways, love is dangerous; it can take away from other things. That's why I didn't get into law school, because instead of studying, I would go out with him. So the things I'm into now, I wouldn't have time to put a guy first.

Anita and Serena both decided to eschew marriage until they establish a firmer professional foothold, but others reached the same conclusion after getting married. At twenty-five, Brianna rued the fact she had allowed her ex-husband to change her occupational course, but saw a silver lining in the breakup:

> I wanted to be an artist, and he really hated it, so I stopped, which I regret. I lost myself during the marriage, so I actually got a lot out of [the breakup]. Now I know what I *don't* want from a relationship. I know what I want from myself. It made me become the person I am, not the person he wanted me to be.

Donna also hit a snag when she learned of her husband's infidelity, but she returned after a temporary separation. Like Brianna, she brought a new determination to take care of herself and never again let a partner undermine her need to survive on her own:

> He thought I would die without him, but I said, "I'd rather be poor and happy than have this and be miserable." I started all over again and did fine for myself. So now I never worry about if I can take care of myself, 'cause I know I can, no matter what.

Those who married early, like those who stayed single, found the loss of autonomy an unacceptable price for a relationship. Even when they decided to stay, they vowed to retain an independent identity and seek their own place in the world of work. Needless to say, the search for self-reliance took on greater urgency for single mothers, where self-reliance became a blueprint for taking care of their children as well as themselves. Some decided having a demanding or unsupportive partner was worse than having no partner at all.[5] Rosa, a single mother at twenty-one, believed she could offer her young son more on her own, even if it meant relying temporarily on public assistance:

> My baby's father was very demanding. He was stuck, and he had me stuck, too. So after two years, I wouldn't take it any more. I feel like I can go faster and have more for our life. I want to finish college and be a social worker.

Also a single mother, Monique's hopes for an equal partnership transformed into a more "realistic" approach when the father of her two sons lost his job and then, in Monique's words, "deserted" them. At twenty-three, she decided she could not let her own and her children's survival depend on someone else. For better or worse, she needed to chart a more independent course:

> I was dependent on my kids' father, and I never want to be dependent on a man ever again. He lost his way, I guess because he lost his job, but I didn't lose my way. So I have the kids now, and I want the job, the career. When I have all that, I can add a man if he's a good guy, and if he's not, let him go.

Whether single or married, childless or a parent, these young women found risks in surrendering a barely achieved autonomy. Partners deemed too demanding, unreliable, or untrustworthy fell short of their egalitarian ideals. When partners threatened to knock a barely launched career off course and undermine an identity in formation, women reacted with a heightened determination to develop their own resources and make their own way in the world. Concerned about losing her independence, Miranda broke off an engagement after the wedding invitations had been sent:

> I compromised much more than I should have, so the breakup was an incredible lesson—something I needed to learn on my own. And it was a very cheap lesson ... just the cost of a wedding dress and a little embarrassment. I learned that nobody dies of not being in a relationship. So that's what I live by, even to this day.

Whatever their differences, these women share a determination to carve out a realm of personal autonomy. Self-reliance appears to offer the surest route to navigate between the ideal of equality and the dangers of dependence. It nurtures the self and provides a safety net no matter what the future might bring. But self-reliance does not preclude commitment. Once on safer ground, they will be in a better position to build the flexible, egalitarian bonds they prefer.

Strategies of Self-Reliance

Most women concluded, in Ashley's words, "You have to depend on yourself." But since there are few well-worn paths that lead toward self-reliance for women, they must blaze new ones. This requires the invention of innovative strategies that offer a measure of practical and psychological independence. Giving concrete form to the notion of "self-reliance," these efforts include establishing a solid base in the world of work, carving out a realm of personal autonomy within intimate relationships, creating a support network of kin and friends, and redefining what it means to be a good mother. Although these are private responses to social dilemmas that seem intensely personal, they reflect a strongly felt need to alter the institutionalized practices of gender.[6] By seeking economic, social, and emotional autonomy, young women are actively redesigning marriage, work, and motherhood.

SEEKING A BASE IN THE WORLD OF WORK

Self-reliant women look to the workplace as the most straightforward route to gaining financial security, social status, and personal identity. Indeed, young women today are just as likely as young men to say they are aiming for greater responsibility at work.[7] Reared by a stay-at-home mother in a middle-class suburb, Angela saw paid work as the way to avoid her mother's situation:

> I would never put myself in that position, ever... I feel like I always have to be ready, like what if my husband leaves me? My dad says, "You want to be able to support yourself and have your own independence," and I agree with him.

Danisha's parents both worked, and she agreed that her economic prospects depend on building a career, not presuming she can live on another person's income:

> Heaven forbid my marriage doesn't work. You can't take a cavalier attitude, so I want to establish myself. Because I don't ever want to have to end up like, "Oh my God, what am I gonna do?" I want to be able to do what I have to do and still be okay.

Sustained work participation appears to offer not only economic survival, but also social integration and personal esteem. After years of training to become a physical therapist, Megan viewed her work as central to her identity and social status:

I want to do more than just support myself. I want to be successful and have some recognition. I definitely think of my work as a career.

Donna dropped out of high school to drive a delivery truck, but her job in this male-dominated world demanded a nonnegotiable respect as important to her as to any man:

My husband tells me to quit my job and go to school, but I *have* to work. This is me; this is who I am. I can't *not* work. I didn't work once for eight months, and I'll never do that again.

Though analysts often distinguish between "needing" to work and "wanting" to work, these women see such distinctions as false and misleading.[8] In their view, work is essential precisely because it offers *both* financial and psychological benefits. Barbara could not separate the search for gratifying work from the search for a well-paid job:

What's most important is fulfillment in my work *and* being able to support yourself. Those go hand in hand. A job can be great in every sense, but only if I'm making what I feel I'm worth.

Despite the glass ceilings they may encounter, these women still see the workplace as the best place to find a measure of control over their destiny. For Danisha, who is planning to study medicine, building a career offers the chance to find something no one can take away:

There are certain things I can have control over, that I can have some hand in guiding my life in a certain direction. A job is something you always have. You can always go to it. So the career is necessary.

Given the erosion of job security in offices as well as factories, it may seem ironic and even misguided to see work as "always yours," to use Danisha's words. But compared to love and marriage, Nancy agreed, at least it is possible to set goals for work and then pursue them in a series of definable steps:

Work is very important because it is something I can strive for, push myself to be better at. There might be frustrations and stress involved at work, but work doesn't break your heart like relationships do.

For self-reliant women, work is both an essential end in itself and a means to other equally important ends. About to graduate from college, Letitia knew that the financial independence offered by a career would make it possible to achieve other markers of middle-class status, like home ownership, that had eluded her poverty-stricken mother. Only then, she reasoned, could she afford to take the apparently riskier step of sharing her life with someone else:

> No doubt, I'm gonna get my degree and have a career in criminal justice. I want my freedom and independence, and then I want to buy a house—so it's mine, no matter what. That's my finished product out of all the hard work, and nobody's ever going to take that away from me. Those are things I'm gonna get. The only thing in doubt is the right man to share it with.

REFASHIONING RELATIONSHIPS

Self-reliant women see two distinct dangers in traditional marriages. First, since marriage no longer promises permanence, they worry about relying too much on another person. Though only twenty, Jennifer assumed that the legal status of marriage offered scant protection from the fleeting emotion of "love":

> Just because you have that piece of paper, it's a false security. Because the other person can still fall out of love with you; they can still cheat on you; all those bad things can still happen. It's nice to believe in it 'cause it's tradition, but that doesn't really promise you anything.

Second, self-reliant women also believe the pressures of unequal marriage will constrain their efforts to establish an independent self. At twenty-six, Catherine was more concerned about losing her hard-won identity than losing a partner's love:

> When it comes down to the wire, my biggest fear is that I will lose the sense of who I am. I know the life I've made for myself, and I know that to make myself happy, I have to have more control over my surroundings. And if I don't have that, I'm not going to make anybody else happy.

Postponing Marriage

Self-reliant women seek to avoid the constraints of traditional marriage while still holding onto the possibility of finding a lifelong partner. First, they plan to avoid early commitments that might undermine self-development. Most eschew early marriage and "premature" commitments. As Danisha explained:

> I want to be stable for myself, so I'm not getting married prematurely. I don't fear growing older. I'll wait till I'm seventy-two if I need to.

Yet postponing marriage does not have to mean avoiding relationships. As the differences blur between marriage and other intimate bonds, self-reliant women view marriage as one of a number of options. Ashley preferred to steer clear of any intense relationship:

> I meet a lot of guys, and I'm pushing them away because I have to take care of myself first. I can't really think about you at this point. You will hold me back.

Most, however, prefer to find a partnership balancing closeness with room to pursue independent goals. Recently divorced, Brianna looked for someone who would respect her need for personal space:

> I have no interest in getting married again, because you do lose an incredible amount of freedom. Now, I'm looking for someone where we don't have to be attached at the hip. I just want to know I can call you up, and you'll be there.

Raising the Standard

By postponing marriage to focus on personal development, self-reliant women hold high standards for an acceptable partner. They want to find someone who will support their need for autonomy and who is also self-directed. As a Wall Street trader, Maria did not relish the idea of supporting her current boyfriend:

> The guy makes thirty-five thousand dollars a year, which is nothing. I always felt like I have to take care of myself, but I just don't want to take care of you. You take care of yourself, I'll take care of myself, and then we can be together.

Letitia did not wish to "settle" by letting her boyfriend support her:

> He's like, "I'm ready to support you." And I don't want anybody to support me. I have my life set already, and I'm not gonna mess it up. I think about marriage and meeting Mr. Right, but I can't settle.

These high standards signal a determination to free the concept of commitment from the strictures of distinct "gender roles." Even in the context of marriage, they deem financial self-sufficiency essential—not just as an insurance policy in the event of a breakup, but also because it offers personal independence within a committed relationship. For Nancy, separate bank accounts are a necessary condition for marital commitment:

I enjoy my financial independence. I would definitely want to have separate accounts and keep our money separate, so I'm not under the financial control of my husband.

Nina used the same rationale to reject her long-term live-in boyfriend's offer to support her while she pursued an MBA:

Tim said I could stop working to complete my MBA. I thought about it for two seconds, but I couldn't do it. I need to have my own money.

Seeing Marriage as Optional and Reversible

Although few wish to remain permanently single, and no one relishes the thought of enduring a breakup, most nevertheless reserve the option to reject marriage or leave an unhappy one. Even married women agree. With a young child and a sporadically employed husband, Louise admitted she would only stay married if he shared both breadwinning and caretaking:

I would like to stay together, but I'm also not going to put up with anything just to accomplish that. If I'm gonna work and take care of the baby and he's not gonna try, then I can be by myself. If he's just gonna lay around and not put in a effort, that's not fair.

Many entertained the option of not marrying. Though not ideal, going it alone looks better than surrendering hard-won autonomy to an unsatisfying relationship. After leaving a marriage in which she felt responsible "for everything," Chrystal decided staying single was better than being let down:

It isn't that I prefer it, but I just don't see myself being married. It doesn't matter whether I'd like to or not. To some degree, I would feel as if something's missing, but if I'm going to be successful in another area, then I wouldn't beat myself up for it.

Maria agreed with Chrystal that she could look to work, friends, and family to fill her life with meaning:

I can't settle. So if I don't find it, do I live in sorrow? To me, it's not one thing that's ultimately important. If I didn't have my family or a career or my friends, I would be equally unhappy. So it's really a circle. Maybe [not getting married] takes away a bit of the pie, but it's still just a slice.

Some women reject legal marriage, but not commitment. However much they wish to fall in love, they do not view marital vows as either a guarantee of lasting love or a legal structure to nourish it. Even though Rachel had grown up with married parents, she put little faith in marriage as an institution:

> Getting married doesn't thrill me in any way, shape, or form. You get to throw a party and have a great dress, but I don't think marriage means you're going to be together forever. And not getting married doesn't mean you're not going to be together forever.

These women see few practical differences between cohabiting and having a marriage license. They are part of a growing group of young people who plan to cohabit either before or instead of getting a marriage license. Pamela Smock reports that the percentage of first-time marriages preceded by cohabitation has risen substantially, from about 10 percent in the mid-1970s to over 50 percent by the mid-1990s, with an even higher percentage for remarriages. Among women, the percentage who cohabited by the time they reached their late thirties rose from around 30 percent to close to 50 percent in the same time period. These "trial marriages," as Sheldon Danziger calls them, are more socially accepted than ever.[9] Claudia echoes this perspective, even though her own parents had a stable marriage:

> People change. So the whole idea of marriage, where you promise to love someone forever, seems sort of unrealistic. If you love someone, getting married is almost incidental.

Not to be derailed from their personal path, these women avoided making early commitments—or, in some cases, left husbands—to focus on self-development.[10] They concluded that being unwilling to "settle" in the short run will help them to find a worthwhile bond in the long run. And there are good reasons to reach this conclusion, since postponing marriage and building a career do appear to confer benefits. In fact, the chance of divorce declines with each year a woman postpones marriage, and educated and high-earning women are less likely to divorce than other women.[11] Shauna agreed, detailing how taking the time to develop an independent self is the best route to building a healthy relationship:

> If you're not happy with yourself, then you can't be happy with someone else. I'm not looking for someone to fill a void. When you're content and happy with who you are, then you can give more of yourself to someone else.

Self-reliant women do not reject commitment; they just wish to redefine it. Instead of seeing marriage as a required and irreversible state, it is a desirable but optional and reversible option that also needs to offer room for personal autonomy and a better life than they can create on their own.[12] Holding onto the possibility of balancing an independent self with a lasting commitment, they are also prepared to go it alone if the right partner never comes along. Miranda explained:

> My boyfriend is a great guy, and I have nothing against marriage. If I meet the person who is perfect, I'll do it. But if it doesn't happen, I have no problem with it either. I'm not afraid of not finding someone.

These women are leading this "generation's redefinition of marriage," as a recent survey of young Americans between the ages of eighteen and twenty-four concluded.[13] They are less likely than men to believe parents must be married (50 percent of women, compared to 63 percent among men), more likely to question marriage as a way of life (45 percent, compared to 26 percent), and more discouraged about the prospects for marriage. Yet they are also increasingly confident that remaining single is not just an option, but a potential route to a good life.[14]

REDESIGNING MOTHERHOOD

As they seek financial independence at work and personal autonomy in relationships, self-reliant women face inevitable questions about the place of motherhood in their lives. Young women and teens overwhelmingly hope to become mothers, with surveys finding that 90 percent say they want to have children and most saying they want at least two.[15] Yet this wish does not necessarily mean endorsing traditional mothering, with its ideology of pure selflessness. Such a construction makes it difficult to see how—or if—motherhood can be reconciled with the search for independence and self-development. Maria saw her personal goals as incompatible with the sacrifices her mother made:

> It would be very hard for me to be a mother, because I could never be—and I don't want to be—the mother [my mother] was. I don't know that I could be that giving. You need to surrender your life. That's what she wanted, but I don't want to give up as much as she gave up.

The answer to the enduring conflict between autonomy and motherhood seems less determined and more contingent for young women than it appeared for their mothers. Megan viewed motherhood as an open question, not a preordained choice:

I don't think my parents had children because they decided to as much as it was the thing to do. Now there are more choices. I expect to have a better career and then decide, rather than having children and then try to struggle along with it.

In redesigning motherhood to better balance selfless devotion with personal autonomy, some young women postponed childbearing, while others found early motherhood a spur to their ambition. Most view marriage as the ideal environment for rearing children, but are nevertheless preparing for other contingencies. Everyone agrees, however, that good mothering can and often must include earning the bread as much as baking it. In all of these ways, self-reliant women are not only redesigning motherhood, but redefining the family.

Postponing Parenthood, or Not

Most self-reliant women plan to postpone motherhood until they can count on a stable work life, but a small group found that early motherhood spurred them to seek a career. For postponing women, developing the "self" is a precondition for having a child. They view motherhood as an optional and contingent choice that depends on a number of prior achievements. Barbara had no doubt that work comes first, even if this means resisting pressures to procreate:

I wouldn't have a child until I was in the right place. So getting the right work is doubly important. It's got to come first, essentially.

Catherine agreed:

I'm twenty-seven and nobody in my family would wait until they're twenty-seven, but this is the real world. So over the next seven or eight years, work would be my agenda. Maybe I'm selfish, but I'm going to put kids off until I'm thirty-five at least.

Other women reversed this sequence, developing a self-reliant outlook after having a child. Some are single and others have husbands with shaky employment ties, but all these young mothers found having a child spurred rather than dampened their aspirations.[16] Louise dropped out of school and married early, but changed her outlook when she realized her child's well-being depended on her efforts:

I'm going to become a nurse, and I have to do it, because I have a daughter, and I want to be able to give her things. I don't want to work as a cashier for the rest of my life.

Theresa underwent the same change:

I'm not working to take advantage of my kids; I'm working for a roof over our heads. So I'm gonna work to better myself, to try to make it out there, so that I can raise my girls in the proper way.

There are clear signs that a "mommy gap" is developing between middle-class women, who defer parenthood, and poor women, who are more likely to become young mothers.[17] In fact, during the period between 2000 and 2006, only 31 percent of women ages twenty-five to twenty-nine with a four-year college degree had borne a child, compared to 62 percent of women with less education.[18] But despite these differences, there are some surprising similarities between affluent and less advantaged women. While middle-class women are increasingly inclined to postpone parenthood and working-class and poor women are more likely to engage in early childbearing, both groups are underemphasizing marriage and placing greater stress on self-reliance.

Separating Marriage and Motherhood

The child-rearing strategies of those who postponed motherhood and those who entered it early are converging despite their social and class differences. While marriage might be the ideal context for rearing children, the uncertainty of relationships requires both groups to prepare for other contingencies. Some are resolved to forgo motherhood if the right person does not come along, but most entertain the possibility of becoming a mother whether or not they marry. For Megan, having a child depended on finding a partner willing to share equally:

I would be willing to make sacrifices, but I would expect my husband to do the same. If he's not willing to do that, I certainly wouldn't want a child.

But Anita, speaking for the majority, planned to pursue motherhood even if she remained single:

I want to have the experience of being a mother, so I want to be in the place where I could, if I needed, have a child on my own. I want to know that I can support a child on my own, that I don't need a man for it.

Indeed, a growing percentage of women from all social backgrounds are either having or are prepared to have children on their own. In fact, in 2006, for the first time in U.S. history, unmarried women accounted for about 40 percent of all births and about half of births to women under thirty (compared to 6 percent in 1960). Even though about half of these births are to cohabiting but unmarried couples, that leaves 20 percent of births to women living without a partner.[19] Self-reliant women may not welcome single motherhood, but they are preparing for it. Letitia hoped for the best, but felt she needed to be ready to care for a child on her own:

> You can't force people to be responsible, and if it happens that way, I would make it the best for my child, whether he's there or not.

And Miranda placed the link between mother and child, with or without a father, at the core of family life:

> I see a family, I look at the mother. If I see her in any kind of way held back, I don't like it. If she looks happy, then I think that's a good family. 'Cause I think she's really the central figure.

Across the educational spectrum, women are willing to reject traditional definitions of family life centered on the bond between wife and husband. In fact, while single motherhood remains more prevalent among those without a college education, college-educated single mothers are growing at a much faster pace. Well-educated single mothers are also more likely to have their first child after age thirty, compared with only about 8 percent overall, but all of these women have decided to have a child without a husband.[20] If industrialism, with its need for a socially and geographically mobile labor force, contributed to the rise of the "conjugal family" with a husband-wife unit at its center, then the rise of postindustrialism has supported the "mother-child" family, where fathers may or may not be present.[21] In a world of fragile marital ties and mothers' employment, bearing and raising a child on one's own may not be ideal, but it is an available option.

Breadwinners Are Good Mothers

With or without marriage, self-reliant women are also reframing their views of good mothering to include breadwinning. Because these women do not wish to depend on another's person's income, they view the financial rewards of a good job as *essential* to being a good mother, not an option or an alternative. Barbara believed that only by establishing her own economic foundation could she secure the well-being of any child she might have:

> I don't know about the marriage, but I definitely picture myself as the breadwinner. If I'm gonna have this child, I have to know that I have "x" amount of dollars coming in or in the bank to support this kid and myself at the level I want.

Yet the desire—and need—for personal autonomy clashes with anxiety about living up to the cultural standard of good mothering. To reduce these internal and external pressures, they perceive the need to challenge the argument that a child's needs should supersede a mother's, reasoning instead that a child's well-being is inseparably intertwined with a mother's happiness. Jennifer saw her own development as a necessary ingredient in rearing happy, well-adjusted children:

> My personal happiness would have to be equal with the children; otherwise there won't be any children's happiness. 'Cause if I'm miserable, they're gonna be miserable too.

Miranda echoed this view:

> There's a different type of growth with a child, but first, I have to make sure I'm okay. Because if the life is getting sucked out of you, how can you give life to someone else?

To lessen the pressure of the ideology that only full-time motherhood will do, they also view employed mothers as excellent models for their children. Catherine declared:

> I have to almost show my children, "Look, this is how people take care of themselves, and mommy can do this." I want that example always.

And Patricia agreed:

> I have a pretty strong work ethic, and I feel it's important for the kids to see work isn't a bad thing.

Making motherhood consistent with carving out a personal space clashes with the widespread and persistent concern that children suffer when their mothers work (even though decades of research have failed to show this). Self-reliant women may not dispel these worries, but they do not acquiesce to them. Social disapproval may leave them feeling uncomfortable, but it does not dictate their strategies. Willing to endure social opprobrium, whether or not it is fair, Brianna did not intend to let this prevent her pursuit of a career:

> I'll be one of those women they talk about in the magazines all the time. Like, "I feel guilty 'cause I'm not home, but I don't want to be home."

Despite having varied backgrounds, self-reliant women seek to reconcile the demands of motherhood with the pursuit of economic self-sufficiency and a strong work identity by making breadwinning a part of good mothering.

They reject the view that mothering demands undiluted altruism and sacrifice, contending that maternal self-development provides children with special benefits. Yet they are also prepared to weather the disapproval it will likely bring, even though they believe pursuing a career need not preclude—and actually enhances—being a good mother.

CREATING CARE NETWORKS

Self-reliant women do not want or expect to do it all by themselves, however. They seek support from a web of friends, kin, and paid help to survive, and even thrive, on their own. For the most part, they focus on women-centered networks. Miranda found that relying on female friends and relations helped her postpone marriage and stick to high standards in the search for a mate:

> I'm always surrounded by very strong women. And because I've had such a great relationship with my family, it's been able to infuse in me a feeling of not needing to be in a relationship.

Rachel drew on a similar safety net of support:

> I want to get married and have children, but I can spend the rest of my life alone. As long as I have my sisters and my friends, I'm okay.

If friends and kin are integral to remaining happily single, becoming a mother makes them even more important. A caretaking network helps mothers combine full-time work with childbearing and, if needed, do so without a steady partner. While working-class women leaned toward calling on family members, and middle-class women more often looked to paid caretakers, they all plan to rely on others. Reliance on her own stay-at-home mom allowed Letitia to plan to work full-time, even as a single mother:

> I have it all planned out—my mom's living next to me because she's going to take care of my kids while I'm working. So to have an unhealthy relationship with a man—I'd never do that—but as long as I've got my mom, I can be the provider, the mother and father.

Suzanne believed the exposure to other children and adults would help her child develop skills that staying home would not:

> Staying at home isn't necessary. Kids get along just as well if they go to nursery school and interact with other people.

For these women, achieving autonomy requires delegating, whether to family members or paid caretakers. Again resisting injunctions for exclusive mothering, they look to a network of caretakers to enhance their own and their children's welfare. Convinced her own mother's isolation contributed to both her depression and her violent actions, Rachel hoped getting help from others would allow her to avoid her mother's mistakes:

> Part of the reason my mother was [physically] abusive—there was no one there. So I want somebody else there. That way, should I ever get to the point where I think I'm going to do anything like what my mother did, I'd be able to remove myself from that situation. If I didn't have a way to make sure, I wouldn't have children.

If pursuing self-reliance means achieving an independent identity and income, it does not mean being isolated or disconnected. John Donne famously declared that "no man is an island," and this is certainly the case for women. In fact, self-reliant women define independence as knowing whom they can depend on for what.[22] As Erica declared, "I don't see leaving it up to one person. As a woman, you have to delegate responsibilities." By creating "chosen families" out of a web of kin, friends, and paid caretakers, self-reliant women want to blend the search for an independent identity with close connection to others.

CONVERGING FORCES

Though their experiences seem personal and idiosyncratic, the strategies of self-reliant women are rooted in a shared understanding that traditional marriages no longer seem secure or appealing. Some, like Maria, understood they are responding to a social context that lowers the chances of finding a relationship like her parents' egalitarian one:

> I would want to have what they had, but I don't think I'll ever have that. I'm twenty-nine and still single, and that's not old, but sometimes I'm forced to ask myself if it's an unrealistic thing. It's a different way to live now.

Whether they emphasize the rewards of self-development or the risks of subordinating their identities and bank accounts, self-reliant women feel caught between domesticity's drawbacks and equality's elusiveness. Though they count on fallback strategies to survive in a less than perfect world, they nevertheless see a silver lining in taking care of themselves. Recalling her grandmother's injunction that, "whatever you have in your brain, whatever you have learned, no one can take that away from you," Miranda knew she could rely on herself. Chrystal took pride in her budding publishing career, her condo, and her ability to care for her young son. Comparing these feats to her parents' lifelong struggles with poverty, she marveled at her own accomplishments:

> Seeing that it's been just me, I think I've accomplished a lot and, not to sound like I'm better than anyone, I can't think of anyone else where I want to be like that person. Because I'm doing pretty well on my own.

By offering protection against the risks of financial dependence, social isolation, and personal stagnation, self-reliant strategies offer insurance against many of women's deepest anxieties. Amid the decline of permanent marriage and "good provider" husbands, they provide another route to economic survival and, for the fortunate, financial security. Amid the rise of new occupational options, they offer new sources of social status and personal esteem. And amid the rise of new childbearing and child-rearing options, they offer alternative ways to create strong family ties. Yet even though these converging social forces make self-reliant strategies seem both necessary and appealing, they still fall short of women's highest ideals.

Falling Back on Domesticity

Not all women are falling back on self-reliance; more than a quarter of those interviewed see independence as more dangerous than domesticity. These women prefer to center their lives around marriage and motherhood rather than risk ending up alone, overburdened, or both.

Why did this sizeable minority reach such a different conclusion about their best chance for the future? Caught between tradition and change, they face obstacles such as resistant partners and inflexible workplaces that make domesticity a more appealing option. Yet even they do not see homemaking as a full-time or permanent pursuit. Though convinced of the need to provide concerted time and attention to child rearing, they still hope to refashion traditionalism by incorporating a scaled-back job or career.

BETTER THAN BEING ALONE

For some women, few fates seem worse than remaining on their own. In fact, watching friends and coworkers who eschewed marriage and motherhood left them determined to follow a different route. Lauren had no desire to emulate a friend who refused to "settle":

A friend of mine hasn't had a good relationship—she's twenty-seven and never been in love. She's very bitter. I think she's looking for Mr. Perfect, and he's not coming. I don't want to be like her, so I'd be almost willing to settle.

Janet believed her boss's decision to put work before marriage held too many long-run dangers:

My current boss, the president of the company, I don't want to be like her. She's had a lot of bad relationships, and she's forty-two. She's not married, with no kids, and she'd like very much to be with a guy.

Women who turned toward domesticity also discovered unexpected stability in relationships, which prompted a newfound confidence in the viability of marriage. A tumultuous childhood left Nicole surprised to find herself happily married at twenty-two:

For the first time in my life, I have a very stable relationship. And a pretty stable self. I'm really enjoying who I am with my husband.

Though her parents' unhappy marriage left Connie with little confidence in the institution of marriage, she met a "wonderful man" who convinced her to change her mind:

I haven't seen evidence of many good marriages, so it wasn't important to me. Then we started discussing having a child, and I felt practically, it's better to be married. I'm a very practical person. Then he surprised me and proposed.

These women shifted their priorities in unforeseen ways. Even ambitious women began to question the primacy of work as they faced difficulties balancing a relationship with building a career. Unwilling to risk the loss of her partner, Lauren changed her focus to motherhood:

When I came out of college, I was so motivated, but it seems now that I would give up work to raise a child. I never would have said that a couple of years ago, but I wouldn't sacrifice this relationship for work. So now I'm thinking I do want to get married and have children and that's more important to me than work.

Traditional partnerships dampened the fear of relying on a partner's paycheck. Connie felt grateful that her husband was prepared to be a primary breadwinner who did not resent her lack of earnings:

It's very clichéd, but I had to separate myself from where I came from. I'm a very practical person, and I found somebody unlike [my] father. He doesn't even care how much money I bring in, so I'm lucky.

Domestically inclined women see single women not as an inspiration but rather as a warning about the costs of putting work first. Their experiences in a traditional relationship also allayed fears about marriage and mitigated concerns about relying on another person's earnings. Faced with giving up a treasured partner or giving up a measure of independence, they began to opt for a more traditional bargain.

AVOIDING OVERLOAD

If traditional partnerships pulled some women toward the home, inflexible workplaces also pushed them there. Whether observing others or reflecting on their own work experiences, these women worry about the escalating time demands of contemporary careers.[23] Even women whose mothers had gone to work every day believed they would have a harder time balancing a job with the rest of their life. Elizabeth fully supported her mother's career, but her own early work experiences left her doubting she could follow in her mother's footsteps:

I thought it was so easy, and now I'm just terrified because it seems so hard. I don't know how my parents did it, actually.

Janet also marveled at her mother's success at combining an administrative career with family responsibilities, but she did not see this as a feasible option in her own life:

It was great [for my mother to work]. I have a lot of respect for that. But, personally, I don't know how people do it. I don't know what you do if you have kids and your client calls with a crisis at six o'clock at night. I would go out of my mind.

Faced with time-intensive workplaces, these women fear that a full-time job will make it difficult to raise a family without succumbing to exhaustion and failure. And since time use studies show that employed mothers have less free time and greater total workloads than stay-at-home mothers, they have good reason to be concerned. In fact, Suzanne Bianchi, John Robinson, and Melissa Milkie report that employed mothers average about 71 hours a week of paid and unpaid work, while mothers without paid jobs average about 52 hours.[24] Aware of this bind, if not the exact details, they reluctantly turned away from the demands of the "ideal worker" ethos and the single-minded devotion to work it requires.[25] Karen did not want to lodge her identity in—or sacrifice her personal life to—the apparently all-consuming requirements of a high-powered career:

> When I started going to work, I didn't want to resign myself to living that way. Because it's starting to make me feel like that's who I am— it's starting to define me—and that's definitely not what I want. So now I'm working in a corporate environment, but knowing that it's temporary, knowing that there's something better.

Since many jobs now require not just full-time but overtime devotion, these women believe they could have a full family life only by rejecting a career. Seeing no alternative to this rigid model, Elizabeth felt she had to choose:

> I keep hoping someday I'll have more flexibility, but I don't see a career as an option. Sometimes you have to sacrifice things, and when I have kids, that will be more important.

BECOMING THE DEFAULT CARETAKER

While the pressure to parent intensively has grown for all women, employed or not, neotraditional women go further. In addition to believing that only a parent can provide an acceptable level of care, they believe they are the only parent available for the job. As Tiffany explained:

> I want to work, but I don't want to have a child in day care. I feel strongly about someone being with the child, and I know it would have to be me.

In contrast to their work-committed peers, they are not prepared to delegate. Instead, motherhood means trading equality for a clear division of family tasks. Jessica declared:

> I know things should be equal, but I want to have a family, so I think I won't be able to work—not for the first few years of their lives. I want to spend time raising them and make sure they're raised properly. I wouldn't want to send them to day care.

Of course, if a father is willing and able to be equally involved, women need not do it all, even if they are reluctant to rely on a nonparental caretaker. But those who fell back on domesticity hold little hope that equal sharing is a realistic goal. Nicole believed she might overcome her husband's resistance, but doubted he had the necessary domestic skills:

I see us both having a very significant role, but I see myself playing much more of the domestic role, just because he's so lousy at it.

Dolores knew the problem was motivation, not ability:

I have changed so much on my husband, and he still will not wash the dishes. He refuses. I guess it's the way he was raised, because he's already set in his ways.

Faced with a resistant partner, these women faced a choice between adding a domestic "second shift" to a demanding job and pulling back from work. Even though Dolores and her husband both worked full-time, "he feels he works harder." When she was offered a promotion at the hospital, where she worked as an administrator, her husband, a jewelry maker, made it clear she could accept the added responsibility—as long as she still took care of matters at home:

Just the way he said, "I have to make up my own mind." He's not going to prevent me. He wouldn't. It's just that I have to make provisions.

Ironically, women face intensified parenting pressures just as they have joined the workplace in unprecedented numbers. The shortage of high-quality, affordable child care, along with men's reluctance to pull back from time-demanding jobs, leave women as the default caretaker.[26] Despite a preference for egalitarian parenting, this "structure of gender" exerts great force on such women, despite their preference for more egalitarian parenting.

FITTING WORK IN

Even though marriage and motherhood take precedence over work or career for traditional women, few wish to be full-time, long-term homemakers. Rather than withdrawing completely or indefinitely from paid work, most plan to "fit work in" even as they put family first. These women are falling back on a "neotraditional" strategy, but only partially and temporarily.

Now that two incomes provide a key way for couples to achieve their desired standard of living, even women who expect to rely mainly on a partner's income feel the need to make a contribution. Dolores's husband felt ambivalent about seeing her advance to a higher level, but valued her economic contributions:

I think it may bother him if I'm moving up the ladder. He may see, "Oh, she's moving up, and I'm staying here." ... [but] there's always difficulties when the money is low, so he wants me to work.

And even though Tiffany had little desire to be the main breadwinner, she felt a personal responsibility to help out financially:

> I wouldn't feel comfortable supporting a man, so he would be the major breadwinner. But I would be a contributor. I want to work, but there would be a period of time where I wouldn't want to work.

Women who put family first still face social and personal pressures to establish an identity beyond those of wife and mother. At twenty-five, Stephanie was prepared to settle for less than she once expected, but she was not prepared to relinquish all her aspirations:

> One expectation, when I was younger, was I'd have my own business. Now, I don't know if I'll ever find the career—or have the time to have the career—that I wanted or was meant for. But I do need to have something for myself, whether it's part-time work or something that I enjoy.

These neotraditional women are juggling the pressure to be a devoted mother with the pressure to help with family finances and claim a separate self. In searching for ways to fit work into their lives without upsetting the domestic balance, they define domesticity as a "time-out," not a way of life.

Scaling Back

Some women scaled back on earlier ambitions, while others could not take advantage of opportunities when they arose. After several years in the corporate world, Lauren gave up on climbing the corporate ladder:

> I became very motivated when I was in high school and just knew that I wanted a lot, but lately I figure I'll do something for a while, but never be the vice president of the company or something.

Dolores did not set out to move up, but her intelligence, dedication, and energy won her a promotion out of the secretarial ranks. But when her job as an executive coordinator required travel that took too much time away from her children, she reluctantly moved back to a lower rung:

> I was doing secretarial work, and then I was a program coordinator. I loved the job. No matter what job I'm in, I bring home work, but the travel time was just too much, and I needed to be closer to my children. So I took a downgrade and became a secretary again. It was a change to a better location, even if it meant making a sacrifice. But hopefully something will go through, and I won't be a secretary anymore.

To offset these sacrifices, neotraditional women define success as the whole package of family and work, not just moving up an organizational chart.[27] For Mariela, the well-being of her children and family meant as much as the size of her paycheck:

> Successful would be the whole marriage thing, kids, a home of my own. I wouldn't have to be successful in my job, because the family comes first—but that I get a good job—meaning I'm getting paid enough to live comfortably with my family.

This definition of success offers the silver lining of "choice." While a neotraditional strategy might constrain the chance to move up, women hope it might expand the chance for work with more intrinsically rewarding pay-offs.[28] In lieu of a substantial paycheck, Karen planned to take a job only if and when the right conditions were present:

> If I do work when I have kids, I want it to be on my own terms. If I have opportunities to work in stuff that I enjoy, then I would like to work, but I'd also like to have time to be with the children.

Just a Time-Out

Though resigned to scaling back, even neotraditional women hope to hold onto work ties in the long run. In contrast to the June Cleavers and Harriet Nelsons of 1950s nostalgia, they define any time they might take off as temporary.[29] For Mariela, taking a "time-out" from the workplace offered a way to parent intensively before eventually establishing a career:

> I would like to be there when they're growing up. I want to see them take their first walk. Later on, I'll go back to work. They're only young for so long.

Kristen even planned to weave back and forth from medical school to stay-at-home motherhood to postgraduate medical training:

> I don't think I'm going to work continuously. I want to go to medical school, and when the child's three or four, do my residency.

Others hope to interweave part-time work with motherhood rather than discontinue work altogether.[30] They seek jobs not requiring long days at the office. Nicole planned to work at home:

> Hopefully, I can write and be there. I feel very strongly about being there the first five or six years. I think it's very important, and I don't believe in full-time help.

Stephanie wanted to blend work with caretaking by working fewer hours:

> As long as financially I don't have to, I won't work a nine-to-five job.
> But I want to put myself in a situation where I can do something, even
> if that means getting some part-time help with the children when I'm
> working.

NOT DÉJÀ VU ALL OVER AGAIN

Since the conflicts between work and family life have intensified, it is not
surprising that a sizeable minority prefer to fall back on domesticity rather
than economic autonomy.[31] Faced with intransigent workplaces, resistant
partners, and pressures to pour time and energy into child rearing, it is surprising that *more* women are not pursuing this course.[32] Lynne felt she had
little choice in a world with so few alternatives:

> It sounds nice to say, "We share everything equally," but I don't think
> that's realistic. So children are my first priority. I'm sure it will wind
> up being like that. It's just the way society is.

Neotraditionalism offers some a better alternative than self-reliance, but
it also represents a reluctant scaling back of earlier aspirations. Karen grudgingly came to the conclusion she could not do it all:

> I think family might come first, and then work. I have this image of
> not working when I have kids, which is funny because of my mom.
> I hate to think that I'm staying home, but there is a sense of having
> to compromise.

Women who stress the primacy of mothering recognize the forces moving
other women toward self-reliance, and these concerns also prompt them to
search for ways to integrate work into their lives. They seek a compromise
between intensive parenting and rigid, demanding jobs by retaining the
hope of ultimately establishing strong work ties and even a career. They also
expect their partners to "help" at home, even if they retain primary responsibility. Stephanie explained:

> With his position, he's home four days. So even though financially
> he'll be the primary breadwinner, he'll still have a big part at home.
> Just from the way he was brought up, I don't think he would be happy
> any other way.

Falling back on domesticity does not signal a return to the 1950s family. It reflects a desire—and need—to refashion this model to fit the social

and economic exigencies of the twenty-first century. Even the most traditional women seek to include some of the advantages work bestows while also avoiding the dual burden that can overwhelm those trying to "do it all."

Blurring Boundaries, Uncertain Futures

Torn between high hopes and deepening doubts, young women are pioneering new strategies for navigating the future. Whether they prefer self-reliance or neotraditionalism, the overwhelming majority of my interviewees (83 percent) agree they have it better than their mothers or grandmothers. But they also take these improvements with a grain of salt. For Connie, the forces of change have created both unprecedented options and difficult new pressures:

> We have it better in that we have more freedom, more independence, more rights, but worse because a lot more is expected of us. When people find out I stay home, they look at me as less of a person. But when they enter the working environment, women still have to work twice as hard to get the same recognition as men. I know I did.

New options have grown alongside persisting obstacles to equality and a lack of institutional supports for combining work and parenting. The clash between demographic shifts and institutional rigidity has created contradictions of work and marriage in addition to the contradictions of motherhood documented by Sharon Hays. In an ironic twist, middle-class married women with good job opportunities and access to high-quality child care are chastised for pursuing careers, while poor single mothers with few job prospects and limited child care are required to take marginal jobs.[33] The implied message is that women should not depend on others for their livelihood, but they also should not work for personal satisfaction or compete for the best jobs. These cultural and structural contradictions leave all women facing unavoidable double binds, where any strategy poses inescapable conflicts. Neither self-reliance nor domesticity can provide an ideal solution to women's search for *both* personal independence *and* lasting bonds. Theresa, who is married and combining full-time work with rearing two children, felt frustrated that *any* choice leaves her facing social disapproval and personal uncertainty:

> They're pushing you to work, but they're not secure with what's going on in day care. Either way, you're messed up. Sometimes I feel like, "What do they want from us?"

Monique, who is rearing two young sons on her own and trying to find a job, agreed:

> I shouldn't *have* to stay home, but I wished we were in a society where I *could* stay home. You shouldn't have to do the impossible, and that's just what I'm doing. I'm making the impossible possible.

In this "damned if you do and damned if you don't" situation, young women focus on different dangers and are developing different strategies for navigating the future. Most view self-reliance as their best protection against the pitfalls of traditional marriage. Coming from all backgrounds, they have learned this lesson from their mothers, other women, and their own experiences. To secure what they deem to be indispensable economic, social, and emotional resources, they are establishing firm ties to paid work, redesigning motherhood to fit their work aspirations, and looking to kin and friends to enlarge their support and, if needed, cushion the absence of an enduring intimate partnership.

Since job and marital opportunities differ by class and race, these differences give self-reliant strategies a different cast. Well-educated women, who hope to establish a promising career, are more likely to postpone motherhood and to expect sufficient financial resources to purchase paid help, but they are also more likely to worry about the time demands of high-status occupations. Working-class and poorer women, with fewer job opportunities, are more likely to become young mothers and to rely on an extended network of relatives and friends. In some sense, African-American women, who overwhelmingly seek self-reliance regardless of their educational level and class position, are the cutting edge of this change.

Yet despite the differences between rich and poor, single and married, and Black, Asian, Latino, and white, women's self-reliant strategies share core elements: work is essential; marriage is optional and reversible; relationships should leave room for autonomy; and good mothering includes earning a living and sharing care. These strategies do not preclude finding a life partner, but they come with high standards for choosing one. Despite the media-driven image of young women turning back the historical clock, large numbers seek new ways to survive, thrive, and establish an independent identity, whether or not they are also able to forge a lasting bond.

Alongside this general trend, however, a notable minority prefer to fall back on domesticity. These women would rather resolve work-family conflicts by making a traditional compromise than by living without a partner or trying to do it all. The needs of children, the inflexible demands of the workplace, the lack of child care, and the difficulties of finding an equally involved partner make domesticity more appealing. Yet, tipping their own hat to the attractions of new options, domestically inclined women still want to fit paid jobs into their lives. They, too, are trying to find a less rigidly gendered balance between home and work.

Despite their differences, both fallback positions involve significant costs for young women. Domesticity, even in the form of neotraditionalism, requires forgone opportunities at work and consequent financial vulnerability. Women who drop out of the workforce, even for short periods, pay a large long-term economic penalty, and the model of a career as full-time, uninterrupted work continues to leave women, and especially mothers, at a disadvantage.[34] Yet self-reliance risks loneliness along with the weight of doing it all. Most women want to enjoy the benefits of enduring commitment, but they do not want marriage to entail working twice as hard.

Aware of these dilemmas, young women know any outlook, no matter how fervently held, may change as their circumstances change. In the face of this uncertainty, they have learned to remain flexible. Miranda's shifting family circumstances left her ready to adapt to unforeseeable developments:

> With my father, I learned we had no chance of making plans because who knows if they were going to happen. I've been doing it for so long, I couldn't live without that. So I keep it really flexible.

Sarah, reflecting on her own lesbian relationship, drew a similar lesson from her parents' resistance to change:

> My parents had to live with the bad consequences 'cause they were not willing to change. They probably didn't feel they were able to change, but they're a generation back.

The search for self-reliance and the turn toward neotraditionalism are both less-than-ideal alternatives. Whether married or single, employed or at home, women are walking on a common ground that may shift without warning and propel them in new directions.

CHAPTER SEVEN | Men's Resistance to Equal Sharing

WHILE GENDER INEQUITIES MAY explain why young women prepare for "second best" options, men are not immune from similar concerns. The increased fragility of marriage, growing time demands and insecurities at work, and women's rising standards for a relationship all confront men with new dilemmas of their own. Though men's responses may differ, they also face options likely to fall short of their ideals.

Young men share women's doubts about their chances of striking a good balance between earning and caring, but they experience this conflict in a different way. If women worry about the economic, social, and psychological risks of depending too much on someone else, men are more apprehensive about their financial ability to support others. And if women worry about having to assume the lion's share of family caretaking whether or not they marry or have a paid job, men face rising pressures to do more at home and earn more at work if they do marry.

Perceiving different obstacles, men form different fallback strategies. Uneasy about the price equality might exact, seven out of ten men look to modified traditionalism, in which they retain the position of a family's main breadwinner while also granting their partner the right, and need, to work. If equality proves impossible or just too costly, these men seek to preserve some distinct gender divisions that most women resist.[1]

The minority of men who do not fall back on modified traditionalism share women's skepticism about traditional marriage. In contrast to women who are preparing to do it all on their own, however, these men are more likely to emphasize freedom *from* family obligations. Anxious about achieving a cultural ideal equating "being a man" with supporting a family, they stress self-reliance as a route to autonomy more than to connectedness. These men are drawn to the freedom side of the tension between commitment and freedom. This tension has pervaded American culture since its inception as a frontier society, but it takes a special form in a world where men face declining economic opportunities and expanding options to reject marriage.[2] This mix of new constraints and opportunities has increased the lure of autonomy, especially for men who doubt they can live up to the cultural injunction to be a breadwinner or the rising pressure to take on more responsibility at home.

Faced with different options and fears, men are adopting fallback strategies that clash with women's. Yet men's outlooks, no less than women's, reflect the need to pursue second-best scenarios because more desirable options seem out of reach. Most men, like most women, prefer a more egalitarian, flexible balance between breadwinning and caretaking. Their aspirations are converging, even if their strategies do not.

It's Hard to Do It All

Today's young men face an uncertain economic landscape and rising expectations for equality in relationships. Each may be a cause for concern, but together, these forces create conflicting pressures. They press men to give more time and energy to both work and family, leaving most to wonder if they can succeed—or even survive—in their jobs or at home. Indeed, a recent study of the American workforce found that 45 percent of employed men report experiencing either "some" or "a lot" of work-life conflict (compared to 34 percent in 1977), and among men in dual-earner couples, that number rises to almost 60 percent.[3] Like these men, Adam worried about whether he could pursue a medical career and also live up to his father's example as an involved parent as well as a successful dentist and good provider:

> I would like to think I'm gonna earn enough money to live a nice life, [but] I'm afraid of not doing as well as my father—either career-wise or family-wise.

Although Mitch's dad was a psychologist who spent plenty of time at home, his own job in banking left him doubtful about the chances of finding work that would allow a similar balance and still ensure a steady income:

> [My dad] certainly set a good example, a paradigm model if you want to call it. In the ideal world, I'd love to work until 4:00, 4:30, then spend time with my family. I want my children to have a real father as

opposed to someone who just kisses them good night. I'd like to have a fairly equal balance, kind of like my dad, but it would be tough to attain because a lot of careers are downsizing, and they want you to work weekends and around the clock.

Men also face new pressures for involvement at home. Although acknowledging the loss, in Sam's words, of a "get out of housework free" card, most focus more on the obstacles to building an equal relationship. Chris hoped to re-create his father's flexible approach, but feared striking such a balance in his own life would be arduous and costly:

I thought you could have just a relationship, and I've learned that you've got to be able to draw that line. It's a difficult thing. And that would be my fear—where am I cutting into my job too much, where am I cutting into the relationship too much, and how do I divide it, and can it actually be done at all?

Lawrence knew even the most rewarding domestic activities would place limits on his independence:

A large part of me wants to have the picket fence, big house, big family, and coach the Little League team and be the head of PTA. And then there's the other side that wants a lot more freedom.

These cross-pressures have raised the stakes on men, leaving them skeptical about whether they can live up to their own ideals or the expectations of others. Reflecting on his hard-working Chinese parents' struggle to keep the family afloat, even though they relied on two incomes, Justin blamed the economy:

You don't want to be in a situation where in order to put food on the table, you can't meet the child's needs in another way. I have a high standard. I don't want to be a sloppy father. So it's a conundrum. I don't think it's as simple as it was in the past.

Joel pointed to his own "high standards," and especially his hope to avoid the pitfalls of his parents' unhappy traditional marriage, but he agreed his goal of equal parenting was on a collision course with successful breadwinning:

I feel sometimes that my standards are too high, and I want it all, and it's just not reasonable or feasible in this world. I don't feel I'm as strong a person as that situation would require—someone who is on top of everything and sort of a superman. It doesn't really seem like I'd be able to keep up that pace.

Young men face trade-offs that mirror those facing women. Like women, they believe the ideal work-family balance will have to give way to a fallback scenario, but men are inclined to fall back on emphasizing their breadwinning rights and duties. Josh felt strongly that, despite his professed support for equality, he could not surrender his duty to be the primary earner:

I'll work as hard as I could to support them. I just think it's a responsibility. It conflicts with what I said about women, but that's just something I feel—that a man's first responsibility is to take care of his family. I know it's kind of contradictory.

Matthew agreed:

I want family life to be the most important thing. If I could have the ideal world, I'd like to have a partner who's making as much as I am—someone who's ambitious and likes to achieve. [But] if it can't be equal, I would be the breadwinner and be there for helping with homework at night.

Yet not all men agree with this view. Some seek more independence than a traditional marriage allows. They neither want to submit to the strictures of conventional jobs nor hope to find a domestically oriented partner. Divorced and on his own in his late twenties, Nick vowed to avoid his father's nine-to-five routine:

I don't want to end up being your every day, run-of-the-mill Joe Commuter, like those uptight people who worry about this bill and that. I don't want to be stuck in one place for twenty-five years. I want to do it my way.

Men's fallback positions reverse rather than mimic women's. Though women disproportionately favor self-reliance, men favor more traditional patterns. They are prone to stress their own economic responsibilities and prerogatives, even if a marriage contains two earners.[4] Figures 7.1 and 7.2 show that a majority of men from all types of backgrounds prefer breadwinning as a fallback, although African-Americans, Latinos, and those from single-parent homes and working-class or poor families are more evenly divided. For these groups, who continue to face more constricted job opportunities, lower rates of educational attainment, and higher incarceration rates, a larger proportion stress freedom from breadwinning, even in the context of an intimate relationship (including slightly more than a third of African-American and Latino men, and close to half of men from single-parent homes).[5]

Because men face different options than women, their versions of both traditionalism and self-reliance also differ. For men, traditionalism means

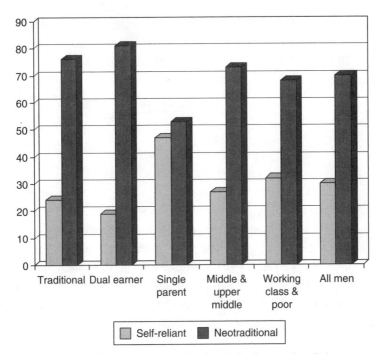

FIGURE 7.1 Men's fallback positions, by family background and class.

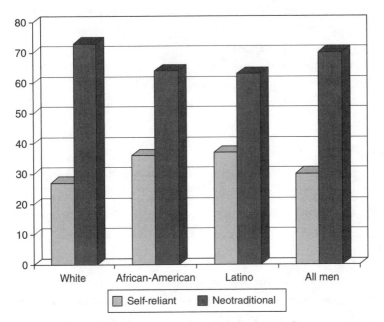

FIGURE 7.2 Men's fallback positions, by ethnic background.

taking on the privileges and responsibilities of primary breadwinning, while self-reliance means *not* being responsible for the care and feeding of a family. Yet even though young men's fallback positions differ from women's, they are "second best" strategies nonetheless.

Falling Back on Breadwinning

Like women who look to domesticity, men who fall back on breadwinning place marriage and family at the center of their plans. For men, this means being a good provider. Parental examples, lessons on the job, and experiences in relationships have convinced them that, when push comes to shove, they need to take responsibility for their family's financial welfare. Some view breadwinning as a privilege, while others see it as an obligation, but they all agree that no matter what the gender revolution prescribes, it is still paramount for men to earn a living and support their families, which also implies taking a backseat as a caregiver.

FATHERS' AMBIGUOUS MODELS

Since over three-quarters of men from both traditional and dual-earner homes, as well as over half of those from single-parent homes, plan to fall back on breadwinning, fathers' choices do not predict sons' strategies. Most harbor mixed reactions to their fathers' choices, but nevertheless see breadwinning as the most reasonable alternative.

Men who grew up in two-parent homes had ambivalent reactions to their parents' arrangements, whether their mothers stayed home or had paid jobs. Jonathan did not share his father's attraction to "the traditional thing":

> I don't want or feel it's right to have a traditional one like my parents, where I was the only one working. Having such a simple, standard, pretty traditional upbringing, I wish it had been more challenging.

Justin had no desire to become an overworked and disengaged parent like his father:

> I don't want to have the type of relationship my father had with me. You get home at 7:00, 7:30. You're wiped out, and [the kids] are ready for bed. That's the greatest fear.

Neither wished to repeat his father's pattern, yet both expected to become primary breadwinners. In the end, they agreed it would be wrong to forfeit the "good provider" mantle or rely on a wife's income, as Jonathan explained:

I like an even relationship, but if it got to the situation where my wife didn't want to work, I need to be able to support [her].

And Justin added:

I saw how hard [my mom] worked, and I didn't feel that was right, so this is the way I'm changing from what my dad did. I realize it's not perfect, and maybe it's paternalistic, but because of the way I grew up, I feel I need to be in a situation where I can take care of her, provide for her.

Sons were even more conflicted when their fathers abandoned the family. Close to half shared women's skepticism about marriage, but the other half agreed with Hank, whose father's departure strengthened his resolve to become a responsible family man:

I'm not afraid to be in a relationship or get married. It's number one. I think I learned that from my father, from his saying "I'm gonna go get cigarettes," and not seeing him till three years later. So I'll be faithful.

Over two-thirds of men reared in a traditional or dual-earner home fell back on breadwinning, yet their enthusiasm is muted. Even men with successful breadwinning fathers were mindful of the dangers. Paul worried about repeating his father's pattern of overwork as a lawyer for an oil company:

I didn't want to go into the corporate world because I saw what it did to my father. He worked all the time. So I realized early on that I didn't want to do that. Unfortunately, I think I'm developing a lot more of these ambitious feelings that I saw in my father growing up and I disliked. I think it's closely tied to the economic comforts that provides.

Although overwork did not concern Manny, he realized he might be unable to support a family on the modest earnings his construction worker father relied on:

Life is scary today, because I know she's my responsibility and the mother of my child.

In a world that questions whether a man who does not carry his own economic weight is "marriageable," having children, a family, and even love seems to hinge on the ability to bring home a "big enough" paycheck.[6] As Jonathan put it:

> Success is getting to the point where you can say, "I've got this great marriage, great kids, this is what I do with my life." But a lot of it's financial—to be able to provide for my family, like I got provided for.

Men from all class backgrounds measured success in market terms. Although those who plan to fall back on autonomy are skeptical about the chances of earning a "good living," most men counted on jobs to ease the way to primary breadwinning. Work opportunities, often invisible or taken for granted, pulled these men into the workplace and away from home. Their routes differ by class and ethnic background, but everyone who turned toward breadwinning focused on their economic prospects.

Invisible Opportunities

Middle-class men largely assumed from an early age that they would enter a demanding occupational niche, while those from more modest economic backgrounds generally took more winding, ambiguous paths. Growing up in an affluent suburb, Adam's professional aspirations emerged early and never wavered:

> I always wanted to be a professional. I would never settle for second-best. Even today, it makes me crazy if I don't do as well as I could have—financially, in a career. That's something that won't go away, and it's my own pressure.

In contrast, Ray, an African-American from a working-class home, became an enthusiastic worker only after he joined the lower ranks of the prison system and rose unexpectedly into management:

> I would do just enough to pass school, but I found out I love work. I became a manager, and I'm so gung ho. So I'm not gonna abuse my job.

Few men attributed their improving prospects to having a gender advantage, but there continues to be an "invisible inequality" in women's and men's occupational opportunities that still allows some men, especially if they are non-Hispanic whites, to "coast" in school and still succeed at work.[7] On average, men continue to earn more than women and to outpace them in professional careers, despite the fact that women are more likely to go to college, earn a college degree, and report studying more and relaxing less.[8] Yet over the long run, most men can still expect to outearn their female peers, and among people with a four-year college degree, the gap between men's and women's pay has actually widened slightly since the mid-1990s.[9] But even those men who drifted through school did not notice these advantages when they found their careers taking off. Jim never liked studying, barely graduated from high school, and dropped out of college after one semester. Yet after "kind of falling into" a job in the court system, he rose up the civil service ladder. Beginning at the "bottom of the barrel" as a guard, he rose to a "supervisory level" by his late twenties and expected to keep moving up:

> What I'm doing, it's pretty much the ideal. I came in as an officer, and now I'm a supervisor. My pay has gone up pretty much within a couple of years. I don't have a college degree, [but] there are a lot of people with college degrees who don't use them. As far as getting ahead, I make more money than my sister, who's an accountant. So I feel very positive about my career. I see myself on the path, and I want to get ahead as far as possible.

Whether anticipated or unexpected, promising careers offer reassurance about the chances of succeeding at breadwinning. But this reassurance comes with a cost, since the demands required to build a career also undermine the chances of striking a balance between work and home.

No Time for "Equal Time"

As financial rewards accrue at work, the heavy time investments required to sustain them make it harder to balance work with the rest of life. The paradigm of a committed worker as someone who works full-time—and overtime—for decades, with no time-outs or even cutting back, creates what Joan Williams calls a "maternal wall" for women, but it leaves men with a shrinking window for sharing at home.[10] Jim believed the need to work "full-time, all the time" meant that, faced with a choice, he would have to spend more time at work:

> Even though I didn't go to school a lot, you can get by in school without being there every day. But now it's different. How are you gonna get ahead if you're not at work? So if somebody's gonna be the breadwinner, it's going to be me. I always feel the need to work.

New economic uncertainties have raised the stakes even higher, making workweeks that extend well beyond forty hours typical in the most demanding professions.[11] In a "winner take all" economy with less room at the top, high- and lesser-earning men alike feel uneasy about taking time away from work.[12] Despite Justin's early financial accomplishments, he felt compelled to work harder and longer just to stay even:

> This society, there's no security. So for a twenty-eight-year-old, I'm successful, but I look around and there are plenty of young people who are successful, too. I'm not the smartest, the brightest, the best, or whatever. So if I'm ahead, then I make a new goal. Once you stop doing it, you start to slide. So everything's relative.

Inexorably escalating job demands, along with intensifying competition for occupational rewards, leave primary breadwinning men with little hope of striking an equal work-family balance. Peter became pessimistic about the possibilities for either balance or equality:

> The biggest challenge is the balance between work and home. I want as even a split as it could be, but with my hours, I don't think it would be very even...because work will be very difficult.

Chris became increasingly wary of a two-career marriage:

> Two careers, it's gonna be very difficult. I see it with the director of our lab. They're both professionals—she's an executive, and I see how he comes in so tired because his wife had to go do her presentation. So I've seen how tricky it gets. It really can run you haggard.

Most greet the prospect of putting so much time into a job with ambivalence and wistfulness. Justin longed to leave his fast-paced corporate career to become a teacher, but felt unable to resist the pressure to "make very good money" for his family:

> If it weren't for money, I would like to be a teacher and live a quiet life. But it's not possible, I'm beginning to realize, because of the financial needs. The more likely scenario [is] I would have to continue in this line of work. I don't feel there's a choice, really.

MOVING TOWARD MARRIAGE

In contrast to self-reliant women, who are skeptical of marriage, breadwinning men are drawn to its benefits. Like women, they are postponing marriage, but most (though certainly not all, as we shall see) view marriage as a goal they want and expect to reach. Some breadwinning men never questioned the attraction of marriage, while others overcame doubts as they grew older. Many were surprised to see their skepticism melt. Ray changed his outlook after a brief but intense period of "wildness":

> I always wanted to have kids, but I didn't want to get married. Then I started quieting down. At twenty-one, I already had money, had traveled, done the wild things. I was tired.

Daniel vowed to be a responsible husband and father after watching his "wilder" brother make mistakes:[13]

> Scott's the divorced one, but he's much different than I am. When he got married, he still wanted to be a drinker and a partyer. That was his problem. I've already gotten rid of those things, so I don't see that being my problem.

Supportive partners also help skeptical men develop a more sanguine view of lasting commitment. Carlos felt fortunate, if surprised, when his girlfriend gave him hope for creating the happy marriage that eluded his parents:

> I was always like, "I'm not ever gonna get married." With her, I can see myself getting married, having kids. She's a real close friend. It's better than my parents, 'cause even when it comes to a point where we're about to disagree, we talk instead of argue.

William went even further. Though he enjoyed the advantages of middle-class affluence, he once feared his life had no direction or purpose. But creating a "real" relationship with his fiancée gave William a newfound faith in himself. At twenty-eight, he marveled at how their relationship had helped him find his way and had given him optimism about the future:

> The course of my life, the past eleven years have not gone the way I think my life ought to have gone. I dropped out of college, diddled around doing this and that. So I'm lucky to be where I am now, just finishing my bachelor's degree. Lindsey is very assertive and has taught me a lot...I'm learning to believe in myself in a real way. I was really unhappy for a long time, but now I'm really happy. Dealing in a more real way with another person in a relationship, a lot of what I went through is getting self-confidence and learning to believe in myself. I look forward to my future, and I'm sure it's going to be great. You've got to understand, it comes after years of dread. You know, I'm never gonna have a midlife crisis.

Eduardo grew up in a working-class Latino home, where neither parent had gone to college, but he had a similar story to tell:

I met Mary six years ago. [It made] a big difference. If it wasn't for her, I wouldn't be here right now. I'd be lost, dreaming somewhere. She's come through with me. She's made me feel really good about myself. She's really important to me and really wants to stay with me.

Supportive partners not only fuel optimism about work and marriage; they also help men anchor their identity in breadwinning by providing moral and practical support. As Manny put it, "I know she's the one 'cause I love the way she takes care of me." For men who fall back on breadwinning, marriage is as a package of commitments that promises intimacy, love, emotional sustenance, and social status. In fact, contemporary men are generally less skeptical about marriage and parenthood than women, who are more supportive of childlessness and hold more cautious views about marriage.[14] Men's more optimistic outlook is well founded, since married men enjoy a range of personal and social benefits, including better health and higher earnings. Not only do married men do better than single men at work, but fathers are more likely than childless men to be hired and offered higher salaries.[15] Ken sensed this advantage when his previous boss, who had remained single well into his thirties, offered an unappealing contrast to his current boss, whose "perfect family" seemed integral to his workplace success:

My former employer, I don't want to be like that. He's about thirty-six and never been married. My current employer is more of a role model. He's got two daughters, a pretty wife, up there in the company, very advanced. He's a great guy, too.

Marriage is clearly associated with benefits for men, but it is difficult to disentangle cause and effect. Does marriage confer advantages, or are healthier, more successful men more likely to marry? In either case, marriage and parenthood help men in myriad ways. At work, they enjoy a wage bonus, and in private life, they are less vulnerable to disease and have larger social networks.[16] Most young men sense this link and hope to create it for themselves.

FROM PARENTING TO MOTHERING

Where do children fit into time-demanding jobs? This question poses the biggest challenge to the ideal of equal sharing. Most agree with Paul, who "always envisioned two earners, but that would obviously be a problem when children start coming into the picture." To resolve this conundrum, breadwinning men distinguish between "equal but different" forms of caring.

They profess support for the ideal of *equal parenting,* but they fall back on the practical advantages of *devoted mothering.*

Only a Parent Will Do

With few exceptions, neotraditional men do not believe mothers are inherently more qualified than fathers to care for children; but they do believe *parents* are inherently more qualified than other caregivers. While Eric assumed mothers and fathers should be equally responsible for children's care, he did not feel caretaking should be delegated:

> I would primarily like it to be a family member—either one of us. I would like for the child to have one or both parents there at the beginning.

Phil echoed this point:

> If children come into the picture, that's when I've got the old, traditional values—not that women should be home, but somebody—one of the parents—should always be there to take care of the kids. Where my part would come, I would deal with it then, but one of us would always be at home.

In principle, a reluctance to rely on babysitters and day care centers does not leave the bulk of parenting to women. Yet few men can envisage finding two flexible full-time jobs or living on two part-time incomes. Phil continued:

> I would like to work certain days and she would work certain days. This way, one of the parents is always there, and it's not always the same. I would like to work my schedule around my kids, but that's not going to happen.

Although the reluctance to delegate coexists with egalitarian principles, its practical implication makes equality close to impossible. Without the option to divide child care equally, neotraditional men look to their partners to pick up an added share of the load.

Market Work and the Gender of Caretaking

Most men feel justified in leaving mothers as the default caretaker because they assume their own market advantages mean their work needs to come first.[17] Although women's yearly earnings, as a percent of men's, have risen from 64 percent in 1955 to 78 percent in 2008, husbands continue to outearn wives in most marriages. Some embrace this circumstance, while others regret it, but they all see it as unavoidable. Justin felt his wife's lower earnings as a freelance writer deprived them both of the option to be equal caretakers:

> She doesn't want to have babysitters, and I agree. If she was in a job that pulls down the same type of money, then either of us could quit. But we don't, so the problem is I have to work, unless she can get another job.

Jim, on the other hand, believed his higher earnings and better job prospects justified an arrangement his wife, a math teacher, did not prefer:

> This may sound sexist, but she'll just have to take time off. As far as a macho thing, if she made a much better salary, it would be different. [But] she's pretty much going to stay at that level, and I'm going to move up as far as I can.

Whether or not they prefer the outcome, an earnings advantage and more promising career prospects lends an air of inevitability to men's reliance on women's caretaking. Yet almost every young man rejected the idea of staying at home, even if it *were* possible.[18] Josh felt it would be irresponsible for him to rely on a woman's paycheck, even if she could earn more:

> I would never stay home. I have a friend who's like that, and I strongly disapprove. The father just stays home. I think it's wrong, 'cause his wife's out there working seven days a week, and he's doing nothing except stay home.

Hank agreed:

> I can't sit home and have a woman pay the bills. Sharing the child care—I would do it once I'm home, but the kids have to have somebody to come home to. So if she makes more than me, then I'll have to get two jobs.

By equating responsible manhood with earning a "good enough" living, breadwinning men relieve their partner of an economic weight that even self-reliant women are reluctant to assume. Coupled with the resistance to delegating child care, however, this view leads inexorably, if unconsciously, to the assumption that a mother will take the main responsibility for the care work. The ideal of intensive parenting becomes the need for *maternal* responsibility. Engaged to be married, Manny moved seamlessly from believing "only a parent will do" to assuming his fiancée would be the one to do it:

Especially at an early age, you don't leave your child with anyone. So she would have to take care of the baby, 'cause I wouldn't like anybody with my child and I'll be working.

Breadwinning in an Age of Women's Work

Though men face powerful incentives to fall back on breadwinning, they cannot ignore the attendant conflicts. Placing paid work first and counting on someone else to do more of the domestic work complicates the search for balance and flexibility, especially when most families need two incomes and most women want to work.[19] This tension prompts neotraditional men to develop mental strategies to resolve the clash. They refashion the core ideals of work-family balance, equal sharing, and the importance of women's work to fit better their need to see themselves as breadwinners first.

BALANCE IS A STATE OF MIND

Breadwinning men have not relinquished the ideal of work-family balance, but they hope to redefine it. In contrast to self-reliant women, who expect to combine work and parenting as best they can, and neotraditional women, who expect to fit paid work around their family tasks, neotraditional men stress how their earnings *substitute* for time and other forms of care. Patrick believed being a good father means giving priority to financial contributions:

> Ideally, my children would be more important than my job. But I need to work to support my family.

Matthew also reluctantly focused on making money before spending time:

> What premium are you going to put on having time or money? Certainly, to give your children any sort of chance takes material things.

To fit "balance" into this framework, some make a mental distinction between time and personal priorities. For Thomas, what matters most is how he *feels,* not what he actually *does:*

> Time-wise, I spend a lot of time on work, so if you slice up the day into a pie, I'll spend more time at work than doing anything else. But in terms of rank in significance, it's fifty-fifty.

Others take a longer view, defining "balance" as a sequence of changing priorities. These men hope putting in long hours early in their careers will pave the way for more family involvement later on. Ken hoped to put work first and then family:

> After I've exhausted my corporate life and saved enough money, it would be very nice to contribute to raising my child. Maybe then [my wife] can work full-time, and I'll go to school and raise the child.

Matthew proposed a similar scenario:

> I'd like to have it such that work dominates my life until my children turn five, six, and then have work taper off such that by the time my kids are in high school, I'll have a job with complete flexibility.

By stressing the long-run nature of the work-family balance, breadwinning men can focus on work in the short run. But these plans presume someone else will pick up the slack in the early stages of child rearing, when the demands of both careers and children are especially intense. For Hank, this meant his wife's presence could stand in for his own:

> I'd never want to work so much that the kids grow up and say, "My father never spent time with me, and that's why I'm a screwup." But if there's someone who represents you at home and doing the same thing I would, hopefully that makes up for it.

Neotraditionalism preserves some semblance of the idea of work-family balance by adopting cognitive strategies that place men's work first. Defining balance as a state of mind helps men resolve inner conflicts between the ideal of involved fatherhood and the reality of time-demanding jobs. Yet this strategy leaves the underlying structure of work unchallenged, leaving genuine balance beyond everyone's grasp.

THE PLACE OF WOMEN'S WORK

Most neotraditional men assume that wives and mothers should be able to pursue careers and see their earnings as important and desirable.[20] Those who fall back on breadwinning do not expect their partners to reject paid work. Although Lucius hoped to be the primary earner, he did not expect or want to be the only one:

> I'm gonna make enough money so that I'll be able to hold it down. But I'd rather that we both work. It helps.

Brian agreed:

It's more on a man to bring home money, but it's not bad if you have the woman bringing home money, too. Otherwise, in twenty years, you've been shelling out money for her.

These men walk a thin line in blending their support for working partners with the image of themselves as good providers. They believe everyone should have a work ethic, but they grant more value to their own paycheck. A partner, they reason, can—and *should*—work, but not in the same way or to the same degree.

Her Job Comes Second

Neotraditional men find value in women's work as a source of income, a protection from boredom, a marker of maturity, and an avenue of personal and social esteem. They neither wish nor plan for their partner to stay home over the long run. Yet even though they frown on full-time homemaking, they nevertheless place women's jobs in a different category than their own. Like notions of women as a "reserve labor force," they view a woman's paid work as something that can ebb and flow depending on family needs.[21] Allen expected to find a career-oriented partner, but hoped she would take time out when children arrived:

Someone I knew would just stay home—that wouldn't be my first choice. I'd like to marry somebody who has a career. But I'd like it if she stayed home for a few years.

Matthew planned for his partner to "shift down":

I'd like to have a partner who's making as much as I am—has a high-powered job where we can put the money aside quickly. So by the time we have a kid, she can shift down. Now she works with the kids and spends her time working for the Humane Society or whatever.

Seeing a partner's career as "extra"—and less essential—helps men discount the costs women (and all these men are heterosexual) bear by putting work on the back burner, even temporarily. Peter argued that pulling back to care for children would not exact a heavy price on his wife's career as long as it did not become a permanent arrangement:

She should work and just adjust her schedule after they're born. After the children reach a certain age, I would feel, if I were her, that if I didn't go on and pursue my own objectives, I would always feel that I missed out on doing something.

And even though Jim recognized the highly professional nature of his wife's accomplishments, he distinguished between her relatively flat career ladder as a teacher and his own plans to move up the civil service ladder:

> She's a professional woman and does very well at her job, so she would go on forever. But to take a year or two off—it's fine, 'cause as a math teacher, it's not gonna be a problem. If she had a job that was more demanding, it would be a bigger problem.

Placing women's work second allows men to affirm a two-earner arrangement without undermining their own identities as breadwinners. It also justifies holding her responsible for domestic work whether or not she holds a job. Although Sam granted his partner the option to work, he did not give himself an offsetting responsibility to share at home:

> If she wanted to work, I would assume it's her responsibility to drop the kids off at grandma's house or something. She's in charge of the kids. If she's gonna work, fine, but you still have responsibilities.

Given most women's determination to preserve their autonomy through paid work, it may be wishful thinking for these men to presume they can find a partner willing to put work aside. As a short-run strategy, it nevertheless allows them to focus on their own economic prospects and identities as family providers. These efforts make room for women's work, but they also represent a pattern that is well short of equal sharing.

DEFINING EQUALITY AS "CHOICE"

How do neotraditional men reconcile the ideal of equality with the identity of a good provider? Alex defined equality as a malleable concept, whose meaning can shift with changing circumstances:

> I would like it to be egalitarian, but I don't have a set definition for what an egalitarian relationship would be like. If she thought, "At this point in my life, I don't want to work, it's more important to stay home," then that would be fine for one person to do more work in some respects.

Because these men believe they should, in Peter's words, "be responsible for the money," they distinguish between a woman's "choice" to work and their own obligation to do so. Dwayne explained that equality means offering a partner the choice *not* to work:

If we're struggling and you're gonna lay around, then I can't see that. But if things is going as they're supposed to and I'm making good money, if you choose not to work, that's on you.

Daniel sounded a similar theme:

It's probably much easier for us to earn the money we're gonna need if both of us are working, but if somehow my job makes enough money, my wife doesn't *have* to work. As long as there's enough money for the family, then it doesn't matter.

Using the language of choice as a frame for women's work narrows men's work options but expands their leverage at home. The responsibility of being the economic mainstay makes it easier to select which forms of domestic work they prefer. It is thus telling that, over the last several decades, men's involvement in child care has risen more substantially than their participation in housework.[22] Lawrence, like most, distinguished between child care and housework:

I can really imagine myself raising kids. It's the housework-type stuff I can't imagine.

Mitch proposed a similar division:

I'd like sharing equally—certainly child raising and also financially. I'd like my mate to be able to balance and maybe switch them, but I do not want to do cooking.

Many also hope to resolve the potential conflicts by delegating the least appealing tasks to a third party. Delegating tasks once performed routinely by wives and mothers is part of a long-term trend of outsourcing household tasks, a process that has been under way since the workplace and children's schooling moved out of the private household.[23] Wayne viewed paid help as a reasonable extension of this process and the best solution to contemporary pressures:

We both gotta work, so I hope we get help. 'Cause I don't want my wife to be working and doing housework chores. And I don't want to be doing it. I did enough of that already.

While self-reliant women define equality as their right to seek independence, breadwinning men typically use the language of choice to distinguish between a partner's option to work and their own obligation to do so. This frame allows men to reconcile the abstract ideal of equal sharing with the real difficulties of putting it into practice, but it also re-creates gender boundaries by preserving personal discretion about how—and how much—to participate at home.[24]

PLUS ÇA CHANGE, PLUS C'EST LA MÊME CHOSE?

Breadwinning men stress the importance of paternal involvement, but they redefine work-family balance as a state of mind. They are prepared to find a work-committed partner, but they expect her to place work in the background if and when needed. They value equality, but frame working as optional for women and their own domestic participation as a matter of choice. These strategies reaffirm men's moral responsibility to support a family while also helping them reconcile the ideals of involved fatherhood and equal sharing with their identity as a good provider. But they also imply that women should be ready and willing to do it all, as Lucius explained:

> I want a woman who knows how to do everything if she has to. She can be independent and domestic at the same time. Independent means a career-minded woman, and domestic means she knows how to take care of home stuff.

Isaiah put it this way:

> Let's say I don't get to that point where I can do it alone, then depending on the situation, I would know that person [can] go either way, whatever they decide. That's why they have to be independent.

By softening the gender boundaries of previous eras without erasing them, these men have developed a neotraditional vision that grants some gender flexibility without surrendering gender distinctions. If most women do not find this "equal, but different" perspective reassuring, most men view it as an unavoidable consequence of circumstances beyond their control. As Lucius acknowledged, "I wouldn't like it if the shoe was on the other foot, but there's a lot of things in life that's unfair."

The same forces pushing and pulling women toward self-reliance prevent a commensurate shift among men toward domesticity. Men, no less than women, understand that market work must come first—not just for survival, but also for self-respect.[25] Because paid work bestows social status as well as economic rewards, few men can sidestep the pressure to measure their own worth in terms of market value. Those who try to resist must cope with pervasive social cues reminding them of its importance. Since care work remains devalued and largely invisible, market logic leaves men with little incentive or opportunity to shift the balance.[26] Despite a professed desire for change, neotraditional men see little alternative to placing the demands of work and the validation it provides before the ideal of equal sharing.[27]

Autonomy through Men's Eyes

Not all men stress primary breadwinning as their fallback strategy. About three in ten of the men I interviewed are wary of marriage as an institution, feel reluctant to assume economic responsibility for another adult, and find a general, if vague, vision of personal freedom more appealing. Thomas contrasted his ideal of a fulfilling relationship with a path that looked achievable:

> My ideal is [to] go through life [with] no philandering, committed to the relationship, going for a decent relationship—no yelling on the sidewalk every day on my way to work. But if not, then I see myself sitting on the beach in the Caribbean, with a swizzle stick in my glass.

While these men do not all plan a life of travel and leisure, they all agree adulthood does not require supporting another adult. As Gabriel put it, "I refuse to support somebody. If I have a kid, yes, but I refuse to support a wife." They stress independence *from* and autonomy *within* relationships.

Like self-reliant women, autonomous men resist the breadwinner-homemaker ethic, even in a neotraditional form. Yet they differ from their female counterparts in crucial ways. Self-reliance offers women protection against the dangers of ceding one's personal identity and economic security to another; autonomy provides men with insulation from the perils of too much financial responsibility. Skepticism about finding secure work and growing doubts about traditional marriage set them on this path.

ECONOMIC UNCERTAINTY AND THE LURE OF SINGLEHOOD

In contrast to the "invisible opportunities" pulling neotraditional men toward time-demanding jobs, about a third of the men expressed substantial pessimism about their career prospects. Most were reared in working-class and minority neighborhoods, including many whose homes teetered on the edge of poverty, but about two-fifths are white men who could look back on a financially secure childhood. Yet economic uncertainties and the demoralizing effects of regimented jobs prompted all of these men to take a different approach to work and family life. If equality proves impossible, they prefer autonomy to the more rigid requirements of breadwinning.

Losing Faith in the American Dream

Although breadwinning continues to form the core of "hegemonic masculinity," the shrinking pool of traditional jobs undermines autonomous men's desire to seek and ability to find steady, secure work. While this view is most prevalent among men with modest economic and educational resources, people from all backgrounds concur.[28] At twenty-nine, Nick believed downsizing and "deskilling" would leave him unable to find the kind of economic security his working-class father enjoyed:

> I'm worried about the future because I am still unemployed. There are a lot of people who are a lot less skilled than I am, [who have] a lot less determination and a lot less communication skills, getting positions because [employers] don't feel like paying the top dollar.

Antonio reached a similar conclusion about his chances of reproducing the middle-class standard he enjoyed as a child:

> In the future, I see a lot of chaos. I wake up with nightmares about the money being gone. We're now middle-class, but that's not gonna exist years from now. You're either gonna be at the top or at the bottom.

If breadwinning men respond to rising competition by vowing to work longer hours, autonomous men are tempted to withdraw from the contest. Demoralized by his low-paying jobs, Jermaine, a high school dropout, decided paid work hardly seemed worth the effort:

> I'm tired of working. I've been working off and on since I was thirteen, fourteen, and I don't have money in the bank. Maybe there's something out there I would like to see through to the end, but nothing comes to mind. Who wants to work twenty-five, thirty years in the same place, and then when it's time to collect a pension, you're too old to enjoy it?

Also in his mid-twenties but with a college degree, Jeff reached a similar conclusion about his more lucrative, but suffocating, career in finance:

> I had plans to be a financial analyst for six, seven years. Now I don't give a shit about any of that. I'd just like to cruise around and say, "screw it all." Most people, they'll stay put somewhere, but I'd like to

maybe go down to Australia [where] I think culturally they're more into anarchy.

Demoralized by poorly paid or overly demanding jobs, autonomous men soured on the goal of building a traditional (male) career and chose riskier paths. Antonio planned to seek his fortune outside the structure of a bureaucratic organization:

Jobs in corporations—I was getting paid, but so what? So I was going late, wasn't enthused to be at the job. I felt like I was selling my soul to this company, like this is gonna be my life now.

Richard sought freedom from the relentless monotony of mainstream work:

I don't want to be stuck here doing the same thing nine-to-five every day for the rest of my life. I just don't know if I want to work. I sound like a dreamer, and I am, but I want lots of time. One summer, I went to Mexico and just painted. I want to be able to do that. I need time to explore and do what I need to do.

Putting Family on the Back Burner

Men's doubts about finding or wanting a steady job foster equally strong doubts about marrying. Comparing his own uncertainty with the opportunities enjoyed by his parents, Angel found family commitments taking a mental backseat:

I really don't know what's gonna happen, if I'm gonna have kids. Before I bring any life to this planet, I want to be well off, situated where I don't have to worry—like my parents.

And Antonio planned to put off becoming a husband or father indefinitely:

I'm not rushin' into marriage. I'm very cynical. Things are gonna get real hard. I wouldn't bring kids into this. If I'm not stable, my kid ain't gonna be stable. I'm more focused on dealing with my own instability, the economic revolution that's going on.

Men stressing autonomy do not view their reluctance to marry as a lack of proper "family values," but rather as a morally responsible response to economic uncertainties. Michael argued it would be irresponsible to marry before achieving financial stability:

I have the correct values—strong family, religious, moral values. I'm gonna do the right thing. But you need [to] make a paycheck so you can afford to do the right thing. Work is not promised to you, and that's what you really have to focus on.

And like a growing number of women, Jermaine viewed independence as a necessary step on the path to self-development:

> I don't want to live with anybody right now. I haven't done anything for *me* yet! If I'm gonna have a place, I want it to be *my* place. I really don't want to be in a relationship...until my feet are firmly cemented in the ground.

Poor work prospects, pessimism about the future, and a desire to avoid stifling jobs prompt men to fall back on autonomy. Some are reacting to the growing time demands and false promises in white-collar careers, while others focus on the dwindling rewards and shrinking opportunities in blue-collar occupations. These different routes lead in a similar direction: men's version of "opting out."

Although the overwhelming majority of Americans eventually marry, marriage rates have declined among most income and ethnic groups. The decline is steeper for the less educated and for members of racial minorities, where men's school and work opportunities are especially squeezed.[29] Indeed, the largest gender disparities in educational achievement are among racial and ethnic minorities, where girls have graduated from high school and college at higher rates than boys.[30] Since half as many African-American men as women now graduate from college, and African-American men have suffered a 12 percent decline in their median income over the last three decades (while African-American women have experienced a 75 percent increase), it is not surprising they have the lowest marriage rate of any racial group.[31] Yet regardless of race or ethnicity, as long as a breadwinning ethic pervades our notions of what makes a man "marriageable," low-earning men with dim job prospects face a declining incentive to marry and better-educated women have similarly low motivation to choose them as a partner.

TYING A LOOSE KNOT

Autonomous men do not reject the possibility of finding a lasting relationship, but they see marriage as only one among a range of alternatives. For David, marriage remained an option, but not a requirement:

> I don't see marriage as an absolute priority. I'm glad that I don't think of it that way. I don't feel pressured.

Jeff also planned to resist the pressure:

I couldn't really set a goal saying I need to be married, because you do that to yourself and all of a sudden you're marrying somebody you're not gonna be happy with.

Accordingly, these men rejected the institution of marriage as the only route to mature manhood.[32] Like self-reliant women, they view marriage an option to be taken only under the most propitious circumstances.

Low on the List

Autonomous men place marriage low on their list of priorities, and, like self-reliant women, set a very high standard for choosing it. Turning the tables on those who argue that singlehood devalues marriage, autonomous men believe they valued it more.[33] Watching his parents stay together throughout his childhood only to divorce after he left home convinced Noah it would be better to remain single than to seek marital ideals he could not achieve:

I would never jump into marriage. I would tell her everything about what my parents were about so she knew what kind of baggage I was carrying. It's the most important decision I might make. We have to spend enough time to see each other at our worst.

Although Joel's parents stayed together, he agreed:

I'll definitely look at my situation and see if I'm in danger of making the same mistakes. It's such a huge commitment, it seems that people don't actually sit down and think of how it's really going to be.

Taking pride in resisting the pressure to marry, these men distinguish between marriage as a legal matter and commitment as a state of mind. Married and divorced by twenty-nine, Nick had good reason to decide that "a piece of paper does not mean you're married." Still in his early twenties and never married, Richard also believed that only a very high standard for marrying would help him avoid divorce:

I haven't found anyone I'd like to marry, and I don't know if she's out there. I'm going to make sure she is 100 percent what I want—because I don't want to go through any divorce. People nowadays take marriage for granted—we'll get married just because we're supposed to. It's a very loose thing. You get married, divorced, no problem. There's no sacred bond anymore. So that's the way it's affected me. I wouldn't get married just for someone I think is really cool.

To avoid making the "wrong" choice, autonomous men set conditions for any relationship to meet. Noah insisted on a prearranged plan to resolve conflicts and "build" a worthy partnership:

> I would make a prenuptial agreement to seek counseling if we ever felt that we would fall apart, and that would be something we'd have to promise to prepare for.

Michael believed any marriage would need a prior blueprint similar to those he drew up as an engineer:

> If you look at it statistically, it doesn't make sense. Over fifty percent of marriages end in divorce. So you have to nurture the kind of marriage you want. You have to draw it out before you can go into it. I want to blueprint how I want marriage to be.

Although most men, and women, do ultimately marry, autonomous men plan to postpone as long as possible. Not concerned about a ticking biological clock, they have the luxury of time. At twenty-five, Jeff vowed to postpone a decision for as long as possible and took no firm position on what that decision might ultimately be:

> I may have thought I would be with somebody at this point, but it's been like, "Stay single as long as possible." And it was always everybody saying, "Don't get married." So I don't feel the pressure.

Blaming his parents' troubles on their rush to marry, Gabriel concurred:

> I'm now thinking it could easily be forty. I want to go into something like that being sure it's what I want to do. There's no reason to rush. [My parents] got married in their early twenties, and I don't want to make the mistake of marrying too young.

In setting a high standard and placing marriage low on their list of priorities, autonomous men seek to avoid the neotraditional bargain outlined by their breadwinning peers. Married or not, they favor relationships where both partners retain a considerable measure of independence.

Seeking a Self-Sufficient Partner

Autonomous men use a metric of equal freedom, rather than equal sharing, to define the ideal of equality. In return for preserving their independence, they grant a large measure of it to others. Luis took pride in giving his ex-girlfriend the same leeway that he reserved for himself:

We were living together, but I always told her, I tell her still, "If it wasn't working out for you, you just had to say so." If you get along well, it works out. If it doesn't, I always felt like I never owned her. So if she wanted to move on, I enjoyed the good times. I'm not a grudge-holding person.

Mark believed his long-term, live-apart relationship succeeded precisely because each could retreat to their own separate space:

The space we have in the relationship—that's a big factor in why we stayed together all these years. I can have my own space, do my own thing, but then I have her there. I'd feel alienated if I was to settle down—the control factor.

Since independence requires a financial base, autonomous men also reject the neotraditional view that employment should be optional or secondary for women. Only a work-committed person would make a suitable mate. With no desire or intention to support a wife, Daniel appreciated knowing the women he dated would never want to depend on him for their livelihood:

If she doesn't work, and she's a deadbeat—I don't think I'd date a girl like that, not for more than two days. Cheryl won't take money from me. I don't see her ever going, "I don't want to work anymore." She hates her job, but she does it because she's earning her own money.

And Mark concurred:

In terms of having a wife who doesn't work, that's a lot of pressure on me to carry the whole weight of the family. I'd rather have a working partner. My girlfriend could never *not* work. That's the farthest thing from her mind.

Work offers a crucial source of psychological as well as financial independence for the women in their lives. These men found it difficult to fully respect a partner who lacks an identity beyond hearth and home. Gabriel could not imagine having a partner who did not have a base outside the home:

I just want, need someone who can stand on their own. I wouldn't mind having someone make more—not for the sake of leeching off her, but so that she was independent. I have to respect her, so she has to be a doer. I need someone to think for themselves.

Richard agreed:

Life is too short, and it shouldn't revolve around a household. There are so many things I need see, do, experience, and I'd feel trapped being in a house. I wouldn't want it for me, so I wouldn't want anyone else to like it.

Men who fell back on autonomy do not reject partnerships, but they seek ones that do not impinge too greatly on their own freedom. This means finding someone with an independent income and identity, who can and will be financially and emotionally self-sustaining.

Paternal Ambivalence

Since it is not possible for children to support or care for themselves, autonomous men are ambivalent about fatherhood. Most plan to postpone parenthood indefinitely, but some are fathers who do not live with their offspring.[34] All of these men reject the view that "being responsible" requires bearing children or living with the children they had borne. At twenty-seven, Luis felt resisting parenthood went hand in hand with resisting breadwinning, since being "child-free" relieved him of having to bring home a big paycheck:

> In ten, twenty years, maybe. 'Cause I like doing my own thing. If something else came along that I wanted to do, all I have to do is make sure someone takes care of the cat. If I had a family, I would have to have a job that's making nice money. If I had kids, I'd have to provide for them.

Single fathers did not have the luxury of postponing parenthood, but they did resist obligations to the mothers of their children. Michael distinguished the importance of having a tie with his daughter from his willingness to support her mother. Though involved in his child's life, he refused his girlfriend's requests to marry or even live together until—and unless—she became secure in her own career:

> I'm very close to Chandra, and I love her mother, but Kim has to get her act together before I consider marrying. Commitment is fine and dandy, but you can't fall into a trap. She's got some bad habits, and one of them is being lazy. Before we move in, I want her to be established in her career, motivated in herself, and not live through me. When she does that, I don't have a problem.

Whether they postponed fatherhood, plan to remain childless, or live apart from their children, these men do not view their choice as irresponsible.

After watching his parents and siblings struggle in unhappy marriages, Nick decided that no one—least of all his son—would benefit from his staying in a forced and flawed union:

> I wanted to stay together, because that's the way my parents did it, but then I realized that I don't believe anybody should stay together because of a child. I've seen that happen with my brother's son. They stayed together just because of him, and now he's seven and in therapy. A lot could have been avoided by not getting married.

Steve, at twenty-six and openly gay, viewed childlessness as the best option as long as he felt unprepared to make the needed sacrifices:

> I don't rule anything out, but even thinking of the future, I'm not planning it. The kid's got to be the priority. When I get to that point, maybe. For now, it's me doing what I want to do for myself.

By remaining childless, becoming a father-at-a-distance, or rejecting a necessary link between paternity and marriage, autonomous men seek to redefine the terms and conditions of fatherhood. This outlook upholds the ideal of personal independence and provides an escape from the pressures of primary breadwinning, but it allows little room for equal parenting.

GENDER AND THE MEANING OF AUTONOMY

Autonomous men, like self-reliant women, view independence as a survival strategy, not an ideal. Yet women view self-reliance as a way to avoid dependence on a man while still being able to care for children and forge ties to others. Autonomous men are more inclined to avoid such ties unless and until they can achieve a level of financial stability that seems not only elusive but hard to define.[35] Concerns that neither economic security nor a lasting relationship will come their way make this starker version of singlehood and independence more acceptable. It nevertheless reflects the continuing strictures on visions of masculinity, which stress men's breadwinning despite the decline in their economic entitlement.[36] Such a strategy reduces an unbearable weight, but it also leaves autonomous men with tenuous social connections, a situation few greeted with enthusiasm.[37] Noah admitted:

> I don't see myself as having a family because I just don't see that progression. If I think about it, that's going to be too much to handle . . . because I'm commitmentless and alone.

Dilemmas and Uncertainties in Men's Lives

In a mirror image of women's outlooks, most men fall back on modified traditionalism, while some favor personal autonomy over breadwinning obligations. Because equal sharing threatens to exact a toll on men's occupational and economic achievement, most men prefer to reassert their place as a primary breadwinner, while leaving room for their partner to make additional contributions. By defining equality as women's "choice" to add work onto mothering, neotraditionalism allows men to acknowledge women's desire for a life beyond the home and also to rely on the financial cushion of a second income. This strategy accepts the end of an era of stay-at-home mothers, but not the disappearance of distinct gender boundaries. Breadwinning men instead define separate spheres of responsibility for fathers and mothers, even if two-earner families are here to stay.

A sizeable minority of men, however, prefer another alternative. Poor work prospects and skepticism about marriage have left them wary of breadwinning and searching for a relationship with a self-sustaining partner who does not depend on their financial support. These men seek independence in lieu of equal sharing, but they give autonomy a different twist than self-reliant women by stressing "freedom from" breadwinning rather than "freedom to" support themselves.

Despite the differences between neotraditional and autonomous men, both outlooks are adaptive responses, not inherent attributes, and they can shift as circumstances change. Autonomous men realize they might welcome marriage and commitment in the long run, especially if their financial prospects improve, while breadwinning men concede the future might not bring the opportunities they anticipate. Brian planned to be a breadwinner, but recognizing "anything could happen," he admitted, "I could be making a lot of money, or I could be out of a job and totally stuck." In contrast, Gabriel harbored strong doubts about marriage, but conceded his skepticism could dissolve if circumstances changed his mind:

> If you asked me five years ago, I'd say there was absolutely no way of ever getting married. Because I didn't know anybody who was happy and married. But even in the last year—meeting and getting involved with Val and just seeing that marriage doesn't have to be like that— came a level of maturity that I've never had.

Whether they fall back on breadwinning or autonomy, young men face an uncertain future that may—and probably will—change at unexpected times and in unexpected ways. Their life paths, like those of women, ultimately depend on the opportunities and obstacles they encounter along the way.

| Reaching across the Gender Divide

THE CHILDREN OF THE gender revolution are preparing for an irreversibly transformed world, in which unpredictable personal and social challenges make gender flexibility and work-family balance not just appealing but essential. Yet the realities of resistant social and economic institutions make these ideals seem distant and elusive. With no way back to a dimly perceived past and no clear path toward their desired goals, young adults must formulate "second best" strategies to cope with an uncertain future. These fallback strategies take women and men in different and potentially clashing directions in their quest for security and personal happiness.

Yet ideals do not perish simply because they are difficult to achieve. Few of my interviewees wish to return to a time when work and family "roles" were clear, distinct, and taken for granted. When asked to compare their options with those of their parents and grandparents, women and men overwhelmingly agree that, despite the obstacles, women are better off today. In response to the question "On balance, do you think women have it better today than they did in the past, worse today, or is there no difference," 83 percent of women and 76 percent of men say today's women have it better.[1] When the same question is asked about men, most agree that men are either better off today or no worse off, with 35 percent of men and 45 percent of women responding that, all in all, men have it better today and another 39 percent of men and 48 percent of women saying there is little change and men have not lost because women have gained.[2]

The one exception to this trend is among African-American men, where large and continuing disadvantages leave half of them saying men—or, more specifically, Black men—have it worse today. Yet they do not attribute Black men's losses to women's gains, but rather to seemingly unrelenting social forces that limit their own opportunities. This agreement among women *and* men offers a potential bridge across the divide that separates self-reliant women and neotraditional men. Even if new gender ideals appear difficult to attain, or even to imagine attaining, they reflect widespread and mounting desires that create a powerful force for change. Even values that are hard to realize matter, because they prompt efforts to overcome social obstacles.

Looking for a Middle Path

Most young women and men do not see the sexes as opposites who possess different capacities and occupy different planets.[3] They reject a forced choice between personal autonomy and lasting commitment, preferring a relationship and a vision of the self that honors both. Though Michelle's two-career parents never resolved their conflicts and ultimately broke up, she hoped to chart a more flexible middle path:

> My parents are sort of closed off, whereas I'm more open-minded about my options. My mom has become very career-driven, and my dad's feeling sorry for himself. I don't think that one side or the other is bad or wrong. They're just at two extremes, and I want to be in a balance.

Sandra's parents remained unhappily wed to a traditional arrangement, but she too hoped to avoid her parents' battle lines:

> Compared to my parents, I want us to have more autonomy and [not] knit into each other. I want a job that satisfies me, and I want someone to get the satisfaction out of their job, but I don't want someone who's a workaholic.

Young women and men know they must create new ways of working and caring in order to find flexibility and balance, and finding the middle path between the "competing devotions" of family and work will not be easy.[4] As Megan observed, the conflicts between earning a living and rearing children make the path ahead difficult to navigate:

> Children are just an afterthought [in this] society. Do I spend more time with my child, or do I work at a job where I can get health care? People shouldn't have to make choices like that.

Although these dilemmas stem from the social organization of earning and caretaking, with undiluted commitment stressed at the workplace and privatized care at home, most of my interviewees are reluctant to rely on collective solutions from either employers or government. While convinced of the need for change, they lack trust in the good faith of large institutions, which seem an integral a part of the problem, and have more confidence in their own ability to control their fate.[5] The preference for private solutions over political action may look like apathy, but it actually reflects a growing need—and potential—for broader institutional change.

MIXED EMOTIONS

Across the political spectrum, young women and men are torn between desiring social change and fearing that collective solutions would prove useless or backfire in dangerous ways. Most believe communities and workplaces should help parents succeed at work without sacrificing their children's well-being. Some say neighborhoods should provide more child care, while others look to the workplace for more flexibility and parenting time.[6] Anita argued that children gain social skills in public settings:

> I'm a big believer in day care. It's great for children to be around other children and learn in a different environment. After having worked in the day care center, I just think it's important for kids to be around other kids and socialize.

Joel contended that employers should place family needs above a narrow focus on short-term profits:

> They should be more realistic and realize that sometimes work has to come second and family needs arise. There's an element of realism that doesn't seem to exist in the workplace. It's like you can't have anything else but the work, but that really isn't true.

Although women and men from a range of backgrounds concur that new realities imply new ways of apportioning public and private responsibility, most are skeptical about the prospects for political change. Those leaning toward political conservatism stress the dangers of government intervention in the private sphere of family life or the economic decisions of employers. Brian worried that the government would tax his hard-earned income to support other families, while legislative mandates would hamper economic growth and impinge on employers' rights:

> I don't want to support people that just wanna sit on their ass and collect checks, not get a job or anything. So the government should just

stay out of it. Just let the economy run itself. People should be left to do what they've gotta do. They've got to run their own business to try to make money and not to please the government.

More surprising, people with liberal views share these doubts. Across the ideological spectrum, then, young women and men are skeptical, even cynical, about whether institutions can change in needed ways, doubting both the competence of governments and the intentions of employers.[7] Most have limited faith that government will act on their behalf or for the common good. Antonio believed valuable resources would be misspent by politicians:

If they wanted to, they could help. They've got something on Mars. But how many homeless people do we have? Things like that get me angry. So much money being wasted.

Employers seem as untrustworthy as politicians and policy makers. Most worry that any support at the workplace will inevitably come with a price. Indeed, a number of studies have shown that workers—whether women or men—fear that family-support options, such as parental leave and flexible scheduling, entail substantial career risks. Though all workers are aware of these penalties, women are more likely to accept them for the sake of family life.[8] Yet women and men alike use camouflage strategies to hide their caregiving activities; rather than acknowledging their involvement in care work, they refrain from requesting flex time and make excuses for absences or missed meetings.[9] They fear, like Noah, that employers who offer support with one hand will take it back with the other:

The problem is once you get something from [an employer], you owe them, and that scares me. Something's going to come up later, and I'm going to be the one who pays. I don't want to have to owe anybody. I just want to work decent hours, for decent pay.

Whether government interference or corporate greed appears to be the culprit, young women and men have mixed emotions about enacting social policies to address the ensuing problems. Even those who acknowledge the institutional sources of their dilemmas lack confidence that organizations will—or can—provide the solutions. Antonio doubted institutions stuck in the past could or would catch up:

I don't look towards these things happening because it's just too much of a change. So it's impossible. Not here, not now.

ON THEIR OWN

Amid concerns that policies developed by employers or public officials will backfire and intensify already serious double binds, the kind of change that looks most possible is change from below. William believed bottom-up approaches would work better than top-down ones:

> It doesn't seem like social engineering works well. The fact that companies are starting to do day care—that's not a company's doing it, it's people saying we want this.

Sarah agreed:

> Can we change it? No, because there's too much keeping it going. It has to be at a whole other level of people changing.

Dubious about collective solutions, young women and men are inclined to turn to private ones. This outlook reveals an especially American approach to social policy, which affirms the ethos of personal responsibility and stresses "equal opportunities" rather than "equitable outcomes."[10] In this context, my interviewees hope sheer determination will help them join the ranks of the "lucky" few. Rather than trying to change the odds, they plan to tailor personal strategies to overcome them. Noah lived in a two-parent, middle-class suburban home and watched his father move up the ladder at a large law firm, but he vowed to reject such a rigid, lockstep path:

> I see the world totally going against me. You work until you drop. Pregnant women working until the last minute and back again before I even knew they were gone. But if that's the way the world is working, I will keep rebelling against it.

Antonio, raised by his mother and grandparents in a Latino enclave, agreed:

> Me and my generation, we're breaking the cycle of their family lifestyle, like work all day, but not going anywhere. The parents want to push you: go get this job, you gotta fit into the world. But I know myself. If I go that route, I'm gonna end up being miserable.

Armed with faith in themselves, women and men alike stress personal control rather than social supports. They hope to fight back against the institutional pressures that put parenting and work on a collision course. These resistance strategies may be uncoordinated, but they reveal a growing need and desire for new ways of working and family building.

Fighting for Control at Work

The mid-twentieth-century model of work defined success as a steady progression up an organizational chart or job security on the shop floor. It presumed the worker (read: male) could count on a partner (read: female) at home and the employer would reward loyalty with loyalty. This model gradually faded as stagnating pay scales undermined men's capacity to subsidize an unpaid domestic spouse, and global competition and market uncertainty undermined the once implicit bargain between employer and employee.[11] Such changes prompt young men—and women—to see this "career mystique" as more myth than reality.[12] Joel valued hard work, but did not wish to work in a large, hierarchical setting:

> When I was with big corporations, I felt taken advantage of. It hasn't soured me on working, but on those situations. They really don't treat you as a person.

Reared by his mother in an African-American working-class neighborhood, Isaiah reached a similar conclusion:

> Everybody works so hard to get so little accomplished. It feels like, "Are you busy being productive, or are you just busy being busy?" It's affected me in that I don't want to have a traditional job. If you don't have a traditional job, you have the time, freedom to do what you think is important.

Amid the fading of bureaucratically organized careers, young workers see danger in putting all their financial eggs in one employer's basket. They hope instead to shape a career trajectory of their own.

IN SEARCH OF WORK AUTONOMY

Young women and men from all backgrounds hope to build careers minimizing dominance from above. Kayla, a college graduate with plans to become a financial analyst, sought some control over the conditions of her labor:

> I want a job where I have autonomy. I want to call the shots at the end of the day, and I want to be able to control what I do. I want to make a contribution to society and to my bottom line.

Carlos returned to community college after barely completing high school, but he also wanted to find a work life with considerable autonomy:

I don't like the idea of having to work for other people. They think 'cause they're your boss, they're over you. If you're the same person as me, who gives you the right? That's why I'd rather be the person running my own business.

These shared goals entail different strategies. Those with middle-class resources and educational credentials focus on professional work and the possibility of upward career mobility, while those with more modest financial and school resources seek ways to avoid hierarchies altogether. Professional work appears to offer the best chance of achieving job autonomy. Megan expected to control her time and work conditions by setting up a private practice as a speech therapist:

That's the big thing for me—something that gives me plenty of flexibility and autonomy as far as when I work and how much I work. With speech pathology, I can take in private clients, have some control over my working environment.

Amanda, perhaps naively, viewed the upper echelons of the corporate world as bestowing similar benefits:

In ten years, [I hope to be] married, probably thinking about children, working hard, but in a position—like vice president—where you don't have to work as hard.

Those with fewer credentials and less interest in professional training look to less hierarchically organized job settings, especially self-employment.[13] After a succession of uninspiring jobs, including an especially demoralizing stint in the mail room of a large newspaper, Antonio left to join a group of friends who were launching their own music engineering firm. He vowed to leave the world of "nine to five" behind:

I need money, but I don't need all the bullshit that comes along with just having the job. I'm not a nine-to-fiver. But I learned you can have your own successful business! We want to have a company, a place we can call our own. We can say we made this work, [rather than] bringing in a little bullshit check every week.

In addition to setting up their own businesses, young people from all class backgrounds hope to find innovative work settings offering more flexibility and personal control than traditional ones. As a computer technician, Luis relished the chance to work at night, when supervisors would not be monitoring his every move:

If they left me alone, that's my ideal job. [That's why] I like to do something with computers. As long as I can make a living and not be too stressed out. My dad's a workaholic, but I'm not.

Even though Miranda worked a long week, she treasured the flexibility to decide when and how to do her job:

I work closer to sixty-hour weeks, but they're focused on what you produce and not on punching a time clock. It takes an open mind and trusting people. I've fallen into a really nice organization. It'll take a while to find something that will beat this.

By relying on some combination of skill and sheer determination, men and women both seek control over the terms of their daily lives. Whether putting in many hours or few, working on one's own or with others, they want to work on their own terms. This opens the possibility for more options at home as well. Mark saw self-employment as a route to greater parental involvement:

If I own my own gym or a business like that, I would have the type of hours where I'd be in and out, and I'd be available. I want to be the type of father to be more emotionally involved, definitely. You control your own destiny in a lot of ways like that.

Carlos hoped building his own business would do more than give him more time with his children; it would also create something he could pass on to them:[14]

I'm gonna open up my own business—audio recording, engineering, stuff like that—so that if I ever do have kids, my kids can take on the family business. I don't want them being nobody else's slave.

Whether these strategies involve rising to the top of a hierarchy, gaining professional skills, or creating a small-scale enterprise, they aim for a level of work autonomy that may prove just as hard to enact as the ideals of family security and work-family balance.[15] Yet because these desires are wide and deep, they are an emerging force for change.[16] Young workers may worry about eroding job security, but they also value the opportunities for self-invention offered in a postindustrial economy.

IT'S *MY* CAREER

Young workers, searching for an alternative to the mid-twentieth-century concept of "career" defined as a series of steps on a fixed organizational chart, continue to value the *idea* of a career, but they define it in a different way.

After watching his father suffer a career-ending layoff after years of service, Joel rejected the notion that remaining a loyal employee would ensure job security or a rising income:

> Twenty-five years in one job and then suddenly losing it! He was figuring to retire with that place. It came as a shock. I used it as a learning experience—that things aren't as stable as you might think, and not to make a choice just because of security. Consciously or subconsciously, I don't want to fall in that situation.

Ashley reached the same conclusion after her mother lost her job:

> I don't want to see myself being downsized, like my mother. So I'm planning postgraduate work in the medical field. If I can't, I'll be on my way to owning something of my own, a business of some kind.

Others did not need their parents' experiences to conclude that stepping off a narrow career track holds intrinsic appeal. Miranda hoped to pursue a variety of jobs, rather than specializing in one:

> The ladder seems kind of old-fashioned. I see myself moving around. And as much as I've changed jobs and done different things, I don't know that I would go back to doing the same thing. I like learning. And just about every job that I've gotten into, I've been over my head, 'cause I've always said "Yeah, I can do it," and then I get in there and learn it and I'm ready to move on. I like the challenge of new stuff.

Richard had a similar plan:

> I want to do more than one thing, and I can see myself doing multiple different things throughout my life—maybe some kind of entrepreneurial stuff, working with different investments, and as a psychologist from time to time.

Among those who set out in traditional jobs, many plan to veer off this course sooner or later by achieving enough early success to launch a more independent work path later on. For Michael, a job as an engineer for a local transit authority marked a beginning in a much longer plan:

> I'm working there to gain experience and knowledge, but my ultimate goal is to start my own business—eventually consulting, making my own hours. Even if I don't make a lot of money, I'll be well off. I want to be happy, take care of my family, be my own boss so I can have control.

Maria, a financial trader, hoped long hours early in her career would provide her with the resources to choose less time-consuming work later on:

> I just want to make enough, and this would avail me the opportunity to have more free time, so then I could stop and do something else.

No longer do young workers assume that a "real" career must follow a predictable series of steps. In place of what Arlie Hochschild once called "the clockwork of male careers," men and women both want to shape their career path by putting a sequence of jobs together in creative and unforeseeable ways.[17]

MONEY ISN'T EVERYTHING

Young workers seek job autonomy, and most are willing to make some sacrifices to achieve it. Thoroughly committed to her promising work as an analyst for a computer products company, Miranda refused to measure her worth by her pay:

> I've worked at jobs I hated and jobs I've loved, and I've actually left better-paying jobs to go to lesser-paying jobs. It's harder financially, but it's better mentally, emotionally. I think it's peace of mind. To work every day at a job that you don't like is just miserable.

It may be less surprising to hear a woman say she is willing to give up some earnings in exchange for more satisfying work, but young men agree. Most hold a more ambivalent view than "human capital" economists who argue that men stress maximizing earnings more than other factors.[18] Although men want to make enough to keep their families secure, few place earnings above all else.[19] Nick held a series of construction and restaurant jobs, but resented the pressure to sacrifice meaningful work on the altar of a high income:

> I am looking society in the face and saying, "You're wrong. Money isn't that important. Self-contentment, happiness is more important. Make sure my family's happy." And that would have to include being able to support them. I'm a very good worker, [but] what appeals to me is being able to do what I want, not looking for the big paycheck.

Justin worked in a high-powered financial service firm, but he felt the same way:

> I'm discovering what my values are, and I question—does money bring happiness? Right now I need it, but I would like to achieve some sort

of success. I would then be very willing to quit and be a teacher and play with [my] kids every day. It won't be the most successful life in terms of money, but it will be a very satisfying life to me.

These aspirations could contravene parental pressures, but even the children of affluence did not assume they would be able or willing to re-create their parents' lifestyles. Mark was reared by professional parents, but preferred to pursue more personally appealing if less financially promising work as a physical trainer who might one day open his own gym:

My mom thinks I have to make a certain amount of money to be successful, but I'm like, "If I'm doing something I hate, how am I gonna be doing that?" It's all right for her; it's just not what I want. I want to have it more balanced. They taught me a lot, but I have my own thing.

Noah's father was a "company man," but Noah was prepared to trade a well-paid but dispiriting public relations job in a corporate conglomerate for the life of a freelance writer:

I'll be happy if I just go from one assignment to another and get paid for it. Could I do with less? The affluence I grew up in—I can honestly say that I don't crave those things.

Just as some middle-class men considered shifting down, hourly wage workers resisted the economic incentives of overtime. Ray deemed time with his two daughters more valuable than the extra income he earned putting in overtime as a prison guard:

You can make fifty thousand easy, that's base, and then you can make sixty, seventy more. This is my sixth year, and I haven't broke fifty yet. I don't do overtime. I tell people, I'm not staying. I like spending time with my kids.

Daniel expected his job as a firefighter to provide both time with his family and enough money to avoid taking a second job:

Maybe I'll do overtime or a second job once in a while—construction or whatever. But if that will interfere with my children, I would never get a second job, unless of course the kids needed the money.

The willingness to trade some money for more time and more satisfying work may not cancel the cultural and familial pressures to emphasize earnings, but it points to cracks in this ethos.[20] It also belies gender stereotypes depicting men, but not women, as earnings specialists. Young workers of all stripes seek economic rewards, but not necessarily income *maximization*. They are searching for work that balances "good enough" earnings with flexibility, autonomy, and time for the rest of life.[21] If social arrangements allowed men and women to enact their values, most would prefer to balance market and nonmarket work rather than specializing in one at the expense of the other.

A NEW IDEAL WORKER?

The occupational shifts of an increasingly fluid and globalized postindustrial economy create opposing forces for young workers. Competition for the best jobs intensifies time demands and psychological pressures, but the decline of an enduring contract between employers and employees leaves workers feeling insecure. This clash prompts young workers to seek more control over the conditions of their daily work and the longer-term course of their careers. They have little choice but to rely on their skills and savvy to guide them through a world that seems both treacherous and rich with opportunity.

Underneath this generational shift in work experiences lies a gender convergence. By claiming the right to build unconventional work trajectories, young people are closing the gap between male "careers" and female "jobs." Women now declare a commitment to lifelong work that embodies ambition but rejects a single-minded devotion to work. If women were the only group seeking this path, it would signal little more than a reframing of their historic place as the primary family caregivers. So the crux of this shift rests with men's fate. By resisting rigid definitions of work and career, young men also pose a challenge to the classic construction of an ideal worker as someone who follows an uninterrupted series of full-time (and overtime) jobs while displaying an unflinching commitment to a "work first" ethos.

After watching their parents struggle to blend work and family, a new generation recognizes the need to restructure the conditions of work if they are to reshape the balance between earning and caring. Many men as well as women prefer to fashion their own career paths, even if this means forgoing some income to gain more control.

Will the effort to build more flexible careers succeed? While there is no going back to the structured work trajectories that offered long-term security to middle- and working-class (white) men, the prospects for the future are uncertain. The converging hopes of young women and men nevertheless signal a new stage in the gender revolution—one where workers of all stripes question the viability of traditional jobs and seek instead to actively shape a more fluid occupational pathway.

Fighting for a Shared Work-Family Career

Flexibility and autonomy at work offer individuals a way to avoid workaholism at one end of the spectrum and full-time domesticity at the other. But two work lives must be coordinated in order to achieve equal sharing. As Rosanna Hertz pointed out several decades ago, egalitarian couples must juggle *three* careers—his, hers, and theirs.[22] Though few receive institutionalized support for this "third career," more young couples are trying—against the odds and without a blueprint—to coordinate a shared "work-family career."[23] As young women redefine an ideal partner to include caretaking men, and young men make a similar shift to include achieving women, together they seek new ways to build a relationship.[24] And by bringing work home and care to work, they also seek ways to break through the spatial and temporal boundaries separating families from workplaces and communities.

REDEFINING THE IDEAL PARTNER

Just as the traditional workplace presumes that caretaking needs do not encumber the ideal worker, the gender-divided family presumes that an ideal partner is someone who specializes in either market or family work. New economic and social realities, however, make these assumptions increasingly untenable, transforming the ideal partner into someone who can and will cross gender boundaries. Women now hold close to half of all jobs, and they are more likely to work in service and white-collar occupations, where the economy is most likely to grow.[25] Most couples now count on two earners, and among two-paycheck families as a whole, women now contribute 44 percent of the income.[26] Many men thus welcomed the chance to find an economically successful partner, even if this tempered their claim as the prime provider. Todd had little problem sharing his life with someone who made more:

> I'd love it if she made money, and it wouldn't bother me if she made more. It wouldn't bother me if she made less. It's a bonus one way and not a problem, hopefully, the other way.

These men also realized that finding a work-committed partner means taking on more at home. And even though the gender gap in housework persists, many men—and especially younger men—are more involved in domestic work than their fathers. While women continue to do more, men's contribution to housework has doubled since the 1960s, increasing from about 15 percent to more than 30 percent of the total, while the time they spend caring for children has increased even more, especially because men are now more likely to multitask by combining leisure and child care.[27] Although Ken was reared in a traditional middle-class family, he knew that searching for a work-committed partner implied providing not just moral but practical support at home:

> [I'm looking for] the opposite of what my parents have—someone who's professional, with mutual admiration and support. Showing respect for what the other person does. Not just saying that you love somebody, but showing it through actions. So I hope we split things right down the middle.

Reared in a two-earner, working-class home where no chores were off-limits to his dad, Daniel expected to be a fully involved caretaker:

> My wife can work as much as my mother worked. The caretaking, I'm willing to take a little more of that. My father raised me to do things for myself. I can cook, do the laundry, change diapers. I got a lot from my father, and I plan to give a lot to my kids.

Some, like Noah, even dreamed of trading places. He was willing to endure the discomfort of depending on a wife's earnings and becoming a contemporary "Mr. Mom" in exchange for the chance to pursue his love of writing:

> To find a nice woman with a good job, I hope that happens, because then all this pressure will fly away and I'll be able to be a person who writes. I might feel guilt that my wife is working all the time—but I don't think we'd be living in this big mansion, so we'd be able to do it. I'll be home with the kids, and she will be out doing whatever she does.

With a growing pool of such men to draw from, young women are better positioned to find a partner who supports—and expects—their achievement outside the home. Catherine's live-in partner refused to let her fall into self-defeating patterns:

> If he sees me feeling sorry for myself, he's like, "I know exactly what you're doing, you're fighting success." He won't let me get away with it. He'll say, "Stop feeling sorry for yourself. You're not gonna get it unless you work hard for it."

Some women also found partners who, like Noah, were willing to be the primary caretaker. Though Theresa did not expect it, her husband became their daughters' designated babysitter when he could not work and she became the main earner:

He's got this disability that prevents him from working. So he takes care of the girls while I'm working. My daughters said, "Let's get something for daddy for Mother's Day." And I said, "You're right; daddy's mommy too."

Nina and her fiancé both worked full-time, but he still took on the nurturing labor in their household:

I feel a need to financially take care of things, and Tim's more, if I had an illness, he'd be there by my bedside taking care. He tells me that as long as he can cook or clean or help out in that way, if that can make me happy, then that makes him happy. Did I expect it? Not to the extent of what he does. I definitely do feel lucky.

Emerging partner ideals prompt more men and women to reject fixed gender divisions and separate spheres. Young men increasingly need work-committed partners who share the financial load, and more young women can find partners who expect them to do so. Indeed, basic economic shifts, such as the contraction of manufacturing and blue-collar jobs, leave men with shrinking opportunities for secure, well-paid, and unionized work.[28] At the same time, women are more likely than men to attend college and earn college degrees, and they are also concentrated in service and white-collar jobs.[29] These occupational and educational shifts make changes in the definition of an ideal—or marriageable—partner even more important. The future of marriage depends in part on women's and men's willingness to seek partners who do not conform to traditional beliefs that husbands should have a higher level of education and earn more than wives.[30] The option to enact new partner ideals depends, however, on redrawing the boundaries between homes, communities, and workplaces.

CROSSING SPATIAL AND TEMPORAL BOUNDARIES

Young women and men also seek new ways to cross the spatial and temporal boundaries separating paid and family work. They hope to find flexible jobs that allow them to bring work home and bring home to work, to pursue unconventional work schedules, and to take turns with partners and other caregivers. Personally tailored careers and less structured work settings offer a chance to blur the divide between home and work. Angela hoped she could conduct her practice as a therapist at home:

I would like a job that [is] flexible or where you can work out of your house. As a psychotherapist, I [can have] an office in my house or something where you don't spend all your time commuting.

Luis, the computer specialist, came to a similar conclusion:

I would really like to work from my house 'cause it's important to be a good father. With computers, you can. I'm trying to build up to it.

Others considered taking their children to work, and not just for one day. In contrast to the employees Arlie Hochschild describes in *The Time Bind,* these young workers view the workplace not as a refuge from family life but as a space where both might coexist.[31] Noah hoped to bring a child along on his assignments as a journalist:

Whatever I do, I want to take a child with me. If I'm on assignment, I'm going to take my kid. And I think if I can do that, I'll have it all.

Once William finished his chemistry degree, he looked forward to joining a small biotechnology firm with a relaxed, child-friendly environment:

I'm hoping to work in a small company which is really informal, so I can bring the kids in the office and play around, work odd hours that make me able to do it all.

When neither bringing work home nor bringing a child to work seem reasonable options, nontraditional work schedules offer a way to reshape the temporal boundaries between working and caretaking. Daniel planned to use the long breaks in his schedule to be an involved parent:

Working as a firefighter, I'm around [home] a lot more than people who have a regular job. As far as daytime, I can be with the kids. So I'm hoping I'll get married and be very happy raising my kids.

Some also considered creating their own caretaking communities, where flexible work schedules for a group of parents would make collective child rearing possible. William hoped to find a community of friends and neighbors who took turns at caretaking:

In the best of all worlds, Lindsey and I would like a time-sharing day care, where it's a community of people who share their kids. And Tuesday, all the kids stay with them; Wednesday, they're yours. I would really like to live in a place where you share with your neighbors, or we'll try to build it.

Finally, many took a longer view. Faced with unpredictable and changing contingencies, Chris focused less on a flexible daily schedule and more on taking turns at paid and family work as circumstances permitted or required over the long run:

> With kids, it would be a function of who has more flexibility with regard to their career, and if neither does, then one of us will have to sacrifice one period and the other for another. It would really be fifty-fifty down the line.

Louise also took this longer view:

> Once I get into nursing, he can take time off to find himself. If he feels he needs to go back to school, I can support everybody. I've always told him, "If I had a very good job, and you wanted to take off time to find something, I have no problem with it."

Men are joining women in efforts to blur the boundaries of space and time. The prospect of flexible jobs and autonomous careers provides hope for a more balanced life. The prospect of finding a partner with similar resources also provides couples with hope for a coordinated effort. Planning to become a freelance travel writer and start her own company, Elizabeth counted on building a partnership where the lines between home and work meshed for everyone:

> Both of us, hopefully, would be working out of the home. Or we'd have our place where, if we have to bring our kids or whatever, we'd be the boss. ,

Brandon had a similar vision about becoming a physical therapist and running a bed and breakfast with his fiancée:

> I could do work four days a week, and with her, something like that also. And if we're running a hotel, it's almost like you can be working and be at home at the same time.

New ways of working—from e-mail to telecommuting to more casual work settings in and close to home—provide options for young workers to pursue these strategies. Like many social shifts, however, blurring the distinction between public and private offers a double-edged promise. Economic and technological changes may make it easier for young workers to coordinate their work and caretaking efforts, but they also make it easier for work to invade the time and space once set aside for private life. As Luis put it, "to be on call twenty-four hours a day—I don't know how to deal with that."[32] If workers have their way, however, women and men will use these changes to overcome the separation of work and family in time and space.[33]

BUILDING A WORK-FAMILY PARTNERSHIP

By redefining the ideal partner and crossing the spatial and temporal boundaries separating public from private life, it is possible to strive for a shared "work-family career." This strategy offers a way to reach across the gender divide, just as crafting a "personal career" offers a route to individual work autonomy. Though these efforts undermine traditional forms of masculinity and femininity, many young people see substantial offsetting advantages. Women increasingly seek men who do housework and whom they consider physically attractive, while men now rank intelligence and education higher than cooking and housekeeping "as a desirable trait in a partner."[34]

Egalitarian marriages also appear to have some distinct advantages for today's couples. Wives are more satisfied and less likely to divorce when they share domestic and paid work with their husbands, and husbands and wives with egalitarian views have higher marital quality and fewer marital problems, even though (or perhaps because) they spend less time together.[35] Yet the ultimate fate of egalitarian strategies depends on whether workplaces and communities provide the necessary support. As Justin put it, "There's no model for this... but if something happened to make it possible, it would change the way I do everything."

Remaking Family Values

Enacting flexible work and family strategies also requires remaking family values. The vast majority of my interviewees reject narrow visions of family life that seem out of touch with their own circumstances and intolerant of the lives of others. Even though Joel grew up in a traditional home, he saw new family forms as a necessary and even natural response to twenty-first-century realities:

> If you're from a different generation, it could be really hard to accept the changes, but if you're growing up now, it seems natural, really. If there's any hope for my generation, we need to be more open.

Shared experiences of gender and family upheavals bind young women and men together in ways that transcend their diverse backgrounds and raise suspicions about narrow, exclusionary views of what makes a good family.[36]

Yet they are also skeptical of a moral framework where anything goes and everything is acceptable. Wary of moral certitude on one side and moral relativism on the other, young adults resist stigmatizing others, but they nevertheless seek a core set of standards for all. This effort points to a softening of the battle lines in the culture and gender wars.

RESISTING JUDGMENT

Whether they experienced shifts in their own families or observed them in the lives of friends, neighbors, schoolmates, and coworkers, young people have witnessed pervasive family changes that leave them reluctant to cast judgment on others' personal circumstances.[37] Those whose own families joined the ranks of dual-earning or single-parent families sympathize with the difficulties facing everyone. Living in a two-income family left Angela determined not to make invidious distinctions between family forms:

> These days, when both parents work, I'm surrounded by situations that reflect more of my situation when I was a child. I'm sure there's families that don't, but now I just say "Hey, that's what it is." I don't judge it at all.

Children raised in stable homemaker-breadwinner homes are equally disinclined to distinguish between "better" and "worse" family types. Though not experienced firsthand, family changes have taken place around them. When Megan filled in as a substitute teacher, she realized her young students lived in a wide range of household arrangements just as "normal" as her own:

> The teacher left a family tree for the kids to fill out, but their families were nothing like this little fill-in-the-blanks thing. If everybody had a traditional family, it might have been something else, but everyone had these crazy branches on their tree. It was amazingly complicated, but it didn't bother them any. It seemed natural and normal.

Simple dichotomies between "good" and "bad" family forms do not appear to do justice to the subtle dynamics of family life nor do they provide a realistic framework for coping with uncertain future contingencies. Though Kevin's parents stayed together, he thought it unfair to oppose divorce in all circumstances, especially since such a policy would leave him ill equipped for an unpredictable turn in his own life:

> I've seen both, and I don't know what I'd do if I was in that situation. I do have an opinion, and it's that I'm unsure. I don't know.

A reluctance to moralize does not, however, preclude making a judgment about the merits of social change. To the contrary, few wish to surrender the wider range of options they now take for granted. Whatever her concern about the future, Patricia held little nostalgia for earlier eras with more restricted choices:

> I don't want to be judgmental, but I really can't conceive of living in the fifties when you didn't have the freedom you have now. It's something I relish.

Reflecting on her own experiences in a home where "the bad stuff" went unacknowledged, Donna did not wish to return to a period when idealized views of family life masked secrets, lies, and unpleasant truths:

> I don't think there's an ideal family. I don't even think it existed. There's no such thing as the Brady Bunch. Everything was secrets years ago. There were all these things going on; it just didn't come out. Then you give kids a complex. They grow up [thinking] "why aren't we like this?" Secrets will kill you.

STRESSING PROCESS, NOT FORM

Rejecting strict definitions of a "good" family, women and men from all types of homes agree that family functioning trumps family form. Kevin lived in a stable, two-parent home, but he did not see it as inherently superior:

> I don't think there's one formula that makes for a successful family. There are lots of families with both parents that are pretty crappy. And there are single-parent families that are wonderful places to grow up. I think it's just all about understanding and being there and caring for each other.

Reared by her mother and grandmother, Keisha took a similar view:

> Everyone has their problems; nothing is ever perfect. I don't feel like I missed out on anything. I had the love and the support. All my sisters and me, that's the end product, and we're real happy.

Instead of judging families according to their composition, women and men reared in all types of homes view families, like individuals, as unique entities facing specific challenges. As Mitch declared:

Those are just big generalizations, and I think it's a function of what one makes of it. A single-parent home has different challenges than a two-parent home, but it can and does work. So I think how well it works is pretty much a function of a case-by-case thing.

This stance does not mean it is inappropriate to judge families, but rather that judgment should depend on different criteria. Drawing on their own experiences, most prefer to stress the *quality* of a family's bonds and the *flexibility* of its members. Joel's parents divided their tasks in stereotypical ways, but he believed an ideal family consists of a web of supportive relationships, not a set of roles or legal ties:

An ideal father is someone who can do the juggling act. Same way for the mother. I really don't want to make any distinctions, like this specified role is for either one. I really don't believe that.

Chrystal, now a single mother, expressed a similar view:

"Family" to me is when you have more than one person who [are] really there for each other, really able to give as well as take, complementing the other people or other person. There are different types of families out there, and it doesn't really matter as long as there's a loving support system in place.

This perspective extends to children's well-being. While everyone agreed an adult's first responsibility, regardless of circumstance, is to provide a supportive, caring context for dependents, they do not believe a child's welfare conflicts with a parent's—and especially a mother's—needs. Looking back on her own parents' shifting ties to each other and to the workplace, Michelle concluded:

As long as the child feels supported and loved, that's the most important thing—whether it's the two-parent home, the single-parent home, the mother is working, or anything.

For this generation, relationships, not roles, make families, and ties of ongoing support, not formal legal obligations, bind them. Redefining families in this way better fits the new options *and* new uncertainties young adults now face. They hope to find a "haven in a heartless world," but this haven does not take the same form for everyone at all times.[38] Indeed, no one type can possibly meet individuals' varied, developing needs or families' changing contingencies.

In a new twist on the classic argument that homemaker-breadwinner households provide the best "fit" for modern societies, postindustrial conditions actually make it more "functional" for people to have a variety of family options as their lives unfold.[39] While a concern for the quality of relationships rather than the composition of a household may seem to some to be a sign of family decline, it actually reflects a more optimistic view. Even those with difficult family experiences prefer to see families as ties that support and uplift as well as bind.

BEYOND THE CULTURE WARS

The search for a more inclusive, less judgmental vision of family life might seem to portend a shift to moral relativism, but those who support new family options do not reject universal principles. The challenge facing new generations is not whether to abandon universal values, but how to balance such contradictory ones as family cohesion and personal freedom within a single moral frame. Brianna was raised by a single mother, but she envisioned a family life blending tolerance and autonomy with duty and commitment:

> I wish we could have the family values that we had in the fifties, but with the open-mindedness we have now. You can not care whether your kid's gay or understand when they have their first sexual experience but still sit down and have dinner together.

Sarah grew up in a traditional home, but hoped to find more balance between individualism and commitment than her parents had achieved:

> To me, an ideal family functions well as a unit but functions well separately, too. I think of it as being very close and nurturing and warm and all those things that we were taught, but also individuated, where my family didn't do so well.

Even those with more traditional outlooks see how new realities require more flexibility. The Pew Research Center reports that the majority of young adults between eighteen and twenty-nine believe divorce is "preferable to maintaining an unhappy marriage," and those reared by two married parents are just as likely as those with divorced parents to agree.[40] With a strict Catholic upbringing, Sam is one of these traditionally reared children, but he recognized the injustice and danger in too rigid a moral frame:

> I don't believe in divorce. But if it's really bad, fighting constantly, then [people] should be separated because that's even a worse

environment—that's more trauma for the kid to grow up in than having a single parent. It depends. There's always exceptions.

In an age of family uncertainty, the challenge is to balance bedrock values with an appreciation of the varied exigencies people face. Single at twenty-seven, Alex felt that "good" families are those prepared to cope with whatever comes:

> If you're realistic, recognizing that the world can be a hard place, a family should be able to respond to that. So it may not be ideal, but that's what the family is there for.

So did Ray, who was thirty and shared the care, feeding, and financial support of his three young children with his wife:

> There is no ideal family. All you can do is handle whatever's given to you.

And Brianna, divorced and living on her own at twenty-five, reached a similar conclusion:

> You get your cards, and you do the best with it you can. So maybe there is an ideal. The ideal is being able to take the punches as they come. And take responsibility. Other than that, it doesn't matter.

For most, "one size fits all" no longer provides a viable moral road map for navigating the shifting terrain of contemporary work and family life. While some cling to settled certainties, the search for a flexible moral frame signals a growing weariness with cultural conflicts pitting different social groups against each other. Reared in a predominantly white working-class suburb where traditional families dominated, Nick took pride in giving his own child the freedoms he did not have:

> Today there are so many different ethnic groups, beliefs, religions. Why is any specific one the way to go? My son is gonna be six in a couple of weeks, and I feel I'm doing a very good job by letting him develop his own personality.

Eric, who has a similar background, agreed:

> I was kind of forced down a road where, whether you believed in it or not, this was the way you were gonna be raised. You had no choice. [So I say] let children develop their own beliefs. Give them the opportunity to see whether they like something or don't instead of saying this is the only right way to live. 'Cause that's not how it is today.

This expansive view of personal development coincides with a concern for the morality of institutions. Many of my interviewees echo the growing chorus of young voices who would like cultural debates to focus on social as well as individual responsibility.[41] As Angel put it:

> There's bigger things to worry about than changes in American families—jobs, homelessness. Why are we so worried about the petty things when there's so much bigger things out there?

Wary of stigmatizing all but a few options, young adults from all backgrounds want a moral frame that respects differences while also providing a guide for individuals, families, *and* institutions. A number of national surveys and polls report a growing fatigue among younger Americans with the culture wars. A Pew survey found young adults are less concerned than older generations about sexual activity before marriage (only 28 percent disapprove, compared to 41 percent for those between 50 and 64) and living together without being married (only 32 percent disapprove, compared to almost half for the older group).[42] This study also revealed that nearly 60 percent of young people agree with the statement, "It is all right for a couple to live together without intending to get married." Similar tolerance exists on matters relating to same-sex relationships, with only 40 percent of young people opposing civil unions, compared to 48 percent for people between 50 and 64, and less than half (46 percent) opposing gay marriage, compared to 63 percent for the older group. Another poll, conducted by Greenberg, Quinlan, and Ross, found even greater acceptance among young adults, with close to 60 percent supporting gay marriage, compared to roughly 30 percent for the rest of the nation.[43] They also found that most of these younger Americans (58 percent) agree the country needs "to work harder at accepting and tolerating people who are different, particularly gays" rather than "work harder at upholding traditional values."

All of these studies show that young Americans are far less divided on social issues than the culture warriors suggest.[44] They attach less moral stigma to family shifts and are loath to pass judgment on other people's private lives. The reluctance to designate one right way to create a family and blend work with caretaking represents an effort to avoid hypocrisy while affirming core values. Young adults now seek a practical morality that balances commitment with autonomy, takes account of situational contingencies, stresses family processes over household forms, embraces diversity, and resists dictating how others should live. This ideological strategy may not help them find the right job or life partner, but it does reframe the discussion to help them cope with an imperfect and highly uncertain world.[45] The alternative is to blame themselves and others for inescapable and irreversible changes beyond their control.

Transcending the Impasse

Superficially, differences of gender, class, ethnicity, and family background point to a widening gap between young women and men, rich and poor, white and nonwhite, and traditional and nontraditional. Yet everyone came of age amid diversifying families, and these shared experiences set the stage for bridging their social divides. Even those who did not experience changes in their own households saw them occurring in the lives of their friends, neighbors, and relatives. They inherited a changing economic and social landscape in which the rise of new family and gender options coincided with the decline of traditional jobs. These basic social shifts have created both new opportunities and new uncertainties, which bind young adults together despite their demographic diversity. In fact, behavioral differences, such as the poor's propensity to marry less often than other income groups, stem more from differences in resources and opportunities than from differences in values.

As they prepare for an uncertain future, young women and men face some shared dilemmas. Convinced that the "organizational career" is a dwindling relic of an earlier era, they hope to tailor their own careers to better accommodate the ebb and flow of family life and to redefine the ideal worker. In search of a new work-family partnership, they hope to blur the boundaries between home and work and to redefine the ideal partner. Facing tough alternatives in their own lives, they resist judging the private choices of others or limiting themselves to a narrow range of options. Searching for a moral framework that retains core values while acknowledging new social realities, they stress the importance of supportive interpersonal processes rather than specific family forms.

These private responses to socially constructed dilemmas offer clues about which collective solutions might reach across the gender divide and transcend the culture wars. Most young adults do not want to turn back the clock; they want instead to combine the traditional value of forging a lifelong commitment with the contemporary values of living a balanced life and creating a flexible, egalitarian partnership. As daunting as the obstacles are, the depth and breadth of these converging aspirations should not be underestimated. They teach us to worry less about the values of new generations and more about how to reduce the institutional barriers to enacting their ideals.

| Finishing the Gender Revolution

It always seems impossible until it's done.

—Nelson Mandela

B ORN INTO AN ERA of tumultuous shifts in the way their parents organized and balanced their work and family lives, the children of the
gender revolution inherited a complicated mix of new options, challenges,
and uncertainties. As they move into and through adulthood, they have an
unprecedented opportunity to create new ways of living, working, and building families, but they also face entrenched patterns of working and caretaking that pose unavoidable dilemmas. This unique position gives their lives
special significance. As a window onto the causes, processes, and limits of
social change, their experiences call on us to reframe the broader debate about
gender, work, and family. How they negotiate life paths amid the persistent
obstacles also provides telling lessons about what social policies will allow
new generations to achieve the lives they seek.

Family Pathways and Gender Strategies

The narratives of these young women and men provide several fundamental
lessons. First, by shifting the focus from static types to families' dynamic processes and pathways, they help us transcend the family values debate. Second,

their experiences show how and why some families are able to respond to and even surmount the inevitable obstacles of twenty-first-century life by fashioning flexible gender strategies for earning and caretaking. Finally, their current actions and future outlooks show how people's "values" are actually a mix of abstract ideals and practical strategies. Enacted values entail a complicated compromise between the lives people want to create and the lives they must construct out of existing social resources and constraints. In all of these ways, the life histories of this generation point toward a general framework for understanding how people negotiate the uncertainties of contemporary adulthood.

FAMILIES—AND LIVES—AS PATHWAYS

American families have become more fluid as well as more diverse than ever before.[1] Regardless of what form a family takes at any moment, it will likely change shape as time passes. Some of these changes are predictable, such as the birth of children and their passage through school and out of the home. But many others are unpredictable. Adult commitments are more voluntary and changeable, work careers less stable, and mothers more committed to the workplace. These new options for adults have created new domestic contexts for their offspring. As today's children grow, their families are prompted, and indeed compelled, to change in ways that are neither determined nor foreseeable.

Fundamental changes in the life course of families underlie the broad categories of family type. Family paths can lead in promising or dismaying directions, but the starting point does not determine the destination. Most no longer move predictably from marriage to childbearing and rearing to the empty nest. From a child's birth to the time she or he leaves home, separation or divorce can transform a two-parent household into a single-parent home, and remarriage can change a single-parent home into a two-parent one. A two-earner home can become traditional if a mother withdraws from the workplace, while a traditional home can shift to a dual-earner one if she takes a paid job. Families are situations in flux, not fixed arrangements. Labels such as "dual-earner," "single-parent," and "traditional" are only snapshots, while family life is a moving picture. Seeing families as pathways captures the ways they encounter a variety of unexpected challenges and undergo a host of unforeseen changes.

Yet obvious changes in family composition tell only part of the story. Despite the conventional wisdom that a family's form determines a child's well-being, my informants report that family support can expand *or* erode amid a variety of domestic contexts and transitions. Seemingly discrete events, such as a parental breakup or a mother's decision to work, can be part of a larger process that undermines a child's emotional or economic security, but they can also put a home on the path toward more security and support. A family's long-term ability to resolve specific conflicts is more consequential than the form a household takes at any one point along the way. Beyond drawing simple—and overly deterministic—associations between forms and outcomes, we need to explore the forces that shape family trajectories.

GENDER FLEXIBILITY IN EARNING AND CARETAKING

Postindustrial life poses risks and challenges to all types of households. Single-parent and dual-earning homes may face difficulties balancing and apportioning paid with domestic work, but sole-breadwinner homes also face perplexing dilemmas when a father feels overburdened at work or a mother feels dissatisfied at home. Though a family's challenges depend on its economic position and current type, few remain immune from intensifying work-family conflicts, rising expectations for intimate relationships, and the persisting devaluation of domestic work.

Why did some children conclude that their homes became more supportive and stable after facing these inevitable challenges? Why did others recount a cascade of destabilizing events? How did some homes overcome the obstacles while others did not? Across diverse family pathways, a child's perception depended on whether parents and other caretakers were able to develop flexible gender strategies in the face of crises and challenges. When families faced economic squeezes and declining parental morale, homes where adults transgressed gender boundaries in breadwinning and parenting were better equipped to meet a child's economic and emotional needs. In some cases, marriages became more stable as a mother went to work and overcame demoralization or helped an overburdened father. In other cases, a parental breakup relieved domestic conflict or led to the departure of an unstable parent, while also prompting a caretaking parent to get back on her or his feet. In still other cases, a more collaborative remarriage provided much-needed financial and psychological support. The common element uniting these different circumstances is the ability and willingness of parents and other caretakers to cross gender boundaries and blur gender distinctions in search of more effective and satisfying ways to bring in money and provide care. Mothers going to work, fathers becoming more involved in child rearing, and others joining in the work of caregiving—all of these efforts helped families overcome unexpected difficulties and create more harmonious homes. They also nourished parental morale, increased a home's financial security, and provided inspiring models of adult resilience.

In contrast, when mothers, fathers, and others could not transcend fixed gender divisions that failed to provide sufficient financial support or personal satisfaction, children watched their caretakers endure unhappy marriages, dissatisfying jobs, and the absence of an economic or caretaking safety net. Sometimes a marriage deteriorated when parents clung to a strict division of labor despite an unhappy mother or a father unable to support the household. Sometimes dual-earner marriages became enmeshed in chronic power struggles and cycles of conflict when a mother had to "do it all" or a father resented egalitarian sharing. Sometimes abandonment—most often a father's—brought emotional turmoil and financial insecurity when the remaining parent—most often a mother—struggled to find new ways to support the family or create an identity beyond wife and mother. Sometimes children (and their parents) lost critical support when nonparental figures were no longer able to provide money or care. Like the paths to improving fortunes, these varied developments also share a common element. The inability to develop more flexible strategies for breadwinning and caretaking left these families unable to sustain an emotionally or economically secure home.

All in all, when families could develop flexible approaches to breadwinning and caregiving, this helped them overcome economic uncertainties and interpersonal tensions. More rigid responses left them ill prepared to cope with unexpected contingencies. Amid a social and economic landscape that is undermining the once clearly drawn divisions between earning and caring, gender flexibility provides an indispensable way for a rising number of families to prepare for and adapt to twenty-first-century uncertainties.

VALUES AS IDEALS AND STRATEGIES

Focusing on family paths and gender strategies helps resolve the debate about the fate of family values. It is easy to see how blurred gender boundaries and unprecedented family diversity prompt some pundits, politicians, and academics to highlight rising culture wars, gender conflict, declining families, and apathetic youth, but those who experienced these changes firsthand tell a different—and more complex—story. These resilient and hopeful, but cautious, women and men are grappling with a clash between their highest ideals and their worst fears.

If we define family values in terms of our highest ideals, then they are not declining. Most women and men from all types of backgrounds hope to build a satisfying lifelong partnership with flexible and egalitarian sharing. In fact, even though marriage has never been more voluntary, it remains overwhelmingly popular. How else to explain the fight for the right to marry among same-sex couples, who aspire to join an institution largely taken for granted by heterosexual couples?[2] By almost any measure, from their desire to marry and have children to their hope to make their partnerships last and their children safe, young women and men overwhelmingly affirm the intrinsic importance of family life.[3]

Once we add people's expectations and strategies to the mix, however, the matter of values becomes more complicated.[4] Left with an ambiguous mix of affirming and demoralizing experiences, most young adults are both hopeful and skeptical. After watching their parents and others contend with marital uncertainty and work-family conflicts, they are guarded about the chances of achieving their own goals. From observing and working in "family-unfriendly" jobs, they know it will be hard to integrate family and work, and with high standards for a relationship, they are reluctant to place their fate in the hands of another. In the end, as Maria declared, planning one's life around a set of elusive ideals may be dangerous and foolish:

> Sometimes I ask myself if it's unrealistic to want everything. I think a lot of people will settle for something that is not what they wished.

And Mark, whose professional parents divorced, sounded a similar note:

> I make decisions based on the best scenario for that time period. Especially in today's world, it's very situational.

Despite their converging ideals, young women and men have reached different conclusions about how to prepare for a future strewn with obstacles and risks. Their divergent fallback positions create a gulf between the many women who fear the dangers of ceding self-reliance and the many men who resist the costs of equal parenting. This mismatch may signal a new gender divide, but it does not reflect a decline in moral values or a deeply entrenched and internalized gender chasm. The gender gap in aspirations has closed to a remarkable degree, with most women wishing to be earners, most men wishing to be involved parents, and most people seeking a balance between the two. If a gap between women's self-reliant strategies and men's neotraditional ones is widening, this stems from intensifying conflicts between time-demanding jobs and a dearth of supports at home.[5]

Whether they grew up in a more flexible home or one with a more rigid division of tasks, women and men desire more balanced and egalitarian lives, but these widely shared ideals have outpaced young people's ability to achieve them. The social organization of work and caretaking, which still largely presumes a caregiver at home and a breadwinner supporting the household, can meet neither the wishes nor the needs of most twenty-first-century families. An unfinished gender revolution has created a conflict between new values and resistant institutions. As long as new generations confront these contradictory pressures, they will move guardedly toward complicated strategies that balance their most idealistic aspirations with their more realistic concerns.

From Individual to Collective Responsibility

Will the children of the gender revolution be able to integrate work and care, or will they remain torn between equally laudable but incompatible goals? Will they be able to create uplifting family paths for their own children or will this desire wilt under the weight of uncertain relationships and insecure jobs? Just as their parents' lives developed during the rise of fluid marriages, work-committed women, and time-demanding jobs, new generations' paths will depend on how arrangements at work, at home, and in their neighborhoods shape their options. They will, to paraphrase Marx's famous declaration, make history, but not under conditions of their own choosing.

Deeply rooted and irreversible forces have undermined both stable marriage and clear gender boundaries. The classic division of moral labor between caretaking women and income-producing men makes little sense in a world where families depend on women's earnings and intimate relationships follow unpredictable paths. If the paradigm of separate spheres divided along gender lines no longer provides a practical guide, its demise also offers an unprecedented opportunity to create a new blueprint. And if we take seriously both the ideals and needs of new generations, this new paradigm will allow individuals and families to blend work and care in flexible, egalitarian ways across their life paths.[6]

How, then, can we create social policies that help transform this new blueprint into real options? To draw on Reinhold Niebuhr's celebrated prayer, creating sound policy depends on having the serenity to accept what we cannot change, the strength to change what we can, and the wisdom to know the difference between the two. Amid an irreversible but unfinished gender revolution, we need to accept the inevitable aspects of change and then create social policies to make change as humane and just as possible. That means helping families successfully negotiate the unforeseen obstacles along their diverse pathways and helping individuals implement their aspirations for equality, flexibility, and balance.

SUPPORTING FAMILY PATHWAYS

No society can guarantee a smooth, stable life path for everyone, but deeply anchored and intertwined social shifts make today's pathways especially uncertain. No social policy can resurrect such mid-twentieth-century arrangements as permanent marriage and stable jobs for men, both of which allowed the homemaker-breadwinner household to become ascendant. But we *can* create social supports to help twenty-first-century families weather the kinds of challenges we know they will face.

Now that most families travel unpredictable paths, we need to help them meet their responsibilities as their circumstances change. To retool social policy to support the fluidity and diversity of actually existing families, we also need to shift from searching for one "best" household type to fostering constructive family processes. This shift takes adult responsibility seriously without imposing one vision on everyone. It holds parents and other caretakers responsible for good care, without judging how such care is provided or who provides it. A focus on family processes also draws attention to the social conditions that make good care possible. How can we help parents stay involved in the lives of their children, whether or not they are married or live together? How can we help mothers and fathers find fulfilling, well-paid jobs that also leave ample space for parenting? How can we help young adults create flexible, egalitarian relationships that do not force them to choose between fixed gender boundaries and going it alone? Since new generations already support these goals, it is time to rethink the structural and cultural logics of work and caretaking to take account of the changes in individual lives.[7]

VALUING EQUALITY, FLEXIBILITY, AND BALANCE

Values reside in institutional practices no less than in individual minds. Yet the institutions inherited by young women and men have not kept pace with their hard-won desires for egalitarian relationships and the flexible integration of earning and caretaking. The collision between institutional logics and individual aspirations creates contradictory forces, and only collective change can provide genuine resolutions.

American political culture has long extolled both the work ethic and the ethic of care, but our social institutions provide few avenues for blending these values.[8] To the contrary, combining work accomplishment with lasting, caring bonds is more a matter of good fortune and ample private resources (enjoyed by the few) than a commonplace social pathway. In an institutional context that penalizes workers for taking out time and devalues care work, whether paid or unpaid, the challenge is not to restore individual morality but to create more moral institutions by restructuring work and the organization of care.

Restructuring Work

In a world where mothers are almost as likely as fathers to work throughout their children's lives, it is time to jettison the outdated model of an "ideal worker" as someone who is willing and able to place his or her job before all else, even during times of great family need. Workers willing and able to live up to this ethos are a dwindling species, even among men. Among those who work the longest hours and draw the largest financial rewards, most say they would choose a better balance if the option were available and would also sacrifice some income for more flexibility and control.[9]

Today's workers need both short- and long-term flexibility. As life expectancy grows and people look forward to many decades in the workplace, it makes little sense to raise the stakes on career-building just as the peak family-building stage arrives. Not only does this shortsighted view handicap women, who continue to bear a larger share of a family's care work, but it also leaves men wary about the costs of equal parenting and leaves families ill equipped to respond to new contingencies. Creating flexible workplaces and child supportive neighborhoods depends on a wide range of policies, although some straightforward measures can begin the process.

Providing genuine work flexibility requires both formal policies and informal work practices that banish the penalties attached to caregiving and give workers more control over when and how to do their jobs.[10] Families as well as individuals need flexibility. Decoupling essential benefits, such as health care, from full-time employment would give households more flexibility in developing their own work strategies. In a similar way, outlawing "family responsibility discrimination" would protect mothers and fathers from hidden penalties for using policies that are formally available but informally stigmatized.[11] Invigorating and enforcing gender antidiscrimination policies would also help bring the importance of work flexibility to the fore. Of course, formal policies are only as effective as the people who implement them, and the key to any policy is creating supportive workplace cultures that emanate from the top and suffuse throughout an organization.[12]

In an era of expanding time obligations and declining job security, replacing greedy jobs with flexible careers is a daunting prospect, but the alternative is a growing chasm between the structure of work and the realities of workers' lives. The good news is that the postindustrial workplace is well suited for flexible approaches that focus on how well a job is done rather than when or where it is performed. Far from harming productivity, flexibility helps workers approach their jobs with more focus and commitment. Indeed, shifts in the nature of jobs and the composition of the labor force make it important that work flexibility is not reserved for parents and caregivers only. Everyone has the right to find a reasonable balance in their lives, and satisfied workers with rich personal ties make better workers whether or not they are responsible for the care of children or other dependents.[13]

Restructuring Caretaking

New generations also need child-supportive communities to help mothers and fathers weather unexpected changes and blend caretaking with earning. Diverse family forms are here to stay, and most will undergo some form of change as their children grow to adulthood. When policies ignore children's increasing exposure to changes in their parents' work and marital ties, they leave children at serious risk. At a minimum, it is time to catch up with the rest of the postindustrial world, where universal day care, mandated parental leave, and other child-supportive arrangements are integral aspects of social policy.

Compared to other postindustrial nations, the United States lags woefully behind in the supports it offers families. Of the twenty-one richest countries in the world, only the United States and Australia do not mandate paid parental leave, and among the industrialized Western nations, only the United States does not mandate paid vacations.[14] France offers mothers paid leave for six weeks before a baby is due and ten weeks after the birth, with a guarantee of return to her job. Fathers can also take up to eleven days of paid leave after the birth of a baby, and parents can share up to three years of leave time without risk of losing their jobs. The French preschool program is available to all children ages three to five, and all teachers have a master's degree and earn a living wage. Closer to home, Canada offers employment insurance for both maternity and paternity leave, allowing a couple to take up to fifty weeks' leave, which can be divided between mother and father.[15]

Parental supports for caretaking are necessary, but they are not sufficient if they reinforce gender inequality in parenting. The most effective policies take fathers' caretaking as seriously as they do mothers'. In France and Sweden, fathers can take seven weeks of paid leave, and another ten countries provide between two days and six weeks for fathers. In these cases, a father's leave is available in addition to a mother's, and, most important, it is not transferrable.[16] By making fathers' participation in child care a matter of national policy, such "use it or lose it" policies provide strong encouragement for men to be involved. Equally consequential, they make it clear that all parents have the right to care for their children without risking their jobs, financial well-being, or work identities.[17]

Egalitarian approaches, which eschew gender divisions, are also the most likely to provide for the collective good. In fact, postindustrial nations that support mothers' employment and fathers' parental involvement enjoy stable fertility rates, while nations with "maternalist" and other policies that encourage mothers' full-time homemaking face a birth dearth. Policies that ignore women's needs for equality invite them to resist public injunctions that are at odds with their own desires.[18]

Alongside supports for parenting equality, children at all life stages, from early childhood to late adolescence, also need wider neighborhood and community supports. Children need a wide network to help them negotiate the unexpected twists and turns in their own lives as well as in their parents' relationships and work circumstances. While recent U.S. social policy has focused on "restoring marriage" rather than providing direct support to children, the causal relationship needs to flow in the other direction. Social programs that foster a wide web of interpersonal ties for children, through after-school and enhanced educational programs as well as community-based child care, will not only help children directly but also enhance their parents' ability to resolve work-family conflicts and strengthen their relationships.[19] Since families take a variety of forms and change their shape as children grow to adulthood, there are many ways to meet children's needs—but assuming that all, or even most, children can depend on a privatized household with a stay-at-home parent is not one of them.[20]

Creating Options, Not Utopia

Social policies can foster the structural and cultural foundations for gender flexibility in public and private life, but they cannot make every marriage succeed or every adult a superlative parent. Private life, by definition, involves developmental conflicts, and postindustrial conditions make the path to and through adulthood unknowable. The once predictable stages of adult life have become an indefinite trajectory in and out of various living arrangements and personal commitments, and no social policy can guarantee an easy path or restore older certainties.

Yet the aim of social policy should not be to create a utopia. One person's perfect life is another's nightmare, and any attempt to impose a singular vision on a complex, diverse society is a recipe for failure that inevitably provokes a backlash. The rise and fall of the idealized homemaker-breadwinner family, which left many feeling confined and others feeling marginalized, should make us cautious about imposing another inflexible blueprint to replace it. We need to resist the temptation to look for uniform solutions to highly personal struggles. The goal of flexibility presumes that people will live in diverse ways and change their behavior as new circumstances permit or require. Equality does not mean sameness, but rather the right to shape and reshape our lives as we deem best in the face of new challenges and opportunities.[21]

Certainly, the children of the gender revolution have learned this lesson. The challenge now is to create institutions flexible enough to support them through inevitable, but unpredictable, crises and to help them prevail when anticipated and unanticipated obstacles emerge. Egalitarian workplaces and child-supportive communities will not usher in a new utopia, but they will help families follow improving paths and avoid declining ones. They will help young adults balance autonomy and commitment in their relationships and integrate work and caretaking in their own lives. They will help young women build family commitments that do not pull them back to an outdated traditionalism or leave them overburdened by having to do it all. They will help young men act in more caring and egalitarian ways at home and at the workplace. They will offer "bridging" supports for families in transition. And they will provide care and economic security for children, whether or not their parents forge a lasting bond or find stable jobs.

No social policy can or should eliminate the intrinsic tensions of growing up, creating an identity, and forging a satisfying life path, but policies fostering gender justice, work-family integration, and community support for children *can* provide the resources to help citizens meet these inevitable challenges. These goals are not just lofty ideals. In the context of irreversible change, they are necessities for individual and collective well-being.

Shifting the Frame

However much it is needed, institutional change needs commensurate cultural change. Amid a widespread and irreversible generational shift, it is time to reframe the debate about its implications. Despite widespread changes in individual aspirations, our public discourse continues to presume old dichotomies—between public and private, earning and caregiving, selfless women and achieving men—that no longer speak to the lives we live or the ideals we seek.

As young women and men grapple with their own conflicts about work, marriage, and parenthood, they are ready to abandon a search for the one best family form and to jettison a rhetoric that blames families for conditions beyond their control. They also wish to transcend a framework of forced-choice options, whether between equality and commitment or personal fulfillment and children's welfare. Despite—or perhaps because of—their diverse experiences, women and men are weary of the judgmental, and ultimately unhelpful, politics of division. They prefer a politics that eschews finger-pointing in favor of a more tolerant vision. And even though they remain skeptical about the prospects for resolving this seemingly intractable political stalemate, their outlooks are converging on a new cultural and political frame that stresses their similar needs rather than putting social groups in conflict. Instead of a stalemated political debate, they long for policy approaches that offer real solutions to their shared problems.[22]

The good news is that across family, gender, class, and ethnic divides, young people share common—and admirable—values, including a desire for balance, fairness, and equality in their public and private lives. These aspirations point toward a more inclusive politics that unites apparently disparate groups and replaces an image of moral decline with a more constructive concern about how to realign our social institutions to meet new personal and family needs. Focusing on institutions rather than individuals affirms our shared values and offers a way to reach across our divides, bringing together men and women, workers and parents, the time-poor and the income-poor around jointly held needs and aspirations. The best family values can only be achieved by creating responsive workplaces that support parental involvement and ensure equal opportunity, by building child-friendly communities that sustain all families, and by helping new generations weather the unpredictable turns their lives will take.

The young women and men who came of age amid the gender and family revolution have little choice but to create innovative pathways. Their lives attest to the ability of ordinary people to overcome life's difficulties, find meaning in their personal strategies, and remain hopeful in the face of daunting obstacles. Most had positive experiences with mothers who worked and parents who strove for flexibility, and those reared with a caring support network and sufficient economic security did well. Regardless of the paths their own families took, most hope to build on the lessons of childhood and early adulthood by seeking equality and flexibility in their own lives.

Yet new generations have good reason to remain cautious about their chances of achieving these ideals. Without social supports for more versatile ways of caretaking and breadwinning, they will have to cope as best they can, searching for private solutions to public problems.[23] If they are to prevail rather than just survive, they need to rely on institutions that support their loftiest goals rather than speaking to their greatest fears.

TABLE A.1 List of Respondents

Name*	Racial identity	Class background	Age
Women			
Alicia	African-American	Working	18
Amanda	Asian	Middle	22
Angela	White	Middle	26
Anita	Latina	Working	26
Annie	White	Middle	23
Ashley	African-American	Working	20
Barbara	White	Poor	26
Brianna	African-American	Poor	25
Catherine	Latina	Middle	26
Chandra	African-American	Middle	19
Chrystal	African-American	Poor	26
Claudia	White	Middle	19
Connie	White	Working	27
Danisha	African-American	Working	21
Dolores	Latina	Working	30
Donna	White	Poor	25
Elizabeth	White	Middle	28
Ellen	White	Working	18
Erica	White	Middle	26
Hannah	White	Middle	26
Isabella	Latina	Working	19

(*continued*)

Name	Racial identity	Class background	Age
Janet	White	Middle	26
Jasmine	African-American	Poor	19
Jennifer	White	Working	20
Jessica	Asian	Middle	19
Karen	White	Middle	27
Kayla	African-American	Middle	23
Keisha	Latina	Poor	23
Kristen	White	Working	18
Lauren	White	Middle	25
Leila	African-American	Middle	20
Letitia	Latina	Poor	19
Louise	White	Working	25
Lynne	White	Working	18
Maria	Latina	Middle	29
Mariela	Latina	Working	19
Megan	White	Working	28
Melissa	Asian	Middle	23
Michelle	Asian	Middle	24
Miranda	Latina	Working	27
Monique	African-American	Poor	23
Nancy	Asian	Middle	24
Nicole	White	Middle	22
Nina	Asian	Poor	26
Olivia	African-American	Working	23
Patricia	White	Middle	20
Rachel	White	Middle	24
Rebecca	White	Middle	24
Rosa	Latina	Poor	21
Samantha	Latina	Poor	24
Sarah	White	Middle	31
Serena	African-American	Working	26
Sharon	White	Middle	26
Shauna	African-American	Working	31
Stephanie	White	Middle	26
Suzanne	White	Middle	18
Tamika	African-American	Working	20
Tasha	African-American	Middle	19
Theresa	Latina	Working	32
Tiffany	Latina	Working	25

Men

Adam	White	Middle	19
Alex	White	Working	27
Allen	White	Middle	18
Andrew	White	Middle	27
Angel	Latino	Working	25
Antonio	Latino	Working	21
Brandon	African-American	Middle	21
Brian	White	Working	19
Bruce	White	Middle	27
Carlos	Latino	Working	18
Chris	Latino	Middle	20
Daniel	White	Working	23
David	White	Middle	25
Dwayne	African-American	Working	24
Eduardo	Latino	Working	20
Eric	White	Middle	24
Gabriel	White	Middle	25
Greg	White	Middle	20
Hal	White	Working	21
Hank	White	Working	26
Howard	White	Working	18
Isaiah	African-American	Poor	21
Jamal	African-American	Poor	20
James	White	Working	18
Jason	White	Middle	26
Jeff	White	Middle	25
Jermaine	African-American	Poor	26
Jerome	African-American	Poor	24
Jim	White	Working	27
Joel	White	Working	21
Jonathan	White	Middle	26
Joseph	White	Working	21
Josh	White	Working	20
Justin	Asian	Middle	28
Ken	White	Middle	24
Kevin	White	Middle	25
Lawrence	White	Middle	21
Lucius	African-American	Poor	23
Luis	Latino	Working	27
Manny	Latino	Working	19

(continued)

Name	Racial identity	Class background	Age
Mark	White	Middle	24
Matthew	White	Middle	25
Michael	African-American	Working	26
Mitch	White	Middle	27
Nate	African-American	Poor	29
Nick	White	Working	29
Noah	White	Middle	25
Patrick	White	Working	20
Paul	White	Middle	26
Peter	White	Middle	27
Phil	White	Working	28
Ray	African-American	Working	30
Richard	White	Middle	20
Sam	White	Working	19
Shawn	African-American	Poor	19
Steve	White	Middle	26
Thomas	White	Middle	27
Todd	White	Middle	27
Wayne	African-American	Poor	25
William	White	Middle	28

*To protect confidentiality and anonymity, all names are pseudonyms.

- Sample size: 120

Racial and Ethnic Distribution			
Non-Hispanic White	African-American	Latino/Latina	Asian
55%	22%	17%	6%

- Gender breakdown: 50% women 50% men

Economic Background		
Poor or near poor	Working class	Middle or upper middle class
16%	38%	46%

- Age 18 to 32, average 24

- 5% lesbian or gay

Single-Parent Home			Stable Two-Parent Home	
40%			60%	
Divorced or never married	Separated and re-united	Parent died	Stable dual earner	Traditional or modified traditional
36%	2%	2%	33%	27%

FIGURE A.I Sample demographics.

APPENDIX 2: STUDYING SOCIAL AND INDIVIDUAL CHANGE

N o single method can provide all we need to know, and each has strengths and limitations. In-depth interviewing relies on smaller sample sizes than do large surveys, and it lacks ethnography's direct observation. But it is especially well equipped to help us explore new and not yet well understood social developments, to discover the meanings underlying statistical trends, and to chart the processes linking social structure with human perception and action.

At the same time, my study sought to follow general principles shared by all scientific methods—the selection of a random (and not self-selected) representative sample of theoretically significant groups, the systematic collection of data, and the careful comparative analysis of similarities and differences. The insights gleaned from this process, like those from other methods, can (and I hope will) be used in service of a common goal: to solve important empirical puzzles, to develop general theories of human behavior and social organization, and to contribute to humane, informed, and effective policy making.

Selecting the Sample

The lives of young adults can tell us about the consequences of a revolution, and their current actions point toward its likely future course. I chose to interview people between the ages of eighteen and thirty-two because they were young enough to have experienced change close at hand, yet old enough to look back on the full trajectory of their childhood as well as forward to their own future. About half of my sample were younger than twenty-five and half were twenty-five or older, but no major differences emerged between these groups.[1] Some younger respondents were understandably tentative when discussing their future plans, but the substantive content of their responses did not diverge from their older peers.

Although practical considerations made it necessary to restrict my sampling to the New York metropolitan area, the randomly selected respondents grew up in all corners of the United States, from Texas and South Carolina to California and Illinois. At the time of the interview, they resided in a variety of neighborhoods, from the suburbs and exurbs to diverse outer- and inner-city communities.[2] While studies in other regions of the country might yield somewhat different percentage breakdowns among different family paths and gender strategies, the *general processes* and *tensions* of change are likely to be similar. Most Americans live in large metropolitan areas, and no region of the country has been insulated from family and gender change.

Two-thirds of my sample was chosen as part of a larger study comparing the children of immigrants to children with native-born parents.[3] To ensure my respondents had been born and reared in the United States, they were drawn entirely from the native-born sample.[4] These names were supplemented with another group of respondents randomly selected from enrollees of a continuing education program, which enlarged the sample to include a sufficient number of college graduates.

After receiving a letter of introduction and a follow-up phone call, 85 percent agreed to participate in a face-to-face interview, which typically took place at the respondent's residence. I personally conducted eighty interviews and relied on two gifted research assistants for the remaining forty. Their help made it possible to enlarge the sample size, and their interviews enriched the insights from my own field work.

Class, Race, and Ethnic Diversity

This sampling procedure yielded respondents who represented the ethnic, racial, and class diversity of twenty-first-century America. Since my goal was to discover how—and, indeed, if—diverse social, cultural, and economic contexts shape childhood experiences and later life chances, it was important to include people with a range of ethnic and racial identities and class backgrounds.

A diverse sample makes it possible to discover the similarities and differences among class and ethnic groups, but it also poses challenges of interpretation when the sample has too few cases to explore subtle differences among subgroups or to subject them to statistical tests of significance.[5] An intensive qualitative study cannot, by definition, include enough respondents to make multiple subgroup comparisons or to draw strict statistical conclusions, but it does offer offsetting opportunities to discover and develop theoretical arguments to explore and test with larger samples. My findings may not foretell the precise breakdowns a large national sample would provide, but they are comparable to the findings of census and opinion surveys.

Rather than focusing on discrete variables, my approach more closely aligns with those who argue for the "intersectionality" of such master categories as race, class, and gender. In contrast to statistical analyses, which strive to isolate the independent effects of specific variables, I sought to understand how markers of difference, such as race, class, and sexual orientation, can operate as holistic packages.[6] As important, my goal was to ascertain how people with varied backgrounds and identities experience broad social shifts in both similar and different ways. The family and gender revolution may have had different consequences for different social groups, but it has swept over everyone like a tidal wave.

Constructing and Conducting Life History Interviews

While surveys with multiple-choice answers have the advantage of large numbers and ethnographies offer direct observation, lengthy, probing interviews provide a uniquely powerful technique for my purposes. Compared to surveys, in-depth interviews make it possible to probe for the nuances in experiences and outlooks, to follow up on unanticipated findings, and to investigate the processes that link "causes" and "effects" identified by quantitative techniques. Compared to ethnographic observation, one-on-one interviews make it possible to explore the whole life span, to discover the meaning and motives for observable behavior, and to chart developmental trajectories.

Since people more easily and accurately recall specific life events when they are placed in a chronological narrative, an open-ended but highly structured questionnaire asked people to describe their lives in sequential order. Starting with early childhood (or, as the questions stated, "as far back as you can remember") and moving to and through adolescence to early adulthood, respondents were asked to recount critical events, stages, and turning points and to reflect on the meaning of these experiences. At each step, the interview probed for the context surrounding an event, the person's immediate reactions, and her or his views today. It also encouraged respondents to express ambivalent reactions and contradictory views.

The interviews were lengthy, lasting from two to more than four hours and averaging about three, and at their best became a conversation in which the respondent reflected not only on the "what and when" of important life events, but also on the "how, why, and with what consequences." As with all self-reporting, answers to these kinds of questions are inevitably colored by a person's particular perceptual lens, and "objective facts" ultimately rest in the eye of the respondent. Self-reports are, by definition, socially embedded constructs that evolve over time, but personal accounts are not invalid because they are subjective. Self-reports take seriously the importance of meaning-making in social life by offering an in-depth look at how people interpret and reinterpret their experiences and how these interpretations inform their actions and worldviews.[7]

Because people possess varying degrees of awareness and insight, they vary in their ability—and willingness—to search for thoughtful answers. Yet, with few exceptions, my interviewees were able to describe important events with remarkable clarity and enthusiasm. Despite the common belief that it is more difficult to report on the past than the present, a temporal perspective often helps people provide more confident answers about life experiences and their significance.[8]

Of course, not all in-depth interviews are equally revealing, but an interviewer's job is to gain as much information as possible from each respondent and then to place them all in a comparative context. The most revealing interviews yielded unexpected findings that did not confirm my own or others' preconceived theoretical assumptions, but every interview contributed to the development of theoretical insights about the link between social forces and individual actions and motives.[9]

Developing a Theoretical Framework

The challenge in analyzing qualitative material is to use thick description to build or reframe theory. This process takes place initially as insights drawn from early interviews help inform later ones and then when all the interviews have been collected, transcribed, and subjected to a comparative analysis.[10] Beyond the many unique, compelling stories, I sought to discover general patterns and to make sense of surprising, counterintuitive findings, especially about the link between social contexts and individual strategies (put differently, between "structure" and "agency") as a person's life took shape and direction. The questionnaire structure provided a frame for charting developmental paths, for distinguishing intended from unanticipated change, and for mapping the links between life events and the meanings people extracted from them and used to formulate life strategies.

Summarizing complex personal biographies and finding the common threads among them is a humbling task, but it can yield new ways of explaining puzzling "social facts." In this study, I soon found that prevailing conceptual frameworks neither accurately described my respondents' experiences nor accounted for their life paths. Like once stylish clothing that has lost its fit, the standard categories that rely on family type did not fit the realities of most people's lives. Even those who lived in a home outwardly resembling a "homemaker-breadwinner," "dual-earner," or "single-parent" home went to great lengths to explain how such a general category did not capture the ways their family life shifted in form and function. In a similar way, in discussing their current outlooks and plans, neither women nor men were comfortable with unidimensional categories contrasting traditional with egalitarian "attitudes."

As the analysis proceeded, my respondents' accounts pointed to a different conceptual framework. Focusing on the paths families took rather than the forms they assumed at any given moment led me to group families by how well—or poorly—they were able to adapt in the face of change. Although this conceptual frame necessarily mixed family types ordinarily seen as fundamentally different, it provided a way to explain the variation *within* traditional demographic categories.[11]

In the analysis of young adult plans and strategies, the more common approach of comparing women's and men's attitudes also yielded puzzling, contradictory results. Both women and men expressed remarkably similar beliefs and convictions, but they were pursuing varied and complex life strategies. Only by teasing out a distinction between professed ideals and practically grounded actions and plans was it possible to make sense of this paradox.

Analysis and Evaluation

Although the task of research is to analyze findings, not evaluate them, my respondents did not shy away from making their *own* evaluations. Some provided uplifting narratives, while others offered disheartening ones. Most drew conclusions about the practices that shaped their lives. Some saw living in a traditional family as a benefit, while others saw it as a disadvantage. Some perceived detrimental consequences following a parental breakup, while others deemed the consequences more beneficial. In short, people reported strikingly different evaluations of similar experiences and remarkably similar judgments about different experiences.

When children looked back over the full scope of their lives, their assessments depended on what happened over time. Since ultimate outcomes could not be known when the events occurred, only the passage of time could provide a vantage from which to draw firmer conclusions. My respondents used this perspective to draw conclusions about the paths their families followed as well as their own development.

People are the historians of their own lives, and perceptions matter because views of the past inform future actions. Since humans are reflexive actors, it is misleading to reduce personal accounts to "mere" subjectivity or "false consciousness." Instead, the challenge is to place individual narratives in a social and comparative context and to explain how and why people see and construct their life paths in both similar and different ways.

NOTES

Chapter One

1. The term "sex role" implies, and often explicitly assumes, that gender differences are intrinsic, static, and necessary for the smooth functioning of families and societies. The concept has its roots in mid-twentieth-century theories of sex differences and especially in the work of Parsons and Bales (1955), which postulates that women are (and should be) the "expressive specialists" and men the "instrument specialists" in families. As feminist sociologists and theorists have shown, the concept is of limited use in explaining gender arrangements. Instead, gender (like class) is a dynamic relationship that is embedded in social arrangements, reflects power differences, and changes its shape across time and space. As Stacey and Thorne (1985) pointed out in an early critique of the "sex roles" framework, we do not refer to "class roles" or "race roles." In my analysis, the term "role" is thus used *only* to refer to others' conceptions of fixed patterns of behavior.

2. As many analysts have noted, it is important to distinguish between the concepts of gender, sex, and sexuality. "Gender" is a social category that is distinct from the biological categories of female and male. It is also multidimensional and can be found at all levels of social life, from the institutional structuring of life chances to the interpersonal dynamics between women and men to people's internalized identities. Gender is linked to both sex and sexuality, but it is important to draw distinctions among them so that we may examine their relationships with each other. See Lorber (2005) for an in-depth discussion of these differences.

3. Because of its ubiquity, I use the term "traditional" to refer to the homemaker-breadwinner household even though the term is misleading in some respects. Although a majority of American households took this form for much of the 1950s, the homemaker-breadwinner family is actually a relatively modern, short-lived arrangement that rose to prominence in the mid-twentieth century, largely as a consequence of post–World War II prosperity. Many groups never conformed to this model, especially in working-class and minority communities where the cultural ideal remained either out of reach or unappealing. In idealizing the "traditional"

household, popular culture has also glossed over its less attractive aspects, such as women's frustrations with making domesticity the true test of womanhood and men's pressures to conform to definitions of manhood stressing loyalty to a job and the "rat race." Despite cultural images of happy homemaking mothers and wise breadwinning fathers, many housewives were dissatisfied, and many fathers did not feel that they knew best. Such families could also be stifling for the children who lived in them and stigmatizing for those who did not. It is no accident that Betty Freidan's *The Feminine Mystique* (1963) and William H. Whyte's *The Organization Man* (1956) both touched a nerve of growing discontent. Indeed, the children born in this period ultimately pioneered more diverse family forms. For a thorough overview of these family trends and misconceptions, see Coontz (1992).

4. U.S. Census Bureau (2007). The Pew Research Center (2007a) reports that the proportion of children born to unmarried mothers is at an all-time high of almost 37 percent, although about half of these nonmarital births are to cohabiting couples (compared to about one-third five years ago). There is also a great deal of variation in children's living situations across racial groups, with the U.S. Census reporting that 17 percent of Asian children, 24 percent of non-Hispanic white children, 34 percent of Hispanic children, and 65 percent of Black children are living with either one parent or neither parent (Blow, 2008).

5. Roberts (2008a, 2008c).

6. The divorce rate rose precipitously during the 1970s and 1980s and then leveled off in the 1990s, with current estimates ranging from a high of 50 percent to lower levels that can drop to around 40 percent. Couples with children living at home are less likely to break up than other couples. The overall divorce rate, moreover, masks differences across generations. The most commonly cited statistic that half of marriages end in divorce actually refers to the expected lifetime divorce rate of people married in the 1970s, but rates are lower for more recently married couples. Among men who married in the 1970s, for example, about 23 percent had divorced by the tenth year of marriage, but men married in the 1990s have a ten-year divorce rate of only 16 percent (Carey and Parker-Pope, 2009).

7. Since many two-parent families represent remarriages, more than half of Americans are likely at some point to live in a stepfamily (Coleman and Ganong, 2008).

8. U.S. Census Bureau (2006a) and Galinsky et al. (2009). This figure is considerably higher than the 57 percent of women without children living at home who are in the labor force, and that group includes older cohorts of women who did not join the workforce in numbers comparable to younger generations. Another way to understand these changes is to look at children's living arrangements. Among all children in 2000, only 21 percent lived in a two-parent household with an employed father and a nonemployed mother, while 59 percent lived with an employed mother, including 41 percent who lived with two employed parents, 3 percent with an employed mother and nonworking father, and 15 percent with an employed single mother (Johnson et al., 2005). The remaining children lived with either a single mother who did not have a paid job (5 percent), a married couple where neither were employed (4 percent), a father-only household (6 percent), or with neither parent (5 percent).

9. Today, women are more likely to work full-time and year-round, whether or not they are employed in historically male professions or are mothers of young children

(Percheski, 2008). Moreover, the definition of "part-time" has expanded, including work-weeks of up to forty hours in some highly demanding professions (Epstein et al., 1999).

10. See, for example, Uchitelle (2006), Greenhouse (2008), Warren and Tyagi (2003), and Kalleberg (2007).

11. Moen and Roehling (2005).

12. Ryder (1965) aptly referred to the life cycle of birth, aging, and death as the "demographic metabolism" and pointed to the central role of young adults in implementing social change.

13. Changes in women's and men's places are at the core of work and family shifts, and these shifts are reflected in the shape of institutions as well as in the actions of individuals. Risman (1998), Lorber (1994), and Acker (1990) discuss how "gender" is far more than an individual trait. West and Zimmerman (1987) see gender as a set of relationships that are created as people "do gender" in their everyday interactions. All of these frameworks stress the ways that gender is an institution and a structure (rather than an immutable individual trait) that creates contradictions and, in Lorber's words, paradoxes.

14. Mills (1959). By drawing an inseparable link between the study of institutions and individual lives, Mills also recognized that theory and method are different sides of the same coin.

15. There are many ways to define class. Since most could not accurately report their parents' incomes, parental occupation provides the most reliable measure of class background. People were classified as middle-class or upper-middle-class when they had at least one parent who worked in a professional, managerial, or similar occupation. They were deemed to have a working-class background if both parents or the only earner worked in blue-collar, pink-collar, or other service or wage work not requiring a college education. Children were considered to have grown up in poverty when one or both parents depended on public assistance for a significant period during their upbringing.

16. Each respondent was asked to identify the group they felt best described their racial identity. Biracial and multiracial respondents were then asked to choose the group with whom they most closely identified.

17. Although I make no claims to exact statistical representativeness, my sample reflects the general contours of U.S. family, class, and race diversity. This is especially important because younger cohorts contain more racial and ethnic diversity than older generations. The Population Reference Bureau reports "a growing racial/ethnic divergence between America's elderly population and younger age groups...While the large majority of people over age 60 are non-Hispanic white, a substantial and growing proportion of young people are racial or ethnic minorities" (Mather, 2007). The Census Bureau reports that in 2000, 61 percent of U.S. children were non-Hispanic white, 15 percent were African-American, 17 percent were of Hispanic origin, and about 4 percent were Asian (Johnson et al., 2005). Appendix 1 presents a list of respondents and summarizes their demographic characteristics, while Appendix 2 discusses the study's design rationale and sampling procedure.

18. Despite a great deal of hand-wringing about the potential dire consequences to children when mothers go to work or parents separate, there has been a surprising lack of curiosity about how children actually perceive and evaluate their parents' actions, especially once they are old enough to have developed a more nuanced

perspective. Ellen Galinsky's 1999 study of children's views of their working parents is a notable and exemplary exception, but adult children were not interviewed. This book thus places the focus squarely on children who are sufficiently mature to reflect on their childhood experience and its consequences. (Appendix 2 considers both the significance and limitations of retrospective reports.)

19. For clarity, the term "work" generally refers to paid labor and the term "care-taking" refers to unpaid domestic tasks. Both are genuine forms of labor, and care work is as essential to a household's survival as is bringing in an income. Indeed, we often pay others outside the household to perform care work. It is nevertheless important to distinguish between work and caretaking in order to analyze the different influences they exert in people's lives. See Folbre (2008).

20. Zerubavel (1991) discusses the advantages of "mental flexibility," which avoids rigidity at one end of the mental spectrum and boundlessness at the other.

21. Anecdotal but high-profile stories have touted an "opt-out revolution," to use a term coined by Belkin (2003). Another *New York Times* article arguing that "Many Women at Elite Colleges Set Career Path to Motherhood" (Story, 2005) made the front page even though it relied on a biased and soon discredited sample. Although the debate about women opting out has centered largely on the reasons for this trend, a number of analysts have shown the "opt-out revolution" to be an urban myth and a highly misleading term. Boushey (2005, 2008), Cotter, England, and Hermsen (2007), Percheski (2008), and Joan Williams (2007) provide ample evidence that such a turn of events has been exaggerated and, in important respects, reflects trends among men as well. Percheski reports, for example, that employment among college-educated women in professional and managerial occupations has increased across generations, with less than 8 percent of professional women out of the labor force for a year or more during their prime childbearing years. Even though women's labor force participation rates have stopped rising, this stall has occurred at a very high level (well over 70 percent), especially compared to several decades ago, when the rate hovered around 30 percent. Today, women's participation stands at almost 73 percent, down from a peak of almost 75 percent in 2000 (compared to men, whose participation rate has dropped from a peak of 96 percent in 1953 to about 86 percent) (Uchitelle, 2008). While mothers with children under the age of one show a small decline in their labor force participation compared to a peak in the late 1990s, mothers whose children are one or older show no similar drop. In fact, the difference in employment rates between mothers and childless women has declined. In sum, while women's march into the workplace may have reached a plateau, there is no widespread exodus of women (at any educational level and marital status) from the world of paid work. Moreover, despite the persisting perception that women leave work for family reasons and men because they lose their jobs, the recent decline in women's employment reflects blocked work opportunities in a worsening economy as women and men join the ranks of the unemployed.

Chapter Two

1. Scott and Leonhardt (2005).

2. Harris (1998) provides a trenchant, if extreme, argument about the limits of parental determinism.

3. Prominent proponents of the "family decline" perspective include Blankenhorn (1995), Popenoe (1988, 1996), Popenoe, Elshtain, and Blankenhorn (1996), and Whitehead (1997). Amato and Booth (1997) describe "a generation at risk" amid family shifts.

4. For rebuttals to the "family decline" perspective, see, for example, Bengston, Biblarz, and Roberts (2002), Coontz (1992, 2005), Kristin Moore et al. (2002), Skolnick (2006), Skolnick and Rosencrantz (1994), and Stacey (1990, 1996).

5. Among the burgeoning literature on how both paid and unpaid care work is devalued, see, for example, England (2005), Folbre (2001, 2008), and Zimmerman, Litt, and Bose (2006). Hochschild (1989) coined the term "stalled revolution" to describe how needed changes in the workplace and men's lives have failed to keep pace with the new demands on women in dual-earner homes.

6. Most research demonstrates that diversity *within* family types, however defined, is as large as the differences *between* them. Acock and Demo (1994) show, for example, that family composition does not predict children's well-being. Parcel and Menaghan (1994) make the same case for different forms of parental employment.

7. The proportion of my respondents who saw their mothers as strongly committed to paid work is lower than the actual proportion whose mothers held a paid job. Even though about two-thirds of American mothers, including those with children under six, now work for pay, fewer are employed full-time over a lengthy period. Over the last several decades, however, women's participation over the course of their lives has come to resemble men's. Despite the recent and relatively small drop among married mothers, most women can expect to work at a paid job throughout their lives.

8. A poll by the Pew Research Center (2007a) reported that many Americans continue to worry that the employment of mothers with children under eighteen, and especially full-time employment, poses problems for children and society at large. Still, most mothers, whether or not they are employed, say they prefer either full-time or part-time work to none at all.

9. Women and men with work-committed mothers are equally likely to believe this was the best choice.

10. Decades of research have found that, on the whole, children do not suffer when their mothers work outside the home. Instead, a mother's satisfaction with her situation, the quality of care a child receives, and the involvement of fathers and other caretakers are more important factors (Harvey, 1999; Hoffman, 1987; Hoffman, Wladis, and Youngblade, 1999; Galinsky, 1999; Clarke-Stewart and Allhusen, 2005; Waldfogel, 2006). Bianchi (2000) and Bianchi, Robinson, and Milkie (2006) report that contemporary mothers, including employed mothers, are actually spending more time with their children, not less. Burchinal and Clarke-Stewart (2007) find that the children of employed mothers do just as well in their cognitive development and, among children in low-income families, they do better. Much research also shows that, despite the difficulties of balancing work and family, employed mothers and two-income homes are, in the words of Barnett and Rivers (1996), "happier, healthier, and better off." Springer (2007) reports significant health benefits for men whose wives work. Those who see having an employed mother as harmful generally point to thin research results that show small, temporary, and nonsignificant negative effects of day care for a small number of children (Crouter and McHale, 2005).

11. In her study of more than 1,000 young people in the third through the twelfth grades, Galinsky (1999) found that only 10 percent of children wished for more time with their employed mothers and only 15.5 percent wished for more time with their fathers. Instead, 34 percent of children wished their mothers would be less stressed and tired, and 27.5 percent wished the same for their fathers.

12. Damaske (2009) shows how mothers rely on a "language of need" to account for a wide range of work strategies, from pursuing a career to staying home to moving in and out of the labor force. Underlying this shared discourse, however, such varied decisions are more likely to reflect differences in women's satisfaction at work and support at home.

13. In the case of one- versus two-parent homes, children living with both biological parents do appear on average to fare better, but most of the difference disappears after taking account of the family's financial resources and the degree of parental conflict prior to a breakup. Most of the negative consequences of divorce can be traced to the high conflict and emotional estrangement preceding a breakup and the loss of economic support often following in its aftermath (Cherlin et al., 1991; Furstenberg and Cherlin, 1991; McLanahan and Sandefur, 1994; Hetherington and Kelly, 2002). In a recent study of the effects of divorce on children's behavior, Li (2007) argues that "the dissolution of some marriages decreases children's behavior problems and the dissolution of others increases children's behavior problems, so that they cancel each other out when I totaled the average effect.... While certain divorces harm children, others benefit them."

14. Amato and Booth (1997, p. 200). Rutter (2004) also finds that children in high-conflict families whose parents divorce fare better than children raised in high-conflict families whose parents do not divorce. See also Li (2007).

15. Wallerstein and Blakeslee (1989), Wallerstein, Lewis, and Blakeslee (2000), and Elizabeth Marquardt (2005) argue that *all* divorces are harmful in the long run, with a "sleeper effect" emerging many years later. In contrast, Ahrons (1994, 2004) and Hetherington and Kelly (2002) point to the large variation in divorce's consequences. In Ahrons' long-term study of divorce and its aftermath, she found that over one-third of the grown children felt their parents' marriage was more stressful than the divorce, which came as a relief when it reduced the long-term daily conflict between parents.

16. Hochschild (1989) shows how gender strategies shape couples' decisions about how to manage "the second shift." She refers to these arrangements as gender strategies, but she focuses primarily on how these strategies reproduce gender divisions in two-earner homes. I adopt a similar approach, but also examine when, how, and why people's strategies can undermine, blur, or change the nature of gender distinctions. In my sample, there is no link between the direction of a family pathway and the race or class backgrounds of respondents.

Chapter Three

1. See Bernard's classic essay, "The Good-Provider Role: Its Rise and Fall" (1981).

2. Hays (1996) describes how an "ideology of intensive mothering" creates double binds for contemporary women, who face strong cultural pressures to shower children with time and attention and concentrate their time on parenting, whether or not they hold jobs outside the home.

3. According to a study by the Center for Economic and Policy Research, the percentage of single-parent homes headed by a father has jumped over the last decade. Single-father families increased by 74 percent between 1990 and 2006, compared to an increase of almost 24 percent in single-mother homes. In 2006, about 4.7 percent of children lived in a single-father household, which is about 17 percent of all single-parent families (Fremstad and Ray, 2006). Broken down by race, about 5 percent of non-Hispanic white children live with a single father, while 4 percent of Black and Hispanic children do so (Blow, 2008).

4. See, for example, Carrington (1999), Risman (1986), and Stacey and Biblarz (2001). My study of the social roots of men's paternal involvement (1993) shows how a breakup can, in some contexts, prompt more involved fatherhood by requiring custodial fathers to develop "mothering" skills. For an early analysis of the concept of "good enough" parenting, see Bowlby (1969).

5. The next chapter considers children's views of how and why "problematic breakups," which conform more closely to our unfavorable images of divorce and single parenthood, trigger or continue a downward slide.

6. In Constance Ahrons's study of how divorced families fared over the long run, about half of the grown children reported a closer relationship with their fathers, who spent more dedicated time with them and attended more of their extracurricular and school activities after the separation (Ahrons, 2004).

7. The next chapter considers what happens when custodial parents are unable to make the journey toward more flexible gender strategies. When parents were unable to master the multifaceted tasks of child rearing, children became more economically and emotionally vulnerable. The more felicitous breakups in this chapter show why such an outcome is not inevitable.

8. See, especially, Furstenberg and Cherlin (1991), Cherlin et al. (1991), and Marsiglio (2004).

9. Only 16 percent report a closer relationship with their biological father than their stepfather, and the remaining 25 percent say they do not have a close relationship with either their stepfather or father (Coleman and Ganong, 2008).

10. Not all remarriages have such beneficial consequences, and the next chapter shows how unsuccessful remarriages can be part of a declining family trajectory. As with marriage, it is important to look beyond the *fact* of a remarriage to its quality. See, for example, Teachman (2008).

11. Waite and Gallagher (2000) argue that marriage conveys benefits to parents and children alike, but they do not sufficiently distinguish between "better" and "worse" marriages or consider how the end of a "bad" marriage creates the chance for ex-partners to enter a better one. Since the overwhelming majority of Americans still choose to marry, and most remarry if the first proves unworkable, it is more telling to compare marriages over the life course of individuals than to make static comparisons between the currently married and the currently single, who are likely to marry or remarry in the future.

12. The debate about whether children need a marriage or a village has a long history, but it gathered steam when Hillary Clinton's *It Takes a Village* inspired neoconservative critics to counter that only a marriage can raise a child. See, for example, Zinsmeister (1996).

13. Stack (1974) remains the classic study of how social networks constitute bonds of reciprocity and help poor and working-class families cope with economic and other uncertainties. See, also, Edin and Lein (1997).

14. Since single parents are overwhelmingly women, and women are more likely to experience a downward economic slide in the wake of divorce, the children of divorce remain economically vulnerable. Debate continues, however, over how much financial fallout divorced women suffer. Weitzman (1985) provided an early and influential argument about such drastic economic declines, but subsequent research and reanalysis has shown how her analysis exaggerated divorce's costs to women. Peterson (1989, 1996) demonstrated that the short-term costs are far less than Weitzman claimed and these costs diminish over time as women get back on their financial feet. A recent study by Elizabeth Ananat and Guy Michaels found that "the average mom who divorces ends up with just as much income as an otherwise similar mom who stays married.... [because] divorced moms are... resilient. They move in with relatives, switch from part-time to full-time work and... 70 percent remarry" (Ananat, 2008).

15. U.S. Census Bureau (2005).

16. Sarkisian and Gerstel (2004, 2008) have shed some light on the class and race differences in helping networks. They found African-American women (and men) are more likely to live with or near relatives than are whites, and African-American women are more involved in helping with housework, rides, and child care, while white women are more likely to give money and emotional support. Yet they also report that African-Americans and whites of the same social class have about the same level of involvement with relatives.

17. Analysts across the political spectrum have pointed to the moral ambiguities of paid care work. In a critique of career-oriented, professional women, Flanagan (2006) has argued that middle-class employed mothers use working-class women to advance their own work ambitions. On the left, Ehrenreich and Hochschild (2002) have expressed similar concerns about native-born Americans relying on immigrant women. The heart of this conundrum, as Folbre (2001, 2008) documents, rests with the fact that care work is routinely undervalued, whether or not it is paid, and it is overwhelmingly performed by women. Hondagneu-Sotelo (2001) points out that since care work is essential and paid care work is here to stay, those who perform this work for pay should be accorded the respect, pay scale, and protections given to other paid workers. But chastising women for seeking help with caretaking is not the answer.

18. A recent Census Bureau study found that 89 percent of preschoolers and 63 percent of school-age children with an employed mother are in some form of regular child care arrangement, and nearly half of American preschoolers receive some kind of child care from a relative. Among children younger than five with an employed mother, 30 percent received regular care from a grandparent, 25 percent received care from their fathers, and around a third spent time in an organized program such as a day care center, nursery, or preschool (U.S. Census Bureau, 2005).

19. Ethnographic studies by Hansen (2005) and Lareau (2003) suggest that unpaid networks of care are more prevalent in working-class communities, while middle-class parents are more likely to rely on paid help. Other studies show that a range of class and ethnic groups rely on help from outside the immediate family. Edin and Kefalas (2005) and Hertz (2006) present rich descriptions of how both poor

and middle-class single mothers create fictive families to help rear their children. In general, nontraditional families of all class and ethnic stripes are turning to both paid and unpaid help to build a diverse array of care networks.

Chapter Four

1. While two-fifths of children with an eroding family path reported a divorce, three-fifths had parents who stayed together. Similarly, about a third had a work-committed mother, but two-thirds had a mother who either never held a paid job or relinquished a career.

2. For incisive accounts of the social pressures leading some mothers to leave hard-won careers, see Stone (2007) and Joan Williams (2000).

3. Hacker (2003) examines how and why women's rising status—and by implication the erosion of some of the privileges men once took for granted—have created tensions in intimate (heterosexual) relationships.

4. Musick, Meier, and Bumpass (2007) report few protections for children when fighting parents remain married, since exposure to marital conflict in biological two-parent families affects children's risk taking whether or not their parents stay together.

5. Marital separation and single parenthood typically lower children's financial resources, although the degree of decline, especially in the long run, remains open to debate. Peterson (1996) has shown the actual decline is not nearly as large as Lenore Weitzman's much-cited book *The Divorce Revolution* (1985) claims. In his own study and in a reanalysis of Weitzman's data, Peterson (1989, 1996) shows that divorce's negative economic consequences decline over time as most women recover and adjust to their new circumstances. Numerous studies also point out that many of the harmful consequences of single parenthood drop substantially and sometimes disappear when analysts control for a family's financial resources. Put differently, the worst consequences of divorce and single parenthood can be traced to the lack of economic stability that often accompanies these circumstances. (See, for example, McClanahan and Sandefur, 1994.)

6. To put single mothers' economic vulnerability in perspective, in 1997 only 53 percent of non-Hispanic white mothers, 44 percent of Hispanic mothers, and 33 percent of Black mothers received full payment of legally awarded child support payments, while 23 percent of white mothers, 33 percent of Hispanic mothers, and 49 percent of Black mothers either received no payment or were not awarded child support (Moore et al., 2002).

7. A number of studies have documented the way humans seek useful lessons out of the raw materials of their experiences. See, for example, Carey (2007) and McAdams (2006). Appendix 2 discusses the meaning and significance of retrospective accounts as a method for understanding how people construct personal narratives to find meaning in their lives.

Chapter Five

1. Some of the most visible liberal proponents of this view include Bellah et al. (1985), Etzioni (1998), and Putnam (2000). Providing a more complicated picture, Cancian (1987) argues that a new paradigm of "interdependence," which balances

commitment with concern for nourishing each partner's separate identity, has emerged alongside the paradigm of independence. Amato et al. (2007) propose that rising individualism and increasing pressures for equality have produced trade-offs in modern marriages.

2. See Gauthier and Furstenberg (2005), Danziger and Rouse (2007), and Furstenberg et al. (2005). Cherlin (1992) refers to the shift toward voluntary marriage as the "deinstitutionalization of marriage." For overviews of the causes, contours, and consequences of marital postponement, cohabitation, and other such changes, see Smock (2000) and Elwert (2008).

3. See Stone (2007) and Joan Williams (2007). Bennetts (2007) and Hirshman (2006) point to the dangers of leaving work and heading home. My findings suggest young women are well aware of these dangers. While a recent survey (Pew Research Center, 2007c) reports that most women prefer part-time work, this finding is more complicated than it appears. Many women, especially in highly demanding professions, define "part-time" as thirty-five to forty hours a week, and many men also say they prefer a similar work schedule. Jerry Jacobs and I (2004) find that most women *and* men generally prefer a workweek of about thirty-five to forty hours, but far fewer can achieve this ideal. Instead, they are increasingly divided between those who are putting in very long days and those who are not working as much as they would like.

4. Beck-Gersheim (2002, p. 42). More specifically, a "major part of any such strategy is thought about the future, a kind of early warning system that can enable risks to be dealt with and rendered harmless. Not by chance has 'prevention,' understood as a combination of foresight and forearming, become such a fashionable keyword in the individualized society. Calculation and control: this planning dimension is forcing individuals into the future as they go about their everyday lives."

5. A long theoretical tradition considers how individuals develop strategies to cope with the conflict between their "values" and their "practices." In *The Second Shift* (1989), Arlie Hochschild uses the term "gender strategies" to capture the internalized ideological and psychological "deep structures" that shape couples' domestic practices. Many cultural analysts point to a distinction between "values" and "strategies." Swidler (1986) argues that culture is not simply a set of values and beliefs, but more fundamentally consists of a "tool kit" of behaviors and practices. Pierre Bourdieu stresses the importance of "habitus," which encompasses the full set of interrelated forces that comprise a person's social world (1977, 1984). In *Abortion and the Politics of Motherhood* (1984), Kristen Luker uses the term "world view" to describe how abortion activists on both sides of the debate develop different perspectives on women's interests. Lamont (1992) and Zerubavel (1991) examine the "symbolic boundaries" that create cultural divisions and inequalities between social groups. Although my approach fits with this tradition, I stress how cultural and structural contradictions create dilemmas that force new generations to innovate (see, for example, Gerson, 2002).

6. Like Max Weber's notion of an ideal type, these categories reflect "aspiration packages" that may not exist in a pure form. Such categories nevertheless shape the way people think about their lives, and they also inform public debate about people's choices.

7. Marc and Amy Vachon (2010) define "equally shared parenting" as the intentional sharing of child rearing, breadwinning, housework, and time for self. They

add that equal parenting need not involve a constant focus on score keeping and that it is not just a way for men to do more or for couples to pursue an abstract principle. In addition to representing the pursuit of equality, egalitarian sharing can have benefits for everyone. Deutsch (1999) and Meers and Strober (2009) also discuss ways of defining and achieving equal sharing.

8. Pew Research Center (2007b).

9. Since same-sex marriage is not (yet) a widely available option, gays and lesbians are the most likely to make the distinction between being legally married and married "in spirit" (as several of my interviewees put it). Recent studies of same-sex couples who enter civil unions show "surprisingly few differences between committed gay couples and committed straight couples" (Parker-Pope, 2008). A Vermont survey comparing same-sex civil unions with heterosexual married couples did find that same-sex relationships, whether between men or women, are somewhat likely to be more egalitarian than heterosexual ones in terms of sharing housework, initiating sex, and having conversations about the relationship. These more equal relationships are also linked with higher satisfaction. The findings that a couple's gender composition makes little difference provides further evidence that inequality in heterosexual relationships is shaped by socially and culturally malleable (rather than inherent) forces. Blumstein and Schwartz (1983) reported similar findings several decades ago.

10. Children choose both positive and negative "role models" from a much wider array than classic socialization theory allows, including a range of people in their social world (Gerson, 1985, 1995).

11. Although younger generations are postponing marriage, rumors of its death, to paraphrase Mark Twain, have been greatly exaggerated. The vast majority of Americans do eventually marry (and if they divorce, most also remarry). In 2005, the majority of men and women (72 percent) had been married by the time they were thirty to thirty-four years old, and 96 percent of Americans over sixty-five had been married (U.S. Census Bureau, 2005). Of course, it remains to be seen if younger generations will ultimately marry at such high rates. Even if they do not attain such high rates of marriage (as seems likely), those who do marry may be more likely to stay married since people who marry after twenty-five are less likely to divorce than those who marry at an earlier age. For careful considerations of the dyamics of marital commitment among contemporary adults, see Byrd (2009) and Cherlin (2009).

12. American Business Collaboration (2004). This survey conducted by the Families and Work Institute for a consortium of American businesses reports that 80 percent of employed, college-educated Gen-Y'ers say they would like to work fewer paid and unpaid hours. Also see Greenberg (2005) and Pew Research Center (2007b).

13. Pew Research Center (2007b). Only faithfulness (93 percent) and having a "happy" sexual relationship (70 percent) ranked higher. For similar findings on the rise of egalitarian ideals, see Musick, Meier, and Bumpass (2007).

14. Teixeira (2009). These findings are from the 2008 National Election study, which asked people to place themselves on a seven-point scale relative to the statement, "Some people feel that women should have an equal role with men in running business, industry, and government. Others feel that women's place is in the home."

15. Hertz (1986).

16. Furstenberg et al. (2004).

17. Jerry Jacobs and I (2004) find a similar "aspiration gap" between women's and men's actual and ideal working times.

18. Merton (1949) formulated the classic framework for understanding how "opportunity structures" can allow, thwart, or redirect individual aspirations. (Also see Stinchcombe, 1975.)

19. Measurement differences have led to some disagreement about current rates of divorce and cohabitation. Some argue that about 50 percent of marriages end in divorce, while others see the rate as closer to 40 percent. Another recent study found that in 2005, unmarried cohabitants comprised 7.6 percent of all couples, compared to 5.1 in 1995 (Popenoe, 2008). In addition, a Census Bureau report shows that "more than half the Americans who might have celebrated their 25th wedding anniversaries since 2000 were divorced, separated or widowed before reaching that milestone" (Roberts, 2007b). For overviews of trends in marriage, divorce, and cohabitation, see Cherlin (2005, 2009), Elwert (2008), and Smock (2000).

20. Greenberg, 2005.

21. Pew Research Center (2007b).

22. Coontz (2005).

23. Wilcox and Nock (2006, 2007) argue that women are happier in traditional marriages, but their evidence actually tells a different story. They find, for example, that wives who work full-time and earn more than their husbands can be unhappy in their marriage *if* they perceive an unfair division of household labor and feel their husbands are not offering sufficient emotional support. When it comes to women's marital happiness, men's practical and emotional support matters most. See Springer (2007) for an alternative to the Wilcox and Nock perspective.

24. The Census Bureau reports that the rise in never-married twentysomethings can be found among both college-educated and high school–educated youth (Jayson and DeBarros, 2007). From 1950 to 2004, the median age of first marriage rose from twenty to twenty-six (Danziger and Rouse, 2007). For women, the median age in 2005 was almost twenty-six, compared to twenty in 1960, and for men, it was over twenty-seven, compared to about twenty-three in 1960. Moreover, in 2006, 29 per cent of women and 33 per cent of men in their early thirties had never been married.

25. Coser and Coser (1974); Moen (2003).

26. Schor (1991) provided an early look at how rising time pressures have affected American workers, while Hochschild (1997) explored the pushes and pulls inside a company with fairly generous family support policies. Jerry Jacobs and I (2004) chart the differences between workers in professional and working-class jobs, showing how working time has become a new form of social inequality.

27. One survey found that 73 percent of young people between the ages of twenty-one and twenty-eight who are either in college or holding a part-time or full-time job worry about balancing work and personal obligations (Blandford-Beringsmith and Musbach, 2009).

28. Among the many studies of the effects of these changes on contemporary workers, see Newman (1992), Ehrenreich (2001), and Moen and Roehling (2005).

29. Lareau (2003) argues that "concerted cultivation" (which involves devoted parenting) is a middle-class development, but Hays (1996, 2003) shows that these

standards, at least as a set of values, can be found in all classes. Warner (2005) presents a popular account of the rising pressures on American parents, especially in contrast to their European counterparts.

30. In his classic article "The Oversocialized Conception of Man in Modern Sociology," Wrong (1961) points out that internalized norms do not guarantee that a person will conform, only that they will feel guilty when they rebel. My study of women's work and mothering decisions (1985) shows this is so for women as well. To extend this argument, transgressing social norms is especially likely when social and cultural cross-pressures force individuals to choose among equally desirable or equally undesirable options.

31. Carol Stack's (1974) classic study of kinship networks in a poor African-American community uses the concept of "survival strategies."

Chapter Six

1. These percentages describe the contours of the sample. Although they do not necessarily indicate the percentage breakdowns that might be found in a larger national sample, they reflect national demographic and social trends. Moreover, most nationally representative surveys report similar findings. Appendix 2 discusses my methods and analytic approach in depth.

2. Joshua Coleman (2005) outlines men's strategies for avoiding their fair share at home, even when their wives work as much as they do.

3. Put differently, these women are determined to avoid what Bennetts (2007) calls "the feminine mistake."

4. While most of these experiences involved heterosexual relationships, those women who self-identified as lesbians also stressed the importance of self-reliance, whether or not they were in a long-term relationship.

5. For rich descriptions of why single mothers stress mothering more than marriage, see Edin and Kefalas (2006) and Anderson (1990, 1999).

6. In the language proposed by Giddens (1979), women's new contingencies prompt them to move beyond "practical consciousness" to "discursive consciousness." Behavior becomes "action" when it requires effort and thought and contributes to social change. Sidel (2006) reports similar strategies among young women from all classes and races.

7. Galinsky et al. (2009) report that 67 percent of men and 66 percent of women under twenty-nine say they want to move up at the workplace.

8. Damaske (2009) finds that both employed and nonworking women use a similar discourse of "family need" to account for their disparate decisions. Women who fall back on self-reliance also argue that their own need to work is compatible with their children's need for both nurturance and economic support.

9. See Smock (2000) and Shapira (2008).

10. Following Cancian's (1987) distinction between "independence," which stresses the development of a separate self, and "interdependence," which involves developing the self in the context of a committed relationship, self-reliant women see independence as a precondition for creating an interdependent relationship.

11. See, for example, Coontz (2008) and Gregory (2007). Mounting evidence also shows that higher earnings help women gain more autonomy in their relationships.

Gupta (2006) reports, for example, that for every $7,500 in additional income, a wife's share of housework declines by one hour per week. Contrary to arguments that economically successful women threaten their spouses so much that wives take on more housework to build up a husband's ego, a woman's share of housework actually depends more on how much she earns and is not related to whether it is more or less than her partner's.

12. Stevenson and Wolfers (2006) have shown that the increased availability of divorce has indeed given women more power. By giving married women an exit option, it has provided stronger incentives for husbands to respect their wishes.

13. Greenberg (2005). This study also reports that 49 percent of women believe that most of the men they know are not responsible enough to get married, compared to 38 percent of men who hold the same view of women they know.

14. Not only are single women among the fastest-growing demographic groups, but a spate of recent studies show that most single women do fine, are satisfied with their lives, and are happy at middle age. See, especially, De Paulo (2006) and Trimberger (2005). Roberts (2007a) offers a journalistic overview of the increase in women who live on their own.

15. Glass (2009). It is instructive to note that while only 10 percent of teens and young women say they want to remain childless, 20 percent of women between the ages of forty and forty-five in 2006 had not borne children. With the birthrate for native-born women hovering around 1.8 children per woman, many are either remaining childless or having only one child. Women's fertility plans and behavior change substantially as they age and many encounter unforeseen obstacles to child-bearing as well as unforeseen attractions to having fewer or no children.

16. In their study of poor single mothers, Edin and Kefalas (2005) report a similar finding. In a three-decade study of more than 300 teen mothers from Baltimore, Furstenberg (2007) finds they did better than most would have predicted and did not fare substantially worse than their peers who postponed childbearing. More than 75 percent finished high school or obtained a GED and 10 percent earned a college degree, outcomes very similar to the equally poor women who did not become teen mothers.

17. Nadis (2006).

18. Shapira (2008). These figures are based on survey data from the National Opinion Research Center on metropolitan areas nationwide, including cities and suburbs. The U.S. Census Bureau also reports that a growing percentage of women are either remaining childless or postponing parenthood well into their forties. Today, about 20 percent of women ages forty to forty-four have no children, double the level of three decades ago, and women in this age group who have children have an average of 1.9, compared with 3.1 in 1976 (Zezima, 2008). While it is too soon to know what younger generations will do, there are strong indications they will continue this trend.

19. The Northwestern University Center for Labor Market Studies (2006) reports that this holds for one-third of births to non-Hispanic white women, 51 percent of births to Latina women, and almost 80 percent of births to black women. A poll conducted by Amick and Hertz (2007) shows that a high proportion of Wellesley undergraduates are prepared to bear a child on their own. At the other end of the economic

spectrum, the Fragile Families Study, a large national study of poor individuals, found that 40 percent of births were to unmarried women, although about half were in a committed relationship (England and Edin, 2007). The U.S. Census Bureau (2006a) reports that 32 percent of births in the year ending in June 2004 were to unmarried women. According to the Center for Disease Control National Center for Health Statistics, 45 percent of all pregnancies in 2004 were among unmarried women, but just 12 percent were to teenagers, compared to 15 percent in 1990, and less than 38 percent were to women under the age of twenty-five, down from nearly 43 percent in 1990 (Fox, 2008).

20. Bazelon (2009).

21. See Goode (1963). Despite Goode's focus on the husband-wife unit, his argument left room for the growth of more diverse family forms. Historical developments such as the need for women to work, the acceptance of sex outside marriage, and the rise of divorce have set the stage for "nonconjugal" families and for conflicts between men's and women's mobility. Hertz (2006) explores the ramifications of this development for middle-class women who choose to become mothers without a partner. In a more popular vein, Dowd (2005) raises the same question.

22. Updating Carol Stack's 1974 study of poor women's care networks, a range of recent research shows how contemporary single women of all classes and races rely on extended networks, from Rosanna Hertz's depiction of middle-class single mothers (2006) to Patricia Hill Collins's analysis of Black women's reliance on "other mothers" (1991) to E. Kay Trimberger's study of middle-aged single women who build friendship networks "in health and sickness, until death did them part" (2005). Gerstel and Sarkisian (2006) report that, contrary to popular belief, singles (especially the never married) are more likely than married couples to socialize with, encourage, and help their friends and neighbors. Hansen (2005) also shows how all parents, including fathers, rely on a much wider network of social and family ties than the image of the "isolated nuclear family" conveys. (Also see Dill, 1994, and Weston, 1991.)

23. For an early analysis of rising time demands, especially in professional and managerial jobs, see Schor (1991). For an alternative perspective, see Robinson and Godbey (1997). In their survey of young workers under twenty-nine, Galinsky et al. (2009) report that a third of these employed women are wary of more responsibility at work, citing concerns about job pressures and a lack of flexibility to manage a personal life.

24. Bianchi, Robinson, and Milkie (2006).

25. Joan Williams (2000) charts how the "ideal worker" ethos discriminates against women and reinforces gender inequality. Blair-Loy (2003) analyzes the "competing devotions" pulling professional women in two directions at once. While Stone (2007) shows how inflexible workplaces and high family demands are the major forces pushing some middle-class professional women out of careers, this analysis also applies to women with less glamorous job options.

26. Although the gender gap in housework and child care has declined in recent decades, it has not disappeared. Bianchi, Robinson, and Milkie (2006) report a gender convergence since the 1960s, but argue that this has slowed in the last decade. Citing national studies, Belkin (2008) reports that "across classes, when wives stay home and husbands are the sole earners, women perform about two-thirds of the housework and even more of the childcare ... In addition, 58 percent of women say

the division of labor in modern families is not fair to them, while 11 percent of men make a similar claim."

27. This process resembles the "emotion work" Hochshild (1979) describes, when people endeavor to shape their feelings to better fit the expectations and demands of their social context.

28. This outlook appears to support the human capital argument preferred by many economists (for example, Becker, 1981). Yet informants who expressed this view are reacting to their situational constraints and limited opportunities. Not only is this a minority outlook, but it does not represent their ideal preferences.

29. Life course analysts point out that, given small family sizes and longer life spans, women are spending a smaller proportion of their lives rearing young children even if they stay home during these years. The much reported rise in the percentage of stay-at-home mothers is misleading, since this statistic typically refers to mothers with children under the age of one. Among mothers with children one or older, the labor force participation rate remains comparable to other women in the same age group at around 70 percent.

30. Garey (1999) offers a perceptive study of how working-class women accomplish this balancing act on a daily basis. Garey argues that these women "weave" work and motherhood in a variety of ways, although she does not focus on the distinction between working at a job and building a career, a feat much harder to integrate with parenting.

31. In *Backlash* (1991), Susan Faludi argues that the rise of mothering standards is part of a backlash against women's fight for equal rights.

32. Despite the popular assertions heralded by some journalists and public intellectuals—for example, Danielle Crittenden (1999) and Elizabeth Fox-Genovese (1996)—that young women prefer domesticity, the preponderance of evidence suggests no such widespread wish to return to traditionalism. While women's work participation may be plateauing rather than continuing to rise, this appears to reflect constricted child care options and work opportunities (Boushey, 2008; Porter, 2006; Uchitelle, 2008; Cotter, Hermsen, and Vanneman, 2004). In the period from 2000 to 2008, the percentage of women with jobs remained relatively stable (dropping about 2 percent) compared to the percentage of men, which dropped more than 5 percent (*New York Times,* 2008).

33. Sharon Hays extends her study of the cultural contradictions of motherhood among middle-class and working-class women (1996) with a study of how these cultural and social contradictions also pose dilemmas for poor women and welfare workers (2003).

34. Rose and Hartmann (2008) and Ann Crittenden (2001).

Chapter Seven

1. For an early statement on why men resist equality, even when it may be in their longer-term interest to support it, see William Goode (1982). In contrast, Robert Jackson (1998) argues that over the long run, most men ultimately support gender equality as part of a larger package of egalitarian movements that are integral to modern social organization.

2. In a brilliant analysis of the tensions of manhood in American culture, Fiedler (1966) charts how great American novels, from *Moby Dick* to *Huckleberry Finn*, involve a male protagonist who forsakes domestic life and heterosexual commitment to find his identity as a man alone. For powerful statements about the dual strains of individualism and commitment in modern American culture, see Swidler (1980) and Bellah et al. (1985).

3. Galinsky et al. (2009).

4. This outlook preserves the essential elements of twentieth-century "hegemonic masculinity" (to use a term coined by R.W. Connell, 1987, 1995), including the assumption of heterosexuality. It is thus not surprising that none of the "neotraditional" men identified as gay.

5. Among the many studies documenting continuing racial disadvantage, see Pager (2007), Manza and Uggen (2006), Massey (2007), and Western (2006).

6. The term "marriageable men," as used by William Julius Wilson (1987), refers to men who earn enough to be a suitable mate. In Wilson's analysis, a dwindling pool of jobs has drastically constricted the pool of acceptable husbands in poor communities. More generally, however, few have questioned the assumption that income should be the primary yardstick for measuring a man's suitability as a husband. As we have seen, women increasingly expect their partner to be a sharing caretaker, but they also want him to be a responsible earner.

7. Annette Lareau uses the concept of "invisible inequality" to distinguish between middle-class and working-class childhoods. Christine Williams (1989, 1995) documents how a "glass escalator" helps men rise in female-dominated fields even though women continue to hit glass ceilings in male-dominated ones. For incisive analyses of continuing discrimination against women at the workplace, see Correll et al. (2007), Correll (2004), Ridgeway and Correll (2004), and Valian (1998).

8. Women now make up 58 percent of those enrolled in two- and four-year colleges and are also the majority in graduate schools and professional schools, although many of these women concentrate in historically female fields that remain underpaid compared to male-dominated ones (Jacobs, 2003). The 2005 National Survey of Student Engagement, which studied 90,000 students at 530 institutions, found that college men are significantly more likely than women to say they skipped classes, did not complete their homework, and did not turn it in on time (Lewin, 2006).

9. Cotter, Hermsen, and Vanneman (2004).

10. Joan Williams (2000).

11. Epstein et al. (1999) show that forty-hour workweeks are now considered parttime in most law firms. Louise Roth's study of Wall Street financial firms (2006) found them more likely to support equal opportunity policies, which give women an equal right to work interminable hours, than to support family-friendly policies, which undermine the principle that work should supersede family needs.

12. See, for example, Frank and Cook (1996). The economic crisis has intensified this concern.

13. The varied outcomes among siblings who grew up in the same household point to the indeterminate nature of family experiences as well as to the diverse influences a father's model can have on sons. Dalton Conley (2004) shows how "within family" differences in adults' income attainment are greater than "between family" differences.

Although he focuses on how parents apportion unequal investments among siblings, I would add that siblings also develop different reactions to similar circumstances and are likely to encounter different opportunities and obstacles in the wider world.

14. Koropeckyj-Cox and Pendell (2007).

15. Glauber (2008), Correll et al. (2007), and Correll (2004).

16. The "case for marriage" (as Linda Waite and Maggie Gallagher put it) appears compelling for men, but much less so for women, who are more likely to pay a price, literally and figuratively, for being a wife and mother. In Correll's experimental research, she also finds that mothers are significantly less likely to be hired and are offered lower salaries than equally qualified childless women. Mothers are rated as less competent, less committed, and less suitable for promotion and training, and they are also held to higher performance standards, while fathers are not rated lower than other men and benefited on some measures. Budig and England (2001) add that mothers suffer a substantial per-child wage penalty not explained by other factors, such as amount of schooling or work experience. In sum, men enjoy a marriage and fatherhood advantage, while women experience a marriage and motherhood penalty.

17. Institute for Women's Policy Research, 2008. Drago, Black, and Wooden (2005) report that approximately 20 percent of couples contain a wife whose earnings exceed her husband's by more than 10 percent, but only about a quarter of these couples remain in this state in the following year. Winslow-Bowe (2006) reports that "although a significant minority of women out earn their husbands in one year, considerably fewer do so for five consecutive years." In sum, although the gender wage gap has declined, a husband's earnings continue to outstrip a wife's in most marriages, especially in the longer run. (Also see Charles and Grusky, 2004; Cotter, Hermsen, and Vanneman, 2004; and Blau, Brinton, and Grusky, 2006.)

18. The percentage of couples relying on a wife as the primary provider (defined as earning 60 percent or more of total couple earnings) remains low, although it increased from 4 percent in 1970 to 12 percent in 2001 (Raley, Mattingly, and Bianchi, 2006).

19. Even though "gender" is an ambiguous category in same-sex partnerships, they face similar work and child-rearing constraints. Same-sex couples tend to create more egalitarian arrangements, but they also tend to devise ways to divide responsibility for caretaking, as Carrington (1999) shows. In her study of African-American lesbian couples, Mignon Moore (2008) finds that biological motherhood shapes parenting strategies and that these couples are more concerned with economic independence than with having an equal distribution of domestic work.

20. Women's earnings are the major reason that contemporary households have maintained a standard of living on a par with the households of several decades ago. Warren and Tyagi (2003) focus on the drawbacks of this trend, while Barnett and Rivers (1996) delineate the advantages of two-income families. Bradbury and Katz (2004) report that in recent decades, families that have moved ahead or maintained their position have had wives with high and rising employment rates, work hours, and pay. In fact, the annual earnings of wives in upwardly mobile families have increased relative to the earnings of their husbands.

21. See, for example, Hartmann (1976). Potuchek (1997) analyzes how dual-earner couples still tend to designate one partner—usually but not always the husband—as

the main breadwinner and how this designation is crucial to shaping the domestic dynamics of contemporary couples.

22. For studies that distinguish among fathers who are helpers, equal partners, and primary caretakers, see Risman (1986, 1998) and my own study of men's parenting and work commitments (1993). Recent decades have seen a notable rise in men's participation in domestic work, but stay-at-home fathers remain a very small group (Smith, 2009).

23. The history of modern family life has been one of continual "outsourcing." This process of "structural differentiation" (a term used by Parsons and Bales, 1955) first involved moving such tasks as raising food, weaving cloth, sewing clothes, and educating the young out of the home. The growing reliance on day care, takeout, and prepared food is a postindustrial extension of this process. If "commodification" has dangers, especially in reinforcing class inequality, it is also a logical and practical response to women's entry into the world of paid work in the absence of a comparable increase in men's domestic involvement. Rather than lamenting the inevitable rise in families' reliance on other caretakers, the larger challenge is to make this shift more equal and fair by increasing the economic and social value of both paid and unpaid care work. See, for example, Hondagneu-Sotelo (2001), Folbre (2001), and Zimmerman, Litt, and Bose (2006).

24. Linda Hirshman (2006) argues that "choice feminism" leaves women short of equality because it does not effectively address the *domestic* glass ceiling.

25. For an overview of how the rise of the market transformed cultural definitions of manhood, see Kimmel (1996). Lamont (2000) richly details the place of work in the lives of contemporary working-class men. See also Sennett and Cobb (1972) and Bourdieu (1984) on the importance of class as a cultural marker, a habitus, as well as an economic status.

26. For compelling analyses of how providing essential, but unpaid or poorly paid, care exacts costs from society as well as from individual care workers and providers, see Folbre (2008) and Ann Crittenden (2001).

27. For an original analysis of how social and cultural arrangements shape market worth, see Zelizer (1994, 2005).

28. Mooney (2008) discusses how economic transformations have undermined young middle-class Americans' ability to achieve their parents' standard of living.

29. See Porter and O'Donnell (2006). Uchitelle (2006) and Greenhouse (2008) document the decline of economic options and the rise of economically squeezed workers, especially at the bottom of the income ladder.

30. Lewin (2008).

31. Jones (2006), *USA Today* (2007).

32. Despite the rise of alternatives to marriage, extended bachelorhood continues to have an aura of immaturity. Many neoconservative analysts argue that marriage exerts a "civilizing" influence on men. In this view, unmarried men are prone to behave badly, while marriage—and by implication, the influence of women—reins in their sexual and violent impulses. See, for example, Nock (1998) and James Q. Wilson (2002). The evidence on the high rates of marital infidelity among both husbands and wives undermines this argument.

33. Popenoe (1988, 1996) argues that declining marriage rates indicate a decline of the family.

34. Given the rising rates of children born to single mothers, it is difficult to ascertain the full contours of unmarried paternity. Not only are some men unwilling to acknowledge it, but others may not be aware that they have fathered children (England and Edin, 2007).

35. Haney (2002) provides an insightful analysis of the culturally variable meanings of "dependency" for women. See also Fraser (1989) and Orloff (2008).

36. Kimmel (2008) and Risman and Seale (2010) analyze the cultural strictures that continue to constrain definitions of masculinity even as women's cultural options expand.

37. Ehrenreich (1983) argues that women's fight for equality also allowed men to flee commitment by making it acceptable for them to remain unmarried. Yet research shows that, in the long run, men who are unconnected to families are more likely to suffer adverse consequences, particularly because they are less likely than women to draw on a wider network of family and friends. McPherson, Smith-Lovin, and Brashears (2006) find that men are especially likely to lack close social ties other than a marital partner. For the classic study of "his and her" marriages, see Bernard (1982).

Chapter Eight

1. Another 15 percent of women and 20 percent of men agree there is no big difference or a mixed difference, and only 2 percent of women and 4 percent of men feel women have it worse today.

2. Only 26 percent of men and 7 percent of women believe men have it worse today than in the past, despite contemporary obstacles.

3. John Gray's best seller, *Men Are from Mars, Women Are from Venus* (1992), offers a popular treatment of gender difference. Using theories that range from classical to feminist to popular, a wide range of writers have posited distinctly different "masculine" and "feminine" personalities. Parsons and Bales (1955) laid out the classic framework, which relied on structural-functional theory to analyze the ascendance of homemaker-breadwinner households in the mid-twentieth century. Particularly influential feminist approaches include Nancy Chodorow's theory of the reproduction of mothering (1978), which offers an incisive critique of Parsons' analysis but nevertheless argues that women have more "permeable ego boundaries" than men possess, and Carol Gilligan's analysis of gender differences in moral reasoning (1982), which argues that women are more inclined than men to stress connectedness rather than abstract principles of justice. Epstein (1988) and Barnett and Rivers (2004) critique this emphasis on gender differences in temperament and personality, outlining the ways social structures and cultural pressures lead to constructing gender as a "dichotomous distinction" despite the substantial variation in personal attributes within gender groups and the large overlap between them.

4. Blair-Loy (2003). The cultural stress on what Zelizer (1985) calls the "pricelessness" of children to their parents is offset by the lack of collective support. As a result, children's fates are privatized, leaving some with abundant resources and others with little. Sadly, privatizing care devalues children in the name of family values.

5. In *The Sociological Imagination*, Mills (1959) makes the classic statement about how public problems are experienced as intensely private troubles.

6. Counter to popular concerns about the dangers of organized day care (see, for example, Eberstadt, 2004), Wrigley and Dreby (2005) report that children are actually less likely to suffer physical harm in day care centers than when they receive in-home care, which is less visible and more variable in quality. Of course, whatever the setting, it is the quality of care that matters most (Rabin, 2008). Gornick and Myers (2003) and Heymann and Beem (2005) document the enormous gap between the child care supports in Europe and around the globe and those in the United States. In a survey of 168 countries, Heymann and Beem report, for example, that the United States is one of only five without mandatory paid maternity leave; the others are Lesotho, Liberia, Papua New Guinea, and Swaziland.

7. Polls show young Americans are becoming more engaged in elective politics and, in the words of some analysts, "leaning left" (Nagourney and Thee, 2007). A 2008 survey found that 28 percent of young people between seventeen and twenty-nine describe themselves as liberal (compared with 20 percent of the general population) and 27 percent call themselves conservative (compared with 32 percent of the general public). In 2008, 35 percent of eighteen- to twenty-nine-year-olds identified as Democratic, 23 percent as Republican, and 32 percent as independent. A Pew study on "Generation Next" reports similar results, with 48 percent of young adults between eighteen and twenty-six identifying more with Democrats and 35 percent leaning toward Republicans (Jayson, 2007). The young women and men in my study hold similarly diverse political orientations and are only slightly less conservative as a group than the general youth population, with 46 percent describing themselves as independent, 39 percent leaning Democratic, and 15 percent leaning Republican.

8. Maume (2006). In a survey of American workers conducted by the Families and Work Institute, women and men of all ethnic groups express concern that asking for family-support policies or using policies already in place will entail long-term career costs (Jacobs and Gerson, 2004).

9. Drago et al. (2006) report, for example, that academic faculty attempt to hide their caregiving activities to avoid bias and discrimination at work.

10. Other rich societies, especially in Northern Europe, are more prone to create universal systems that guarantee a baseline level of support for all citizens. See Gornick and Myers (2003, 2009) and Wilensky (1974).

11. As its title makes clear, Whyte's *The Organization Man* (1956) presumed this conformist worker was a man.

12. Whether termed "the career mystique," as Phyllis Moen and Patricia Roehling propose, or "the ideal worker," as Joan Williams argues, this ethos presumes that an undiluted dedication to work will bestow upward mobility and economic security. It leaves little room for the ebb and flow of personal responsibilities outside the workplace as they arise during the day or over the span of a working life.

13. Dwyer (2006) reports that "more workers are choosing a self-directed career, leaving behind company politics and gaining flexibility." The Bureau of Labor Statistics found that independent contract workers made up 8 percent of the workforce in 2005, which is likely to be an underestimate due to the measuring procedure. For in-depth considerations of the rise and appeal of self-employment, see Arum (2004).

14. A number of studies have shown that wealth is a greater source of U.S. inequality than income. See Oliver and Shapiro (1995) and Conley (1999).

15. Friedson (1998) pointed out that autonomy in professional jobs, though substantial compared to other occupations, is nevertheless under assault in late modern societies. Also see Abbott (1988).

16. Pitt-Catsouphes et al. (2009) report that 80 percent of younger Gen X'ers (age twenty-seven to thirty-five) and 71 percent of Gen Y'ers (twenty-six or younger) believe that job flexibility contributes a great or a moderate amount to work success. Even more telling, 92 percent of the Gen X'ers and 86 percent of the Gen Y'ers believe flexibility at work contributes a great or a moderate amount to the overall quality of life. Yet they also report that 65 percent of younger Gen X'ers and 59 percent of Gen Y'ers believe that employers view workers who use flexible options as less serious about their careers than those who do not.

17. Hochschild (1975). For an example of how young people are reconsidering the contours of careers, see Kossek and Lautsch (2007), who describe three types of "flexstyles," including integrators, who blend work and family; separators, who keep work and family separate; and volleyers, who are in between. Since no one best way is right for everyone, they argue, people need to have enough options to choose what works best for them. See also Benko and Weisberg (2007).

18. Gary Becker laid the framework for this view in his classic book *A Treatise on the Family* (1981), which applied the principles of human capital economics to family decision making. The views of my respondents, however, belie the basic argument that men are more inclined to specialize in market pursuits while women prefer to trade earnings for a family-friendly job. "Tastes" do not necessarily drive choices, since no one makes choices in a constraint-free context. Whether conscious or unconscious, the act of choosing always involves deciding among alternatives that are shaped by social contexts.

19. In a related debate, some analysts, such as Schor (1996), stress the role of outsized consumption desires in fueling the trends toward long working hours, while others (for example, Warren and Tyagi, 2003) argue that the rising costs of essential goods, especially housing, are forcing Americans to work more than they would prefer.

20. In a survey of young adults age eighteen to twenty-four, Greenberg (2005) reports, for example, that among those seeking work, a large majority (60 percent) say the most important factor is finding a job they enjoy, while only 17 percent say it is making a good amount of money, and an additional 11 percent place having an opportunity to advance at the top. Economic realities can nevertheless temper this outlook. Among those who call themselves "mature adults," a smaller proportion (48 percent) place job enjoyment first, and a larger group (26 percent) stress the importance of "making good money." Groups with pronounced economic strains—married youth and high school dropouts—are more likely to stress finding a job with a good salary.

21. A survey of 351 law students found that the vast majority of men and women are willing to trade money for the time to achieve a better balance between family and work (Rankin, Taubman, and Wu, 2008). A Families and Work Institute survey of American workers also found that most workers would be willing to sacrifice some income for flexible scheduling, fewer working hours, and other family-friendly options (Jacobs and Gerson, 2004). Also see Galinsky, Kim, and Bond (2001) and Galinsky et al. (2005).

22. Hertz (1986). See also Moen and Chesley (2007).

23. Garey (1999) proposes the image of "weaving" to describe women's efforts to combine work and motherhood. Egalitarian sharing, however, means fathers and mothers need to weave these activities as a couple.

24. These views undermine received patterns of "doing gender." In addition to examining how gender is reproduced, we also need to understand when, how, and why some are motivated and able to "redo" or "undo" gender as an organizing principle in relationships.

25. Rampell (2009). Although the recession has accelerated the growth in women's share of all jobs, this process has been under way for decades as service sector and white-collar occupations have gradually but inexorably supplanted manufacturing and blue-collar occupations. Unfortunately, the jobs women hold are likely to pay less and to offer fewer benefits or long-term security. The gender wage gap has declined from 60 cents on the dollar in 1980 to 78 cents on the dollar in 2008, but it still persists and has cumulative effects that make a bigger difference in the long run (Rose and Hartmann, 2008).

26. Galinsky et al. (2009).

27. Sullivan and Coltrane (2008). See also Bianchi, Robinson, and Milkie (2006), Barnett and Rivers (2004), Coltrane (1996, 2004), Coltrane and Ishii-Koontz (1992), and Sullivan (2006). Deutsch (1999) finds a close relationship between being an equal couple and having friends who are also egalitarian.

28. Indeed, men's stagnant earnings account for much of the decline in the gender pay gap (Bernhardt, Morris, and Handcock, 1995; Coy, 2008; Hennessy-Fiske, 2006). Unions now account for only 8 percent of jobs in the private sector and 37 percent in the public sector.

29. In 2007, about 33 percent of young women twenty-five to twenty-nine held a bachelor's degree or higher, compared with 26 percent of their male counterparts (U.S. Census Bureau, 2008).

30. This is especially so for men who lack college degrees, whose relative earnings have declined over the last three decades along with their marriage rates.

31. Hochschild (1997).

32. Zerubavel (2006) argues that rotating schedules and turn-taking provide flexible time structures and better correspond with the mental flexibility needed in postindustrial contexts. As a counterpoint, however, Presser (2003) charts how the rise of shift work and nonstandard working hours has created disruptions that leave couples scrambling for time together.

33. By blending work and family, these strategies hearken back to the preindustrial "family economy." This may be a case of going "backward" to the future (Stacey, 1992).

34. See Press (2004) and Coontz (2008), respectively. The rise of more egalitarian marriages also signals a new form of "assortative mating," in which achieving women and men choose each other. Some argue this attraction of like to like increases class inequality by compounding educational differences in economic opportunities. The percentage of couples who share a similar level of educational attainment has reached its highest point in forty years (Paul, 2006). Unfortunately, this view pits one form of inequality against another. The more pressing challenge is to create a win-win scenario

for working couples in all class groups. Because women in all income brackets need an independent base, the answer is not to return to an inequality that gives men a leg up, but to allow all people to thrive and then choose the partners they want.

35. Cooke (2006) and Amato et al. (2007).

36. In his classic article "The Cohort as Concept in the Study of Social Change," Ryder (1965) shows how during periods of rapid social change, the shared experiences of young adults may trump other social divisions.

37. Greenberg (2005) reports, for example, that 82 percent of young people between eighteen and twenty-four know at least one gay person and a third know a gay or lesbian whom they consider a "close friend." In a New York Times/CBS News poll, 57 percent of people under forty said they support same-sex marriage, compared with 31 percent of those over forty (Nagourney, 2009).

38. See, for example, Shorter (1975).

39. In addition to the argument made by Parsons and Bales (1955) that homemaker-breadwinner couples are particularly "functional" in modern societies, Goode (1963) proposed that the "conjugal family," with the husband-wife bond at its core, provides an especially good "fit" with industrial society's need for geographic and social mobility.

40. Pew Research Center (2007b).

41. Witness the rise of new concerns among younger Evangelicals, who wish to extend the traditional focus on private matters such as gender dynamics and sexuality (where their outlooks remain quite conservative) to also include social issues such as poverty. See, for example, Kirkpatrick (2008) and Greeley and Hout (2006).

42. Pew Research Center (2007b).

43. Greenberg, Quinlan, and Ross (2005).

44. Also see Wolfe (1999) and DiMaggio, Evans, and Bryson (1996).

45. See the discussion in Gerth and Mills (1953) of how people develop "vocabularies of motive" to explain their actions to themselves and others, as well as that in Scott and Lyman (1968) of the "accounts" people create to justify actions that are "subjected to valuative inquiry." Howard Becker (1964) also discusses how a series of seemingly small "side bets" have unintended consequences that foster change in adult commitments.

Chapter Nine

1. Coontz (2005) argues that marriage has changed more in the last thirty years than it did in the previous five millennia.

2. See, for example, Green (2006).

3. For evidence that younger generations of women and men are converging, not diverging, on a variety of fronts, see Barnett and Rivers (2004), Mooney (2008), and Cameron (2007).

4. A number of theorists argue that "culture" is embodied in actions, skills, and "tool kits," even more than in beliefs and ideologies. See, especially, Swidler (1986), Lamont (2000), Lareau (2003), and Bourdieu (1977, 1984).

5. See, for example, Hacker (2003). Hacker also notes how this "mismatch" spans racial groups, as families of all races have diversified. In 1960, for example,

91 percent of non-Hispanic white households were headed by a husband and wife, compared to 67 percent of African-American families. But by 2000, the figure for white families had dropped to 80 percent, and births to unmarried white mothers had risen to 22.5 percent by 2001, compared to 2.3 percent in 1960. The gender revolution has both created new divides that undermine a system of "complementary roles" enshrined in notions of husbands' and wives' separate spheres, and also created grounds for lessening those divides. Jackson (1998) argues that the underlying forces of industrialism and postindustrialism set the stage for achieving gender equality, although not for achieving class and economic equality. For a wide-ranging look at both sides of this debate, see Blau, Brinton, and Grusky (2006).

6. Gerson (2002). For an excellent summary of the changing views and hidden benefits of juggling "multiple roles," see Barnett (2008). Despite the common belief that men and women are better off when they specialize in work and family, respectively, Barnett shows that the preponderance of research does not support this view. To the contrary, when the quality is high, shouldering the multiple roles of partner, parent, and employee is beneficial to the individual, the partner, and the partnership.

7. Drago (2007) examines how a care gap (in which children and other dependents do not receive the care they need) is rooted in a "motherhood norm" expecting women to provide care alone, an "ideal worker norm" expecting workers to put in long hours, and an "individualism norm" relieving government of the responsibility to help. Albelda and Tilly (1997) point out that women executives and welfare mothers have much in common—job discrimination, lower pay than men, and primary responsibility for unpaid care work. If we can see beyond class and gender boundaries, it becomes clear that public policies need to provide economic equality to women and support for all families. See, also, Rayman (2001) and Harrington (1999). All of these writers see such policies as paid family leave, early childhood education and child care financing, guaranteed health care, and financial security as crucial to meeting contemporary family needs.

8. From Alexis de Tocqueville to Robert Bellah and his colleagues, cultural theorists have spoken of the conflict between freedom and commitment, individualism and community (Bellah et al., 1985; De Tocqueville, 2006). Cerulo (2008) extends this argument by showing how American "values and beliefs are 'a multiplex system' [in which] the prioritization of one value over another…shifts [with] social events and structural conditions."

9. Bradbury and Katz (2004); Bond and Galinsky (2004).

10. Kelly (2009) points out that genuine work flexibility involves employee, not employer, control and moves beyond accommodation to embrace widespread change in workplace culture, especially when it comes to caretaking needs. Webber and Williams (2008) add that the concept of flexibility can be used in different ways, some of which enhance employer rather than employee preferences. In low wage service jobs, for example, flexibility can be a euphemism for scheduling work according to an employer's needs.

11. There are signs of headway for the concept of protecting caretakers from workplace discrimination. Joan Williams (2007) reports that "caregiver discrimination" cases increased 400 percent in the last ten years and that the U.S. Equal Employment

Opportunity Commission recently issued guidelines on what might constitute illegal discrimination against workers with family obligations.

12. For analyses of the critical role of workplace culture and organizational leadership, see, for example, Premeaux (2007) and Gerson and Jacobs (2001).

13. For this reason, many argue that we need to develop "work-life" policies that are need-blind and available to all (Casper et al., 2007). In 2002, the United Kingdom established a right for workers caring for children under six (or under eighteen if disabled) to request flexible work arrangements, and in 2006, it expanded this right to those caring for adults. Although this law does not obligate an employer to accept a request, surveys show that the vast majority of requests are granted and that employers and employees both see benefits (Boushey et al., 2008). Ford et al. (2007) show that when organizations foster positive family relationships, improvements in employee satisfaction and commitment make such investments worth their cost.

14. Ray et al. (2008). In 2008, California was the only state with a paid family leave policy, with Washington State joining in 2009. California's policy offers six weeks of leave and up to 55 percent of pay to care for a new baby or ill family member (Hawkins, 2008).

15. Heymann (2006). For thorough analyses of current and needed workplace policies, see Bailyn (2006), Glass (2000, 2004), and Kalleberg (2007). For more popular treatments focusing primarily on high-achieving women, see Hewlett (2007) and Mason and Ekman (2007). Jerry Jacobs and I (2004) propose a combination of "work-facilitating" and "family-supportive" policies that speak to new gender and family needs while also reaffirming such core American values as equal opportunity, personal responsibility, and community cohesion.

16. Ray et al. (2008).

17. In addition to policies that actively encourage fathers' involvement, such as parental leaves that only fathers can take, it is also important to provide day care and other child care supports that help mothers return to their jobs within a reasonable time period. Misra et al. (2007) find that maternal leaves of over three months decrease women's longer-term work involvement and even leave them at greater risk of falling into poverty.

18. Glass (2009). Countries with gender-divided policies that also have worrisomely low fertility rates include Italy, Greece, Japan, and Germany. In contrast, the Scandinavian countries, with more egalitarian policies and less concern for the marital status of cohabiting parents, have notably higher fertility rates. The United States birthrate has remained stable, but only because higher rates among immigrants have made up for lower rates among other women, including the children of immigrants.

19. Furstenberg (2005).

20. As a number of scholars have pointed out, the welfare state no longer supports the stay-at-home mother in any case. See, for example, Alstott (2005), Bergmann (1986), Fraser (1989), Mink (1998), and Orloff (2008). For overviews of child care policies, see Heymann (2006) and Heymann and Beem (2005).

21. Jessica De Groot (2008), who heads the Third Path Institute and has spent decades promoting what she calls "shared care," explains that "there is no one-size-fits-all solution for families, and shared care does not demand that there be one. Even

within one family, over time patterns that worked once will be modified, priorities will change, and shared care will evolve and change just as life does."

22. Acknowledging the diversity of American lives, while also emphasizing shared ideals, is a message that resonates with young people's experiences. When Barack Obama says "we may have different stories, but we share common hopes," he is drawing on this vision. Accordingly, a full 66 percent of voters between the ages of eighteen and twenty-nine voted for Obama, with similar or higher majorities among youth in all ethnic groups. And it would also be a mistake to presume that this more inclusive vision is confined to liberals and progressives. Among eighteen- to twenty-nine-year-olds who identify as evangelical and born-again Christians, 32 percent cast their vote for Obama, compared to 16 percent for John Kerry in 2004. Banerjee (2008) reports that "younger evangelicals [are] representative of a new generation [who] say they are tired of the culture wars [and] want to broaden the traditional evangelical agenda." Surveys by the Pew Forum on Religion and Public Life find only 40 percent of eighteen- to twenty-nine-year-old evangelicals identify themselves as Republicans, down from 55 percent in 2005, while 32 percent say they are independents (up from 26 percent in 2005) and 19 percent say they are Democrats (up from 14 percent in 2005) (Kuo and DiLulio, 2008). Teixeira (2009) also finds that the more tolerant outlooks of younger generations auger a substantial decline in the resonance of politically divisive cultural wedge issues. Sarah Palin's selection as the Republican vice presidential nominee is also telling and ironic, and not simply because she is a woman. Religious conservatives embraced her candidacy even though she had young children and an unmarried teenage daughter who became pregnant. Cultural fault lines remain strong, especially around issues such as abortion and gay rights, but future candidates who claim to represent so-called values voters will find it more difficult to indict employed mothers.

23. As C. Wright Mills pointed out fifty years ago in *The Sociological Imagination* (1959), there are social roots to these "private troubles."

Appendix 2

1. I use the term "generation" to refer to a group of people born within a historical period that binds them together in socially meaningful ways. Since the interviews were conducted throughout the mid- to late 1990s and early 2000s, the sample includes both younger members of "Generation X" and older members of "Generation Y," who are also called "Millennials." Yet analysts often disagree about the proper birth date for designating membership in one group or the other, with some starting as recently as 1983 to mark the dividing line and others going as far back as 1979. For my purposes, younger Gen X'ers and older Millennials share a common set of experiences that transcend such distinctions and make these labels arbitrary and potentially misleading. I thus refer to my respondents as young adults or, more colloquially, as twenty- and thirty-somethings. Carlson (2009) points out that Generation X, which he argues includes those born up to 1982, is the first generation with a greater share of women than men graduating from college. Its members have also delayed marriage and parenthood more than any other generation in the twentieth century. Although only a minority of Millennials are old enough to have left their parents' home or to be considered young adults, those who have reached

adulthood show patterns of schooling, marriage, parenting, and work that are similar to younger Gen X'ers. While the interviews were conducted before the economic crisis, the findings have even more relevance in its wake.

2. To ensure the sampling of communities with a diverse range of social and political outlooks, neighborhoods with Republican elected officials were included to balance the preponderance of Democratic majorities in the Northeast. Respondents grew up in all regions of the country.

3. The methodological procedures of the Study of the Immigrant Second Generation in Metropolitan New York are fully reported in Kasinitz, Mollenkopf, Waters, and Holdaway (2008). There is no overlap between my interviews and those conducted by the Second Generation project, which by agreement provided only names, contact information, and brief screening information. Members of the ISGMNY project had access to my interviews (without individual identifiers) to provide a contrast between those with immigrant parents and those growing up with native-born parents.

4. Since my purpose was to understand the experiences of children who grew up in the United States and were reared by parents who were also exposed to American work and family changes, the children of immigrants were largely excluded from my sample. None of the respondents were reared by a same-sex couple, but close to 5 percent hope to do so in their own lives.

5. Tables summarizing important frequency distributions are used to describe the contours and relationships, or lack thereof, in the sample—not as a representation of larger national samples.

6. See, for example, Patricia Hill Collins' analysis of the intersection of race, class, and gender in the lives of African-American women (1991) as well as Candace West's and Sarah Fenstermaker's discussion of "doing difference" (1995).

7. Gerth and Mills (1940) long ago pointed to the importance of understanding how people use "vocabularies of motive" to account for their own and others' actions. Scott and Lyman (1968) went on to propose we investigate how people develop "accounts" to explain behavior that is necessarily "subjected to valuative inquiry."

8. The methodological question is not whether accounts of the past are valid, but whether any form of self-reporting is reliable. If not, then many of our most important research tools, including surveys, would need to be jettisoned. Fortunately, this is not the case.

9. As Glaser and Strauss (1967) point out in their classic discussion of the discovery of grounded theory, qualitative research can use unexpected findings to produce new ways of theorizing. When the field work produces no more analytic surprises, a researcher has achieved "saturation" and can leave the field.

10. The interviews were transcribed verbatim, and most of the selected quotes are presented verbatim as well, including some that contain grammatical errors. Some have been edited lightly, but only for clarity and brevity. All names were changed to protect anonymity.

11. Theoretical concepts are "ideal types" that cannot correspond perfectly with every piece of data, but they provide useful categories to explain empirical outcomes.

REFERENCES

Abbott, Andrew. 1988. *The System of Professions: An Essay on the Division of Expert Labor*. Chicago, IL: University of Chicago Press.

Acker, Joan. 1990. "Hierarchies, Jobs, and Bodies: A Theory of Gendered Organizations." *Gender & Society* 4: 139–158.

Acock, Alan C., and David H. Demo. 1994. *Family Diversity and Well-Being*. Thousand Oaks, CA: Sage.

Ahrons, Constance R. 1994. *The Good Divorce: Keeping Your Family Together When Your Marriage Comes Apart*. New York: Harper Collins.

————. 2004. *We're Still Family: What Grown Children Have to Say about Their Parents' Divorce*. New York: Harper Collins.

Albelda, Randy, and Chris Tilly. 1997. *Glass Ceilings and Bottomless Pits: Women's Work, Women's Poverty*. Boston, MA: South End Press.

Alstott, Ann. 2005. *No Exit: What Parents Owe Their Children and What Society Owes Parents*. New York: Oxford University Press.

Amato, Paul R., Alan Booth, David R. Johnson, and Stacey J. Rogers. 2007. *Alone Together: How Marriage in America Is Changing*. Cambridge, MA: Harvard University Press.

Amato, Paul R., and Alan Booth. 1997. *A Generation at Risk: Growing Up in an Era of Family Upheaval*. Cambridge, MA: Harvard University Press.

American Business Collaboration. 2004. *Generation and Gender in the Workplace*. Boston: October 5.

Amick, Emily, and Rosanna Hertz, 2007. "Generation eXXception," *The Huffington Post*, November 6. http://www.huffingtonpost.com/emily-amick-and-rosanna-hertz/generation-exxception_b_71453.html

Ananat, Elizabeth O. 2008. "Single Parenting: Some Richer, Some Poorer." *Atlanta Journal Constitution*, April 24.

Anderson, Elijah. 1990. *Streetwise: Race, Class, and Change in an Urban Community*. Chicago: University of Chicago Press.

————. 1999. *Code of the Street: Decency, Violence, and the Moral Life of the Inner City.* New York: W.W. Norton.

Arum, Richard. 2004. "Entrepreneurs and Marginal Laborers: Two Sides of Self-Employment in the United States." In *The Resurgence of Self-Employment: A Comparative Study of Self-Employment Dynamics and Social Inequality,* edited by Richard Arum and Walter Mueller, 170–202. Princeton, NJ: Princeton University Press.

Bailyn, Lotte. 2006. *Breaking the Mold: Redesigning Work for Productive and Satisfying Lives.* Ithaca, NY: Cornell University Press.

Banerjee, Neela. 2008. "Taking Their Faith, but Not Their Politics, to the People." *New York Times,* June 1.

Barnett, Rosalind. 2008. "On Multiple Roles: Past, Present, and Future." In *Handbook of Work-Family Integration: Research, Theory, and Best Practices,* edited by Karen Korabik, Donna S. Lero, and Denise L. Whitehead, 75–94. New York: Academic Press.

Barnett, Rosalind C., and Caryl Rivers. 1996. *She Works/He Works: How Two-Income Families Are Happier, Healthier, and Better-Off.* San Francisco, CA: Harper San Francisco.

————. 2004. *Same Difference: How Gender Myths Are Hurting Our Relationships, Our Children, and Our Jobs.* New York: Basic Books.

Bazelon, Emily. 2009. "2 Kids + 0 Husbands = Family." *New York Times Magazine,* February 1.

Beck-Gernsheim, Elisabeth, and Patrick Camiller. 2002. *Reinventing the Family: In Search of New Lifestyles.* Malden, MA: Polity Press.

Becker, Gary S. 1981. *A Treatise on the Family.* Cambridge, MA: Harvard University Press.

Becker, Howard S. 1964. "Personal Change in Adult Life." *Sociometry* 27: 40–53.

Belkin, Lisa. 2003. "The Opt-Out Revolution." *New York Times Magazine,* October 26.

————. 2008. "When Mom and Dad Share It All." *New York Times Magazine,* June 15.

Bellah, Robert N., et al. 1985. *Habits of the Heart: Individualism and Commitment in American Life.* Berkeley and Los Angeles: University of California Press.

Bengston, Vern L., Timothy J. Biblarz, and Robert E. L. Roberts. 2002. *How Families Still Matter: A Longitudinal Study of Youth in Two Generations.* New York: Cambridge University Press.

Benko, Cathleen, and Ann Weisberg. 2007. *Mass Career Customization: Aligning the Workplace with Today's Nontraditional Workforce.* Cambridge, MA: Harvard Business School Press.

Bennetts, Leslie. 2007. *The Feminine Mistake: Are We Giving Up Too Much?* New York: Voice/Hyperion.

Bergmann, Barbara. 1986. *The Economic Emergence of Women.* New York: Basic Books.

Bernard, Jessie. 1982. *The Future of Marriage.* New Haven, CT: Yale University Press.

————. 1981. "The Good-Provider Role: Its Rise and Fall." *American Psychologist* 36: 1–12.

Bernhardt, Annette, Martina Morris, and Mark S. Handcock. 1995. "Women's Gains or Men's Losses? A Closer Look at the Shrinking Gender Gap in Earnings." *American Journal of Sociology* 101: 302–328.

Bianchi, Suzanne M. 2000. "Maternal Employment and Time with Children: Dramatic Change or Surprising Continuity?" *Demography,* 37 (4): 401–414.

Bianchi, Suzanne M., John P. Robinson, and Melissa A. Milkie. 2006. *Changing Rhythms of American Family Life.* New York: Russell Sage Foundation.

Blair-Loy, Mary. 2003. *Competing Devotions: Career and Family among Women Executives.* Cambridge, MA: Harvard University Press.

Blandford-Beringsmith, Linda, and Tom Musbach. 2009. "What Millennial Workers Want." Yahoo! Hotjobs: February 28. Available at http://www.hotjobsresources. com/webinars/ProductionInfo/022808yahoo.html

Blankenhorn, David. 1995. *Fatherless America: Confronting Our Most Urgent Social Problem.* New York: Basic Books.

Blau, Judith, Mary Brinton, and David Grusky. 2006. *The Declining Significance of Gender?* New York: Russell Sage Foundation.

Blow, Charles M. 2008. "Talking Down and Stepping Up." *New York Times,* July 12.

Blumstein, Philip, and Pepper Schwartz. 1983. *American Couples: Money, Work, Sex.* New York: Morrow.

Bond, James T., and Ellen Galinsky. 2004. *When Work Works: Flexibility, A Critical Ingredient in Creating an Effective Workplace.* New York: Families and Work Institute.

Bourdieu, Pierre. 1977. *Outline of a Theory of Practice.* New York: Cambridge University Press.

———. 1984. *Distinction: A Social Critique of the Judgement of Taste.* Cambridge, MA: Harvard University Press.

Boushey, Heather. 2005. "Are Women Opting Out? Debunking the Myth." Washington, DC: Center for Economic and Policy Research, briefing paper, November.

———. 2008. "'Opting Out'? The Effect of Children on Women's Employment in the United States." *Feminist Economics* 14 (1): 1–36.

Boushey, Heather, Layla Moughari, Sarah Sattelmeyer, and Margy Waller. 2008. "Work-Life Policies for the Twenty-First Century Economy." Washington, DC: The Mobility Agenda.

Bowlby, John. 1969. *Attachment and Loss.* New York: Basic Books.

Bradbury, Katharine, and Jane Katz. 2004. "Wives' Work and Family Income Mobility." Boston, MA: Federal Reserve Bank of Boston, Public Policy Discussion Report No. 04–3, July.

Brines, Julie. 1994. "Economic Dependency, Gender, and the Division of Labor at Home." *American Journal of Sociology* 100: 652–682.

Budig, Michelle, and Paula England. 2001. "The Wage Penalty for Motherhood." *American Sociological Review* 66: 204–225.

Burchinal, Margaret, and Alison Clarke-Stewart. 2007. "Maternal employment and child cognitive outcomes: The importance of analytic approach." *Developmental Psychology* 43: 1140–1155.

Byrd, Stephanie E. 2009. "The Social Construction of Marital Commitment." *Journal of Marriage and the Family* 71 (May): 318–336.

Cameron, Deborah. 2007. *The Myth of Mars and Venus: Do Men and Women Really Speak Different Languages?* New York: Oxford University Press.

Cancian, Francesca M. 1987. *Love in America: Gender and Self-Development*. New York: Cambridge University Press.

Carey, Benedict, and Tara Parker-Pope. 2009. "Marriage Stands Up for Itself." *New York Times* (June 28).

Carlson, Ellwood. 2009. 20th-Century U.S. Generations. *Population Bulletin* 64 (1).

Carlson, Marcia, Sarah McLanahan, and Paula England. 2004. "Union Formation in Fragile Families." *Demography* 41: 237–261.

Carr, Deborah. 2005. "Mothers at Work." *Contexts* 4 (2): 51.

Carrington, Christopher. 1999. *No Place Like Home: Relationships and Family Life among Lesbians and Gay Men*. Chicago: University of Chicago Press.

Casper, Wendy J., David Weltman, and Eileen Kwisega. 2007. "Beyond Family-Friendly: The Construct and Measurement of Singles-Friendly Work Culture." *Journal of Vocational Behavior* 70: 478–501.

Cerulo, Karen. 2008. "Social Relations, Core Values, and the Polyphony of the American Experience." *Sociological Forum* 23: 351–362.

Charles, Maria, and David Grusky. 2004. *Occupational Ghettos: The Worldwide Segregation of Women and Men*. Stanford, CA: Stanford University Press.

Cherlin, Andrew J. 1992. *Marriage, Divorce, Remarriage*. Cambridge, MA: Harvard University Press.

———. 2005. "American Marriage in the Early Twenty-First Century." *The Future of Children* 15: 33–55.

———. 2009. *The Marriage-Go-Round: The State of Marriage and the Family in America Today*. New York: Alfred A. Knopf.

Cherlin, Andrew J., Frank F. Furstenberg, Jr., P. Lindsey Chase-Lansdale, K. E. Kiernan, P. K. Robins, D. R. Morrison, and J. O. Teitler. 1991. "Longitudinal Studies of the Effects of Divorce on Children in Great Britain and the United States." *Science* 252 (June): 1386–1389.

Chodorow, Nancy. 1978. *The Reproduction of Mothering: Psychoanalysis and the Sociology of Gender*. Berkeley and Los Angeles: University of California Press.

Clarke-Stewart, Alison, and Virginia D. Allhusen. 2005. *What We Know About Child Care*. Cambridge, MA: Harvard University Press.

Clinton, Hillary R. 1996. *It Takes a Village: And Other Lessons Children Teach Us*. New York: Simon & Schuster.

Cohen, Phillip N., and Suzanne M. Bianchi. 1999. "Marriage, Children, and Women's Employment: What Do We Know?" *Monthly Labor Review* 122: 22–31.

Coleman, Joshua. 2005. *The Lazy Husband: How to Get Men to Do More Parenting and Housework*. New York: St. Martin's Press.

Coleman, Marilyn, and Lawrence Ganong. 2008. "Remember Stepfathers on Father's Day." Chicago, IL: Council on Contemporary Families, June 2.

Collins, Patricia Hill. 1991. *Black Feminist Thought: Knowledge, Consciousness, and the Politics of Empowerment*. New York and London: Routledge.

Coltrane, Scott. 2004. "Fathering: Paradoxes, Contradictions and Dilemmas." In *Handbook of Contemporary Families: Considering the Past, Contemplating the Future*, edited by Marilyn Coleman and Lawrence Ganong, 224–243. Thousand Oaks, CA: Sage Publications.

———. 1996. *Family Man: Fatherhood, Housework and Gender Equity.* New York: Oxford University Press.

Coltrane, Scott, and Masako Ishii-Koontz. 1992. "Men's Housework: A Life Course Perspective." *Journal of Marriage and the Family* 54: 43–57.

Conley, Dalton. 1999. *Being Black, Living in the Red.* Berkeley and Los Angeles: University of California Press.

———. 2004. *The Pecking Order: Which Siblings Succeed and Why.* New York: Pantheon Books.

Connell, R. W. 1987. *Gender and Power.* Stanford, CA: Stanford University Press.

———. 1995. *Masculinities.* Berkeley: University of California Press.

Cooke, Lynn P. 2006. " 'Doing' Gender in Context: Household Bargaining and Risk of Divorce in Germany and the United States." *American Journal of Sociology* 112 (2): 442–472.

Coontz, Stephanie. 1992. *The Way We Never Were: American Families and the Nostalgia Trap.* New York: Basic Books.

———. 2005. *Marriage, a History: From Obedience to Intimacy, or How Love Conquered Marriage.* New York: Viking.

———. 2008. "The Future of Marriage." *Cato Unbound,* January 14.

Correll, Shelley J. 2004. "Constraints into Preferences: Gender, Status, and Emerging Career Aspirations." *American Sociological Review* 69: 93–133.

Correll, Shelley J., Stephen Benard, and In Paik. 2007. "Getting a Job: Is There a Motherhood Penalty? *American Journal of Sociology* 112 (5): 1297–1338.

Coser, Rose. 1974. "The Housewife and Her Greedy Family." In *Greedy Institutions: Patterns of Undivided Commitment,* edited by Lewis A. Coser, 89–166. New York: Free Press.

Cotter, David A., Paula England, and Joan Hermsen. 2007. "Moms and Jobs: Trends in Mothers' Employment and Which Mothers Stay Home." Chicago: Council on Contemporary Families, May 10.

Cotter, David A., Joan M. Hermsen, and Reeve Vanneman. 2004. "Gender Inequality at Work." In *The American People: Census 2000,* 1–32. New York and Washington, DC: Russell Sage Foundation and Population Reference Bureau.

Coy, Peter. 2008. "Slumping Economy: It's a Guy Thing." *Business Week,* May 8.

Crittenden, Ann. 2001. *The Price of Motherhood: Why the Most Important Job in the World Is Still the Least Valued.* New York: Metropolitan Books.

Crittenden, Danielle. 1999. *What Our Mothers Didn't Tell Us: Why Happiness Eludes the Modern Woman.* New York: Simon & Schuster.

Crouter, Ann C., and Susan M. McHale. 2005. "Work Time, Family Time, and Children's Time: Implications for Youth." In *Work, Family, Health, and Well-Being,* edited by Suzanne Bianchi, Lynne Casper, and R. B. King, 49–66. New York: Routledge.

Damaske, Sarah. 2009. "Having It All? Explaining Women's Work Pathways." Unpublished dissertation, Department of Sociology, New York University.

Danziger, Sheldon, and Cecilia E. Rouse. 2007. *The Price of Independence: The Economics of Early Adulthood.* New York: Russell Sage Foundation.

De Groot, Jessica. 2008. Personal correspondence.

De Paulo, Bella M. 2006. *Singled Out: How Singles Are Stereotyped, Stigmatized, and Ignored, and Still Live Happily Ever After.* New York: St. Martin's Press.

Deutsch, Francine. 1999. *Halving It All: How Equally Shared Parenting Works*. Cambridge, MA: Harvard University Press.

DiMaggio, Paul, John Evans, and Bethany Bryson. 1996. "Have Americans' Social Attitudes Become More Polarized?" *American Journal of Sociology* 102: 690–755.

Dowd, Maureen. 2005. *Are Men Necessary?: When Sexes Collide*. New York: G.P. Putnam's Sons.

Drago, Robert. 2007. *Striking a Balance: Work, Family, Life*. Boston, MA: Economic Affairs Bureau.

Drago, Robert, et al. 2006. "The Avoidance of Bias Against Caregiving: The Case of Academic Faculty." *American Behavioral Scientist* 49 (9): 1222–1247.

Drago, Robert, David Black, and Mark Wooden. 2005. "Female Breadwinner Families: Their Existence, Persistence, and Sources." *Journal of Sociology* 41: 343–362.

Draut, Tamara. 2006. *Strapped: Why America's 20- and 30-Somethings Can't Get Ahead*. New York: Doubleday.

Dwyer, Kelly Pate. 2006. "Workers Warm to Contract Jobs." *New York Times*, January 22.

Eberstadt, Mary. 2004. *Home-Alone America: The Hidden Toll of Day Care, Behavioral Drugs, and Other Parental Substitutes*. New York: Sentinel.

Edin, Kathryn, and Maria Kefalas. 2005. *Promises I Can Keep: Why Poor Women Put Motherhood before Marriage*. Berkeley and Los Angeles: University of California Press.

Edin, Kathryn, and Laura Lein. 1997. *Making Ends Meet: How Single Mothers Survive Welfare and Low-Wage Work*. New York: Russell Sage Foundation.

Ehrenreich, Barbara. 1983. *The Hearts of Men: American Dreams and the Flight from Commitment*. New York: Anchor Books.

———. 2001. *Nickel and Dimed: On (Not) Getting By in America*. New York: Metropolitan Books.

Ehrenreich, Barbara, and Arlie R. Hochschild. 2002. *Global Woman: Nannies, Maids, and Sex Workers in the New Economy*. New York: Metropolitan Books.

Elwert, Felix. 2005. "How Cohabitation Does—and Does Not—Reduce the Risk of Divorce." Unpublished manuscript. Department of Sociology, Harvard University.

England, Paula. 2005. "Emerging Theories of Care Work." *Annual Review of Sociology* 31: 381–399.

England, Paula, and Kathryn Edin, editors. 2007. *Unmarried Couples with Children*. New York: Russell Sage Foundation.

Epstein, Cynthia F. 1988. *Deceptive Distinctions: Sex, Gender, and the Social Order*. New Haven; New York: Yale University Press; Russell Sage Foundation.

Epstein, Cynthia F., Carroll Seron, Bonnie Oglensky, and Robert Saute. 1999. *The Part-Time Paradox: Time Norms, Professional Lives, Family, and Gender*. New York: Routledge.

Etzioni, Amitai. 1998. *The Essential Communitarian Reader*. Lanham, MD: Rowman & Littlefield.

Faludi, Susan. 1991. *Backlash: The Undeclared War against American Women*. New York: Crown.

Ferree, Myra Marx. 1990. "Beyond Separate Spheres: Feminism and Family Research." *Journal of Marriage and the Family* 52: 866–884.

Fiedler, Leslie A. 1966. *Love and Death in the American Novel*. New York: Stein and Day.

Flanagan, Caitlin. 2006. *To Hell with All That: Loving and Loathing Our Inner Housewife*. New York: Little, Brown.

Folbre, Nancy. 2001. *The Invisible Heart: Economics and Family Values*. New York: New Press.

———. 2008. *Valuing Children: Rethinking the Economics of the Family*. Cambridge, MA: Harvard University Press.

Ford, Michael T., Beth A. Heinen, and Krista A. Langkamer. 2007. "Work and Family Satisfaction and Conflict." *Journal of Applied Psychology* 92: 57–80.

Fox, Maggie. 2008. "Typical Unwed Mother Is Not a Teen, Study Says." *Boston Globe*, April 15.

Fox-Genovese, Elizabeth. 1996. *Feminism Is Not the Story of My Life*. New York: Anchor Books.

Frank, Robert, and Phillip J. Cook. 1996. *The Winner-Take-All Society: Why the Few at the Top Get So Much More Than the Rest of Us*. New York: Penguin Books.

Fraser, Nancy, ed. 1989. *Unruly Practices: Power, Discourse, and Gender in Contemporary Social Theory*. Minneapolis: University of Minnesota Press.

Fremstad, Shawn, and Rebecca Ray. 2006. "Fast Facts for Father's Day: Lone-Father Families and Economic Insecurity." Washington, DC: Center for Economic and Policy Research, June 12.

Friedan, Betty. 1963. *The Feminine Mystique*. New York: W.W. Norton.

Friedson, Eliot. 1998. "Professionalization and the Organization of Middle-Class Labour in Postindustrial Society." *Sociological Review Monograph* 20: 47–59.

Furstenberg, Frank F. 2005. "Can Marriage Be Saved?" *Dissent* 52: 76–80.

———. 2007. *Destinies of the Disadvantaged: The Politics of Teenage Childbearing*. New York: Russell Sage Foundation.

Furstenberg, Frank F., and Andrew J. Cherlin. 1991. *Divided Families: What Happens to Children When Parents Part*. Cambridge, MA: Harvard University Press.

Furstenberg, Frank F., Sheela Kennedy, Vonnie C. McLoyd, Ruben G. Rumbaut, and Richard A. Settersten, Jr. 2004. "Growing Up Is Harder to Do." *Contexts* 3: 33–41.

Furstenberg, Frank F., Ruben G. Rumbaut, and Richard A. Settersten Jr. 2005. "On the Frontier of Adulthood: Emerging Themes and New Directions." In *On the Frontier of Adulthood: Emerging Themes and New Directions*, edited by Richard A. Settersten, Frank F. Furstenberg, and Ruben G. Rumbaut, 3–25. Chicago: University of Chicago Press.

Galinsky, Ellen. 1999. *Ask the Children: What America's Children Really Think about Working Parents*. New York: William Morrow.

Galinsky, Ellen, Stacy S. Kim, and James T. Bond. 2001. *Feeling Overworked: When Work Becomes Too Much*. New York: Families and Work Institute.

Galinsky, Ellen, James T. Bond, Stacy Kim, Lois Backon, Erin Brownfield, and Kelly Sakai. 2005. *Overwork in America*. New York: Families and Work Institute.

Galinsky, Ellen, Kerstin Aumann, and James T. Bond. 2009. "Times Are Changing: Gender and Generation at Work and at Home." New York: Families and Work Institute.

Garey, Anita I. 1999. *Weaving Work and Motherhood.* Philadelphia: Temple University Press.

Gauthier, Anne H., and Frank F. Furstenberg. 2005. "Historical Trends in Patterns of Time Use among Young Adults in Developed Countries." In *On the Frontier of Adulthood: Theory, Research, and Public Policy,* edited by Richard A. Settersten, Jr., Frank F. Furstenberg, and Rubén G. Rumbaut, 150–176. Chicago: University of Chicago Press.

Gerson, Kathleen. 1985. *Hard Choices: How Women Decide About Work, Career, and Motherhood.* Berkeley and Los Angeles: University of California Press.

———. 1993. *No Man's Land: Men's Changing Commitments to Family and Work.* New York: Basic Books.

———. 1995. "The Uses and Limits of Socialization Theory." Paper presented at the annual meeting of the Eastern Sociological Society. Philadelphia, PA: March.

———. 2002. "Moral Dilemmas, Moral Strategies, and the Transformation of Gender: Lessons from Two Generations of Work and Family Change." *Gender & Society* 16: 8–28.

Gerson, Kathleen, and Jerry A. Jacobs. 2001. "Changing the Structure and Culture of Work: Work-Family Conflict, Work Flexibility, and Gender Equity in the Modern Workplace." In *Working Families: The Transformation of the American Home,* edited by Rosanna Hertz, and Nancy L. Marshall. Berkeley and Los Angeles: University of California Press.

Gerstel, Naomi. 2000. "The Third Shift: Gender, Employment, and Care Work Outside the Home." *Qualitative Sociology* 23: 467–483.

Gerstel, Naomi, and Natalia Sarkisian. 2006. "Marriage: The Good, the Bad, and the Greedy." *Contexts* 4 (5) (November): 16–21.

Gerth, Hans, and C. Wright Mills. 1953. *Character and Social Structure.* New York: Harcourt.

Giddens, Anthony. 1979. *Central Problems in Social Theory: Action, Structure, and Contradiction in Social Analysis.* Berkeley and Los Angeles: University of California Press.

Gilligan, Carol. 1982. *In a Different Voice: Psychological Theory and Women's Development.* Cambridge, MA: Harvard University Press.

Glaser, Barney, and Anselm Strauss. 1967. *The Discovery of Grounded Theory.* Chicago, IL: Aldine.

Glass, Jennifer. 2000. "Envisioning the Integration of Family and Work: Toward a Kinder, Gentler Workplace." *Contemporary Sociology* 29: 129–143.

———. 2004. "Blessing or Curse? Work-Family Policies and Mother's Wage Growth over Time." *Work and Occupations* 31 (3): 367–394.

———. 2009. "Can Work-Family Policies Help Women Achieve Their Family Aspirations?" Council on Contemporary Families Conference on Relationships, Sexuality, and Equality. University of Illinois at Chicago: March 17–18.

Glauber, Rebecca. 2008. "Gender and Race in Families and at Work: The Fatherhood Wage Premium." *Gender & Society* 22 (1): 8–30.

Goldin, Claudia. 1990. *Understanding the Gender Gap.* New York: Oxford University Press.

Goode, William J. 1963. *World Revolution and Family Patterns.* New York: Free Press.

Gornick, Janet C., and Marcia K. Meyers. 2003. *Families That Work: Policies for Reconciling Parenthood and Employment*. New York: Russell Sage Foundation.

———. 2009. *Gender Equality: Transforming Family Divisions of Labor*. New York: Verso Books.

Gray, John. 1992. *Men Are from Mars, Women Are from Venus: A Practical Guide for Improving Communication and Getting What You Want in Your Relationships*. New York: HarperCollins.

Greeley, Andrew, and Michael Hout. 2006. *The Truth about Conservative Christians*. Chicago: University of Chicago Press.

Green, Adam. 2006. "'Until Death Do Us Part?': The Impact of Differential Access to Marriage on a Sample of Urban Men," *Sociological Perspectives* 49 (2): 163–189.

Greenberg, Anna. 2005. "Coming of Age in America, Parts I and II." Washington, DC: Greenberg Quinlan and Rosner Research (September).

Greenhouse, Steven. 2008. *The Big Squeeze: Tough Times for the American Worker*. New York: Alfred A. Knopf.

Gregory, Elizabeth. 2007. *Ready: Why Women Are Embracing the New Later Motherhood*. New York: Basic Books.

Gupta, Sanjiv. 2006. "Her Money, Her Time: Women's Earnings and Their Housework Hours." *Social Science Research* 35: 975–999.

Guzman, Lina, Laura Lippman, and Kristin A. Moore. 2003. "Public Perception of Children's Well-Being." Washington, DC: Child Trends Working Paper (July).

Hacker, Andrew. 2003. *Mismatch: The Growing Gulf between Women and Men*. New York: Scribner.

Haney, Lynne. 2002. *Inventing the Needy: Gender and the Politics of Welfare in Hungary*. Berkeley: University of California Press.

Hansen, Karen V. 2005. *Not-So-Nuclear Families: Class, Gender, and Networks of Care*. New Brunswick, NJ: Rutgers University Press.

Harrington, Mona. 1999. *Care and Equality: Inventing a New Family Politics*. New York: Alfred A. Knopf.

Harris, Judith R. 1998. *The Nurture Assumption: Why Children Turn Out the Way They Do*. New York: Free Press.

Hartmann, Heidi. 1976. "Capitalism, Patriarchy, and Job Segregation by Sex." *Signs* 1: 137–169.

Harvey, Lisa. 1999. "Short-Term and Long-Term Effects of Early Parental Employment on Children of the National Longitudinal Survey of Youth." *Developmental Psychology* 35 (2): 445–459.

Hawkins, Stacy Ann. 2008. "California Paid Family Leave: Moving Forward with Our New Moms Study." *Berger Institute for Work, Family, and Children Newsletter* Spring (9): 10.

Hays, Sharon. 1996. *The Cultural Contradictions of Motherhood*. New Haven, CT: Yale University Press.

———. 2003. *Flat Broke with Children: Women in the Age of Welfare Reform*. New York: Oxford University Press.

Hennessy-Fiske, Molly. 2006. "Gender Pay Gap Narrows—For Unexpected Reasons." *New York Times*, December 3.

Hertz, Rosanna. 1986. *More Equal Than Others: Women and Men in Dual-Career Marriages*. Berkeley and Los Angeles: University of California Press.

———. 2006. *Single by Chance, Mothers by Choice: How Women Are Choosing Parenthood without Marriage and Creating the New American Family*. New York: Oxford University Press.

Hetherington, E. Mavis, and John Kelly. 2002. *For Better or For Worse: Divorce Reconsidered*. New York: W.W. Norton.

Hewlett, Sylvia Ann. 2007. *Off Ramps and On Ramps: Keeping Talented Women on the Road to Success*. Cambridge, MA: Harvard Business School Press.

Heymann, Jody. 2006. *Forgotten Families: Ending the Growing Crisis Confronting Children and Working Parents in the Global Economy*. New York: Oxford University Press.

Heymann, Jody, and Christopher Beem, eds. 2005. *Unfinished Work: Building Equality and Democracy in an Era of Working Families*. New York: The New Press.

Hirshman, Linda R. 2006. *Get to Work: A Manifesto for Women of the World*. New York: Viking.

Hochschild, Arlie R. 1975. "Inside the Clockwork of Male Careers." In *Women and the Power to Change*, edited by Florence Howe, 47–80. New York: McGraw-Hill Books.

———. 1983. *The Managed Heart: Commercialization of Human Feeling*. Berkeley and Los Angeles: University of California Press.

———. 1989. With Anne Machung. *The Second Shift: Working Parents and the Revolution at Home*. New York: Viking.

———. 1997. *The Time Bind: When Work Becomes Home and Home Becomes Work*. New York: Henry Holt.

Hoffman, Lois. 1987. "The Effects on Children of Maternal and Paternal Employment." In *Families and Work*, edited by Naomi Gerstel and Harriet E. Gross, 362–395. Philadelphia, PA: Temple University Press.

Hoffman, Lois, Norma Wladis, and Lise M. Youngblade. 1999. *Mothers at Work: Effects on Children's Well-Being*. Cambridge, UK: Cambridge University Press.

Hondagneu-Sotelo, Pierrette. 2001. *Doméstica: Immigrant Workers Cleaning and Caring in the Shadows of Affluence*. Berkeley and Los Angeles: University of California Press.

Hulbert, Ann. 2003. *Raising America: Experts, Parents and a Century of Advice about Children*. New York: Alfred A. Knopf.

———. 2005. "Post-Teenage Wasteland?" *New York Times,* October 9.

Institute for Women's Policy Research. 2008. "The Gender Wage Ratio: Women's and Men's Earnings." Washington, DC: IWPR Fact Sheet No. C350 (February).

Jackson, Robert Max. 1998. *Destined for Equality*. Cambridge, MA: Harvard University Press.

Jacobs, Jerry. 2003. "Detours on the Road to Equality: Women, Work and Higher Education." *Contexts* 2: 32–41.

Jacobs, Jerry A., and Kathleen Gerson. 2004. *The Time Divide: Work, Family, and Gender Inequality*. Cambridge, MA: Harvard University Press.

Jayson, Sharon. 2007. "Gen Y's Attitudes Differ from Parents.'" *USA Today,* January 9.

————. 2008. "More View Cohabitation as Acceptable Choice." *USA Today,* June 8.

Jayson, Sharon, and Anthony DeBarros. 2007. "Decline of Married Twenty-Somethings: Young Adults Delaying Marriage." *USA Today,* September 12.

Johnson, Julia O., Robert Kominski, Kristin Smith, and Paul Tillman. 2005. "Changes in the Lives of U.S. Children: 1990–2000." Washington, DC: U. S. Census Bureau.

Jones, Joy. 2006. "Marriage Is for White People." *Washington Post,* March 26.

Kelly, Erin. 2009. "Changing Times, Changing Lives: Creating More Supportive Work Organizations." Council on Contemporary Families Conference on Relationships, Sexuality, and Equality. University of Illinois at Chicago: March 17–18.

Kalleberg, Arne L. 2007. *The Mismatched Worker.* New York: W.W. Norton.

Kasinitz, Phillip, John H. Mollenkopf, Mary C. Waters, and Jennifer Holdaway. 2008. *Inheriting the City: The Children of Immigrants Come of Age.* Cambridge, MA: Harvard University Press.

Kimmel, Michael. 1996. *Manhood in America: A Cultural History.* New York: The Free Press.

————. 2008. *Guyland: The Perilous World Where Boys Become Men.* New York: HarperCollins.

Kirkpatrick, David D. 2008. "Huckabee Splits Young Evangelicals and Old Guard." *New York Times,* January 13.

Koropeckyj-Cox, Tanya, and Gretchen Pendell. 2007. "The Gender Gap in Attitudes about Childlessness in the United States." *Journal of Marriage and Family* 9: 899–915.

Kossek, Ellen Ernst, and Brenda Lautsch. 2007. *The CEO of Me: Creating a Life That Works in the Flexible Job Age.* Philadelphia, PA: Wharton School Press.

Kuo, David, and John J. DiLulio. 2008. "The Faith to Outlast Politics." *New York Times,* January 29.

Lamont, Michèle. 1992. *Money, Morals, and Manners: The Culture of the French and American Upper-Middle Class.* Chicago: University of Chicago Press.

————. 2000. *The Dignity of Working Men: Morality and the Boundaries of Race, Class, and Immigration.* Cambridge, MA: Harvard University Press.

Lareau, Annette. 2003. *Unequal Childhoods: Class, Race, and Family Life.* Berkeley and Los Angeles: University of California Press.

Leonhardt, David. 2006. "Gender Pay Gap, Once Narrowing, Is Stuck in Place." *New York Times,* December 24.

Lewin, Tamar. 2006. "At Colleges, Women Are Leaving Men in the Dust." *New York Times,* July 9.

————. 2008. "Girls' Gains Have Not Cost Boys, Report Says." *New York Times,* May 20.

Li, Allen J. 2007. "The Kids Are OK: Divorce and Children's Behavior Problems." Rand Working Paper: WR 489.

Lorber, Judith. 2005. *Gender Inequality: Feminist Theories and Politics.* Los Angeles: Roxbury.

————. 1994. *Paradoxes of Gender.* New Haven: Yale University Press.

Luker, Kristin. 1984. *Abortion and the Politics of Motherhood.* Berkeley and Los Angeles: University of California Press.

Manza, Jeff, and Christopher Uggen. 2006. *Locked Out: Felon Disenfranchisement and American Democracy*. New York: Oxford University Press.

Marquardt, Elizabeth. 2005. *Between Two Worlds: The Inner Lives of Children of Divorce*. New York: Crown.

Marsiglio, William. 2004. *Stepdads: Stories of Love, Hope, and Repair*. Lanham, MD: Rowman & Littlefield.

Mason, Mary Ann, and Ekman, Eve Mason. 2007. *Mothers on the Fast Track: How a New Generation Can Balance Family and Careers*. New York: Oxford University Press.

Maume, David J. 2006. "Gender Differences in Restricting Work Efforts Because of Family Responsibilities." *Journal of Marriage and Family* 68 (1): 859–869.

McAdams, Dan P. 2006. *The Redemptive Self: Stories Americans Live By*. New York: Oxford University Press.

McLanahan, Sara, and Gary D. Sandefur. 1994. *Growing Up with a Single Parent: What Hurts, What Helps*. Cambridge, MA: Harvard University Press.

McPherson, Miller, Lynn Smith-Lovin, and Matthew E. Brashears. 2006. "Social Isolation in America, 1985–2004." *American Sociological Review* 71 (3) (June): 353–375.

Meers, Sharon, and Joanna Strober. 2009. *Getting to 50/50: How Working Couples Can Have It All by Sharing It All*. New York: Bantam.

Merton, Robert K. 1949. *Social Theory and Social Structure: Toward the Codification of Theory and Research*. Glencoe, IL: Free Press.

Mills, C. Wright. 1959. *The Sociological Imagination*. New York: Oxford University Press.

Mink, Gwendolyn. 1998. *Welfare's End*. Ithaca, NY: Cornell University Press.

Misra, Joya, Stephanie Moller, and Michelle J. Budig. 2007. "Work-Family Policies and Poverty for Partnered and Single Women in Europe and North America. *Gender & Society* 21: 804–827.

Moen, Phyllis, ed. 2003. *It's About Time: Couples and Careers*. Ithaca, NY: ILR Press/Cornell University Press.

Moen, Phyllis, and Patricia Roehling. 2005. *The Career Mystique: Cracks in the American Dream*. Lanham, MD: Rowman & Littlefield.

Mooney, Carolyn. 2008. "Vive la Similarité." *Chronicle of Higher Education*, February 1.

Mooney, Nan. 2008. *(Not) Keeping Up with Our Parents: The Decline of the Professional Middle Class*. Boston, MA: Beacon Press.

Moore, Kristin A., Rosemary Chalk, Juliet Scarpa, and Sharon Vandiverre. 2002. "Family Strengths: Often Overlooked, But Real." *Child Trends Research Brief*. Washington, D.C.: Annie E. Casey Foundation.

Moore, Mignon R. 2008. "Gendered Power Relations among Women: A Study of Household Decision Making in Black, Lesbian Stepfamilies." *American Sociological Review* 73 (April): 335–356.

Musick, Kelly, Ann Meier, and Larry Bumpass. 2007. "Influences of Family Structure, Conflict, and Change on Transitions to Adulthood." CCPR Working Paper No. 011–06, University of California, Los Angeles.

Nadis, Steve. 2006. "The Mommy Gap," *Kennedy School Bulletin,* Spring.

Nagourney, Adam. 2009. "Political Shifts on Gay Rights Lag Behind Culture." *New York Times,* June 27.

Nagourney, Adam, and Megan Thee. 2007. "New Poll Finds That Young Americans Are Leaning Left." *New York Times,* June 27.

Newman, Katherine S. 1993. *Declining Fortunes: The Withering of the American Dream.* New York: Basic Books.

Nock, Steven. 1998. *Marriage in Men's Lives.* New York: Oxford University Press.

Oliver, Melvin, and Thomas Shapiro. 1995. *Black Wealth, White Wealth: A New Perspective on Racial Inequality.* New York: Routledge.

Orloff, Ann. 2008. "Farewell to Maternalism?: Welfare Reform, Ending Entitlements for Poor Single Mothers, Expanding the Claims of Poor Employed Parents." Unpublished manuscript.

Pager, Devah. 2007. *Marked: Race, Crime, and Finding Work in an Era of Mass Incarceration.* Chicago: University of Chicago Press.

Parcel, Toby L., and Elizabeth G. Menaghan. 1994. *Parents' Jobs and Children's Lives.* New York: Aldine de Gruyter.

Parker-Pope, Tara. 2008. "Gay Unions Shed Light on Gender in Marriage." *New York Times,* June 10.

Parsons, Talcott, and Robert F. Bales. 1955. *Family, Socialization, and Interaction Process.* Glencoe, IL: Free Press.

Paul, Annie Murphy. 2006. "The Real Marriage Penalty." *New York Times Magazine,* November 19.

Percheski, Christine. 2008. "Opting Out? Cohort Differences in Professional Women's Employment from 1960 to 2005." *American Sociological Review* 73: 497–517.

Peterson, Richard R. 1989. *Women, Work, and Divorce.* Albany: State University of New York Press.

———. 1996. "A Re-Evaluation of the Economic Consequences of Divorce." *American Sociological Review* 61: 528–536.

Pew Research Center. 2007a. "Generation Gap in Values, Behavior: As Marriage and Parenthood Drift Apart, Public Is Concerned about Social Impact." Pew Research Center Social and Demographic Trends Report, July 1.

———. 2007b. "How Young People View Their Lives, Futures and Politics: A Portrait of the 'Generation Next.'" New York: Pew Research Center.

———. 2007c. "From 1997 to 2007: Fewer Mothers Prefer Full-time Work." New York: Pew Research Center.

Pitt-Catsouphes, Marcie, Christina Matz-Costa, and Elyssa Besen. 2009. "Workplace Flexibility: Findings from the Age & Generations Study." Chestnut Hill, MA: Sloan Center on Aging & Work.

Popenoe, David. 1988. *Disturbing the Nest: Family Change and Decline in Modern Societies.* New York: Aldine de Gruyter.

———. 1996. *Life without Father: Compelling New Evidence that Fatherhood and Marriage Are Indispensable for the Good of Children and Society.* New York: Martin Kessler.

———. 2008. "Cohabitation, Marriage, and Child Well-Being: A Cross-National Perspective." Piscataway, NJ: The National Marriage Project.

Popenoe, David, Jean B. Elshtain and David Blankenhorn. 1996. *Promises to Keep: Decline and Renewal of Marriage in America.* Lanham, MD: Rowman & Littlefield.

Porter, Eduardo. 2006. "Stretched to Limit, Women Stall March to Work." *New York Times,* March 2.

Porter, Eduardo, and Michelle O'Donnell. 2006. "Facing Middle Age With No Degree, and No Wife." *New York Times,* August 6.

Potuchek, Jean L. 1997. *Who Supports the Family? Gender and Breadwinning in Dual-Earner Marriages.* Stanford, CA: Stanford University Press.

Premeaux, Sonya F., Cheryl L. Adkins, and Kevin W. Mossholder. 2007. "Balancing Work and Family: A Field Study of Multi-Dimensional, Multi-Role Work-Family Conflict." *Journal of Organizational Behavior* 28: 705–727.

Press, Julie. 2004. "Cute Butts and Housework: A Gynocentric Theory of Assortative Mating." *Journal of Marriage and Family* 66: 1029–1033.

Presser, Harriet B. 2003. *Working in a 24/7 Economy: Challenges for American Families.* New York: Russell Sage Foundation.

Putnam, Robert D. 2000. *Bowling Alone: The Collapse and Revival of American Community.* New York: Simon & Schuster.

Rabin, Roni Caryn. 2008. "A Consensus about Day Care: Quality Counts." *New York Times,* September 15.

Raley, Sara B., Marybeth J. Mattingly, and Suzanne M. Bianchi. 2006. "How Dual Are Dual-Income Couples? Documenting Change from 1970–2001." *Journal of Marriage and the Family* 68: 11.

Rampell, Catherine. 2009. "As Layoffs Surge, Women May Pass Men in Job Force." *New York Times,* February 6.

Rankin, Nancy, Phoebe Taubman, and Yolanda Wu. 2008. "Seeking a Just Balance: Law Students Weigh in on Work and Family." New York: The Work and Family Legal Center (June).

Ray, Rebecca, Janet C. Gornick, and Steve Schmitt. 2008. "Parental Leave Policies in 21 Countries: Assessing Generosity and Gender Equality." Washington, DC: Center for Economic Policy Research.

Rayman, Paula M. 2001. *Beyond the Bottom Line: The Search for Dignity at Work.* New York: Palgrave.

Ridgeway, Cecilia, and Shelley J. Correll. 2004. "Motherhood as a Status Characteristic." *Journal of Social Issues* 60: 683–700.

Risman, Barbara J. 1986. "Can Men 'Mother'? Life as a Single Father." *Family Relations* 35: 95–102.

———. 1998. *Gender Vertigo: American Families in Transition.* New Haven, CT: Yale University Press.

Risman, Barbara J., and Elizabeth Seale. 2010. "Betwixt and Be Tween: Gender Contradictions Among Middle Schoolers." In *Families As They Really Are,* edited by Barbara J. Risman. New York: W.W. Norton.

Roberts, Sam. 2006. "It's Official: To Be Married Means to Be Outnumbered." *New York Times,* October 15.

———. 2007a. "51% of Women Are Now Living without Spouse." *New York Times,* January 16.

———. 2007b. "25th Anniversary Mark Elusive for Many Couples." *New York Times,* September 20.

————. 2008a. "Most Children Still Live in Two-Parent Homes, Census Bureau Reports." *New York Times,* February 21.

————. 2008b. "In a Generation, Minorities May Be the U.S. Majority." *New York Times,* August 14.

————. 2008c. "Two-Parent Black Families Showing Gains." *New York Times,* December 17.

Robinson, John P., and Geoffrey Godbey. 1997. *Time for Life: The Surprising Ways Americans Use Their Time.* University Park: Pennsylvania State University Press.

Rose, Stephen J., and Heidi I. Hartmann. 2008. "Still a Man's Labor Market: The Long-Term Earnings Gap." Washington, DC: Institute for Women's Policy Research.

Roth, Louise. 2006. *Selling Women Short: Gender and Money on Wall Street.* Princeton, NJ: Princeton University Press.

Rubin, Lillian B. 1996. *The Transcendent Child: Tales of Triumph over the Past.* New York: Basic Books.

Rutter, Virginia. 2004. "The Case for Divorce." Unpublished dissertation. Seattle, WA: University of Washington.

Ryder, Norman B. 1965. "The Cohort as a Concept in the Study of Social Change." *American Sociological Review,* 30 (6): 843–861.

Sarkisian, Natalia, and Naomi Gerstel. 2004. "Kin Support Among Blacks and Whites: Race and Family Organization." *American Sociological Review* 69 (4) (December): 812–837.

————. 2008. "The Color of Family Ties: Race, Class, Gender, and Extended Family Involvement." In *American Families: A Multicultural Reader,* 2nd ed., edited by Stephanie Coontz, Maya Parson, and Gabrielle Raley, 447–453. New York: Routledge.

Schor, Juliet. 1991. *The Overworked American: The Unexpected Decline of Leisure.* New York: Basic Books.

————. 1996. *The Overspent American: Upscaling, Downshifting, and the New Consumer.* New York: Basic Books.

Scott, Janny, and David Leonhardt. 2005. "Shadowy Lines that Still Divide." *New York Times,* May 15.

Scott, Marvin, and Stanford Lyman. 1968. "Accounts." *American Sociological Review* 33: 46–61.

Sennett, Richard, and Jonathan Cobb. 1972. *The Hidden Injuries of Class.* New York: Alfred A. Knopf.

Shapira, Ian. 2008. "Bringing Up Babies, and Defying the Norms: Some Young College Grads Embrace Parenthood as Their Peers Postpone It." *Washington Post,* January 15.

Shorter, Edward. 1975. *The Making of the Modern Family.* New York: Basic Books.

Sidel, Ruth. 2006. *Unsung Heroines: Single Mothers and the American Dream.* Berkeley and Los Angeles: University of California Press.

Skolnick, Arlene. 2006. "Beyond the 'M' Word: The Tangled Web of Politics and Marriage." *Dissent* (Fall): 81–87.

Skolnick, Arlene, and Stacy Rosencrantz. 1994. "The New Crusade for the Old Family." *The American Prospect* (Summer): 59–65.

Smith, Jeremy A. 2009. *The Daddy Shift: How Stay-at-Home Dads, Breadwinning Moms, and Shared Parenting Are Transforming the American Family*. Boston: Beacon Press.

Smock, Pamela. 2000. "Cohabitation in the United States: An Appraisal of Research Themes, Findings, and Implications." *Annual Review of Sociology* 26: 1–20.

Springer, Kristen W. 2007. "Research or Rhetoric? A Response to Wilcox and Nock." *Sociological Forum* 22 (1): 111–116.

St. George, Donna. 2007. "Part-Time Looks Fine to Working Mothers: 60% Prefer It to Full-Time or No Job." *Washington Post,* July 12.

Stacey, Judith. 1990. *Brave New Families: Stories of Domestic Upheaval in Late-Twentieth-Century America*. New York: Basic Books.

———. 1996. *In the Name of the Family: Rethinking Family Values in the Postmodern Age*. Boston: Beacon Press.

Stacey, Judith, and Timothy Biblarz. 2001. "(How) Does the Sexual Orientation of Parents Matter?" *American Sociological Review* 66: 159–183.

Stacey, Judith, and Barrie Thorne. 1985. "The Missing Feminist Revolution in Sociology." *Social Problems* 32 (4): 301–316.

Stack, Carol B. 1974. *All Our Kin: Strategies for Survival in a Black Community*. New York: Harper and Row.

Stevenson, Betsey, and Justin Wolfers. 2006. "Bargaining in the Shadow of the Law: Divorce Laws and Family Distress." *Quarterly Journal of Economics* 121: 267–288.

Stinchcombe, Arthur. 1975. "Merton's Theory of Social Structure. In *The Idea of Social Structure: Papers in Honor of Robert K. Merton,* edited by Louis A. Coser, 11–33. New York: Harcourt Brace Jovanovich.

Stone, Pamela. 2007. *Opting Out? Why Women Really Quit Careers and Head Home*. Berkeley and Los Angeles: University of California Press.

Story, Louise. 2005. "Many Women at Elite Colleges Set Career Path to Motherhood." *New York Times,* September 20.

Sullivan, Oriel. 2006. *Changing Gender Relations, Changing Families: Tracing the Pace of Change over Time*. New York: Rowman & Littlefield.

Sullivan, Oriel, and Scott Coltrane. 2008. "Men's Changing Contribution to Housework and Child Care." Chicago, IL: Council on Contemporary Families Briefing Paper (April 25).

Swidler, Ann. 1980. "Love and Adulthood in American Culture." In *Themes of Love and Work in Adulthood,* edited by Erik H. Erikson and Neil J. Smelser, 120–147. Cambridge, MA: Harvard University Press.

———. 1986. "Culture in Action: Symbols and Strategies." *American Sociological Review* 51: 273–286.

Teachman, Jay. 2008. "Complex Life Course Patterns and the Risk of Divorce in Second Marriages." *Journal of Marriage and Family* 70 (2): 294–305.

Teixeira, Ruy. 2009. "The Coming End of the Culture Wars." Washington, DC: Center for American Progress.

Tierney, John. 2006. "The Happiest Wives." *New York Times,* February 28.

Tocqueville, Alexis de. 2006. *Democracy in America*. Edited by J. P. Mayer. Translated by George Lawrence. New York: HarperPerennial.

Trimberger, Ellen Kay. 2005. *The New Single Woman*. Boston: Beacon Press.

USA Today. 2007. "Downward Mobility Trend Threatens Black Middle Class." November 19.

U.S. Census Bureau. 2005. "Who's Minding the Kids? Child Care Arrangements." Washington, DC: Spring.

———. 2006a. "Current Population Survey Annual Social and Economic Supplement: Families and Living Arrangements: 2005." Washington, DC.

———. 2006b. "Families and Living Arrangements." Washington, DC: June 19.

———. 2007. "Single-Parent Households Showed Little Variation since 1994." Washington, DC.

———. 2008. "Educational Attainment in the United States: 2007." Washington, DC: January.

Uchitelle, Louis. 2006. *The Disposable American: Layoffs and Their Consequences.* New York: Alfred A. Knopf.

———. 2008. "Poor Economy Slows Women in Workplace." *New York Times,* July 22.

Vachon, Marc, and Amy Vachon. 2010. *Equally Shared Parenting: Rewriting the Rules for a New Generation of Parents.* New York: Perigee.

Valian, Virginia. 1998. *Why So Slow? The Advancement of Women.* Cambridge, MA: MIT Press.

Waite, Linda J., and Maggie Gallagher. 2000. *The Case for Marriage: Why Married People Are Happier, Healthier, and Better Off Financially.* New York: Doubleday.

Waldfogel, Jane. 2006. *What Children Need.* Cambridge, MA: Harvard University Press.

Wallerstein, Judith S., and Sandra Blakeslee. 1989. *Second Chances: Men, Women, and Children a Decade after Divorce.* New York: Ticknor & Fields.

Wallerstein, Judith S., Julia M. Lewis, and Sandra Blakeslee. 2000. *The Unexpected Legacy of Divorce: A 25-Year Landmark Study.* New York: Hyperion.

Warner, Judith. 2005. *Perfect Madness: Motherhood in the Age of Anxiety.* New York: Riverhead Books.

Warren, Elizabeth, and Amelia W. Tyagi. 2003. *The Two-Income Trap: Why Middle-Class Mothers and Fathers Are Going Broke.* New York: Basic Books.

Weber, Max. 1962. *Basic Concepts in Sociology.* New York: Philosophical Library.

Webber, Gretchen R., and Christine L. Williams. 2008. "Mothers in 'Good' and 'Bad' Part-Time Jobs: Different Problems, Same Results." *Gender & Society* 22: 752–777.

Weitzman, Lenore J. 1985. *The Divorce Revolution: The Unexpected Social and Economic Consequences for Women and Children in America.* New York: Free Press.

West, Candace, and Sarah Fenstermaker. 1995. "Doing Difference." *Gender & Society* 9: 8–37.

West, Candace, and Don H. Zimmerman. 1987. "Doing Gender." *Gender & Society* 1 (2): 125–151.

Western, Bruce. 2006. *Punishment and Inequality in America.* New York: Russell Sage Foundation.

Whitehead, Barbara D. 1997. *The Divorce Culture.* New York: Alfred A. Knopf.

Whyte, William H. 1956. *The Organization Man.* New York: Simon & Schuster.

Wilcox, Bradford, and Steven Nock. 2006. "What's Love Got to Do with It? Equality, Equity, Commitment and Women's Marital Quality." *Social Forces* 84: 1321–1345.

————. 2007. "'Her' Marriage after the Revolutions." *Sociological Forum* 22: 354–362.

Williams, Christine. 1989. *Gender Differences at Work: Men and Women in Nontraditional Occupations.* Berkeley: University of California Press.

————. 1995. *Still a Man's World: Men Who Do Women's Work.* Berkeley: University of California Press.

Williams, Joan C. 2000. *Unbending Gender: Why Family and Work Conflict and What to Do About It.* New York: Oxford University Press.

————. 2007. "The Opt-Out Revolution Revisited." *The American Prospect* ("Mother Load" Special Report: 12–15).

————. 2007. "Enforcement Guidance: Unlawful Disparate Treatment of Workers with Caregiving Responsibilities." Unpublished report (May 23). San Francisco: Center for Work-Life Law, Hastings Law School.

Wilson, James Q. 2002. *The Marriage Problem: How Our Culture Has Weakened Families.* New York: Harper Collins.

Wilson, William Julius. 1987. *The Truly Disadvantaged.* Chicago: University of Chicago Press.

Winslow-Bowe, Sarah. 2006. "The Persistence of Wives' Income Advantage." *Journal of Marriage and Family* 68 (4): 824–842.

Wolfe, Alan. 1999. *One Nation, After All: What Middle-Class Americans Really Think About God, Country, Family, Racism, Welfare, Immigration, Homosexuality, Work, the Right, the Left, and Each Other.* New York: Viking.

Wrigley, Julia, and Joanna Dreby. 2005. "Fatalities and the Organization of Child Care in the United States, 1985–2003." *American Sociological Review* 70: 729–757.

Wrong, Dennis. 1961. "The Oversocialized Conception of Man in Modern Society." *American Sociological Review* 26: 183–193.

Zelizer, Viviana. 1985. *Pricing the Priceless Child.* New York: Basic Books.

————. 1994. *The Social Meaning of Money.* New York: Basic Books.

————. 2005. *The Purchase of Intimacy.* Princeton, NJ: Princeton University Press.

Zerubavel, Eviatar. 1991. *The Fine Line: Making Distinctions in Everyday Life.* Chicago: University of Chicago Press.

————. 2006. "Flexible Structures: Time, Work, and Identity." Annual meeting of the American Sociological Association. Montreal, Canada: August.

Zezima, Katie. 2008. "More Women Than Ever Are Childless, Census Finds." *New York Times,* August 19.

Zimmerman, Mary K., Jacquelyn S. Litt, and Christine E. Bose. 2006. *Global Dimensions of Gender and Carework.* Stanford, CA: Stanford University Press.

Zinsmeister, Karl, editor. 1996. "It Takes a Marriage, and Other Lessons Families Teach Us." Special issue, *The American Enterprise* (May/June).

INDEX

children
  aftermath shaping views, 32
  care gap, 261n.7
  embracing work ethic, 24
  gaining involved caretaker, 56–57
  gender revolution, 3, 103, 189
  ignoring parents' problems, 75
  lessons and experiences, 15, 39–40
  "lost fathers," 87–88
  parental breakups, 30–33
  relief and sadness, 31
  role models, 247n.10
  single parents, 30, 56
  stable childhood vs. happy home, 35
  staying together for sake of kids, 29
child support, father refusing to provide, 48
Chodorow, N., 256n.3
"choice," defining equality as, 176–178, 188
"choice feminism," 255n.24
"chosen families," creation, 147
Clarke-Stewart, A., 241n.10
class
  defining, 239n.15
  men's fallback positions, 162, 163
  studying social and individual change,
    232–233
  women's fallback positions, 126–128
  work and family ideals, 106, 107
  young people sharing values, 225
Clinton, H., It Takes a Village, 243n.12
"clockwork of male careers," Hochschild, 198
Cobb, J., 255n.25
cohabitation, 116, 140, 248n.19
Coleman, J., 249n.2
Coleman, M., 238n.7, 243n.9
Collins, P. H., 251n.22, 264n.6
Coltrane, S., 259n.27
commitment
  affirming value of, 11
  balancing, with autonomy, 212–213
  children of divorce seeking, 108–109
  gender roles, 138
  men's optimistic outlook, 170
  parents sharing, 74
  rearing children, 10–11
  remarriages, 62–63
  seeking lifelong, 107–110
  "work first" ethos, 200
communitarians, concerns, 103
community decline, 103
"competing devotion," 251n.25

"concerted cultivation," 248–249n.29
conflicts
  easing, after breakups, 61
  high- and low-conflict marriages, 29–30
  intensive parenting, 121
  men's and women's mobility, 251n.21
  parental separation, 85
  persistence of work-family, 123
  work and family shifts, 7
  work-life, of men, 160
  young people shifting focus, 224–226
"conjugal family," 144, 260n.39
Conley, D., 253n.13, 257n.14
Connell, R. W., 253n.4
consequences, long-run, framing views, 32
constant fighting, 31–32, 69
contingency plans, self-reliant women, 126
contradictions
  and conflicts, 7
  cultural and structural, 156, 239n.3,
    246n.5, 252n.33
Coontz, S., 241n.4, 249n.11, 259n.34,
    260n.1
Correll, S. J., 253n.7
Coser, Louis and Rose, "greedy institution,"
    118
Cotter, D. A., 240n.21, 252n.32, 254n.17
Coy, P., 259n.28
Crittenden, A., 255n.26
Crittenden, D., 252n.32
Crouter, A. C., 241n.10
"culture," embodiment, 260n.4
culture wars, moving beyond, 210–213

"daddy's little girl," fear of losing place as,
    39
Damaske, S., 242n.12, 249n.8
Danziger, S., 140, 246n.2, 248n.24
daughters, lessons about mothers, 97–98
day care, dangers of organized, 257n.6
DeBarros, A., 248n.24
debate, "family values," 16–17
De Groot, J., 262–263n.21
deinstitutionalization, marriage, 246n.2
Demo, D. H., 241n.6
Democrats, young Americans, 257n.7
"demographic metabolism," life cycle,
    239n.12
De Paulo, B. M., 250n.14
"dependency," women, 256n.35
De Tocqueville, A., 261n.8

still parents, 60–61
unprepared to "do it all," 88–90
"worst case," 85–90
parental estrangement, two-earner marriage, 28
parental figures, caretakers, 66–67
parental separation, belief of action, 25
parenthood, postponing, 142–143, 186–187
parenting, 170–173
parents
    "acting out roles," 31
    ambiguities of breakups, 30–32
    "American dream" focus, 40–41
    distribution of tasks, 34
    pressures, 120–121
    quality of bond forged, 29
    reluctant traditionalism, 79–82
    self-imposed roles, 35–36
    "separate roles," 36–37
    sharing duties and economic security, 74
    still, when not partners, 60–61
    stuck "in a rut," 35
    together and apart, 25–33
    vs. other caregivers, 171
Parker-Pope, T., 238n.6, 247n.9
Parsons, T., 237n.1, 255n.23, 256n.3, 260n.39
partnerships. *See also* relationships
    building work-family, 206
    dual-earner arrangement, 52–53
    new forms of adult, 3–4
    raising standards for acceptable, 138–139
    seeking egalitarian, 112–114
    skepticism, 121–122
"part-time," definition, 239n.9
paternal ambivalence, fathers, 186–187
pathways. *See* family pathways
Percheski, C., 238–239n.9, 240n.21
Peterson, R. R., 245n.5
Pew Forum on Religion and Public Life, 263n.22
Pew Research Center
    children of employed mothers, 241n.8
    divorce and marriage, 210
    faithfulness and sexual relationship, 247n.13
    nonmarital births, 238n.4
    politics, 257n.7
    sex and marriage, 212
    women and part-time work, 246n.3
Pitt-Catsouphes, M., 258n.16

politics, young Americans, 257n.7, 263n.22
Popenoe, D., 241n.3, 248n.19, 255n.33
Population Reference Bureau, 239n.17
Porter, E., 252n.32, 255n.29
postindustrialism, 144, 200, 216
Potuchek, J. L., 254n.21
power struggle, dual-earner marriages, 82–83
pregnancy, out-of-wedlock, 104–105
Premeaux, S. F., 262n.12
Press, J., 259n.34
Presser, H. B., 259n.32
public assistance, 37, 55
Putnam, R. D., 245n.1

quality
    bond forged by parents, 29
    family bonds, 209
    organized day care, 257n.6
    remarriages, 62, 243n.10

race, survey respondents, 8, 227–230, 232–233
Raley, S. B., 254n.18
Rampell, C., 259n.25
Rankin, N., 258n.21
Ray, R., 243n.3, 262n.14
Rayman, P. M., 261n.7
relationships. *See also* partnerships
    experience as teacher, 132–134
    fragility of modern, 123, 124
    loss of autonomy and, 133–134
    postponing marriage, 137–138
    raising standards for partner, 138–139
    refashioning, 137–141
    same-sex, 212
    second chances, 99
    uncertainty in, 116–118
reluctant traditionalism, parents, 79–82
remarriages
    family shifts in, 90–92, 93
    new and improved, 61–64
    quality, 62, 243n.10
    stepparents, 63–64
reproductive mothering, Chodorow theory, 256n.3
Republicans, young Americans, 257n.7
responsibility, individual to collective, 219–224
Ridgeway, C., 253n.7